Class
Warfare

Class Warfare

Besieged Schools, Bewildered Parents,
Betrayed Kids and the Attack on Excellence

J. MARTIN ROCHESTER

ENCOUNTER BOOKS
SAN FRANCISCO

KH

First edition published in 2002 by Encounter Books, an activity of Encounter for Culture and Education, Inc., a nonprofit tax-exempt corporation.

Encounter Books website address: www.encounterbooks.com

Manufactured in the United States and printed on acid-free paper.

The paper used in this publication meets the minimum requirements of ANSI/NISO Z39.48-1992 (R 1997) (*Permanence of Paper*).

FIRST EDITION

Library of Congress Cataloging-in-Publication Data

Rochester, J. Martin.
    Class warfare : besieged schools, bewildered parents, betrayed kids and the attack on excellence / by J. Martin Rochester.
    p. cm.
    Includes bibliographical references and index.
    ISBN 1-893554-53-8 (alk. paper)
1. Education—United States. 2. Public schools—United States. I. Title.

    LA217.2 .R64 2002
    371.01'0973—dc21
    2002028606

10 9 8 7 6 5 4 3 2 1

11/22/04

I dedicate this book in heartfelt thanks
to those remarkable U. City and Clayton teachers,
not facilitators, my sons had the great fortune
to learn from, and in the hope that
they are not a dying breed.

CONTENTS

Author's Note

There is a war going on today in K-12 education in America. It is occurring all across the country, with conflict ranging from modest skirmishes to full-scale rebellions. This is a cold war, fought with words rather than swords, although it has been heating up lately, as reflected in the 2002 passage of the "No Child Left Behind Act" in Congress and in the U.S. Supreme Court decision approving the use of vouchers in religious and other private schools. Much is riding on the outcome of this contest: not only the future of every individual child, whose success in life will depend largely on the quality of the schooling he or she receives, but also the future of American society as a whole, whose prosperity will depend more than ever on a well-educated citizenry able to acquire, process, and evaluate information. Commentator after commentator has noted that human, intellectual capital will be the single most important factor of production in the knowledge-based global economy of the twenty-first century. But a fight rages over what this means for our education systems and what is the essence of a world-class school. In my judgment, despite some glimmers of progress, we are moving in the wrong direction. The war is being lost. I think it could still be won, or I would not be writing this.

I have found myself a combatant in this conflict, both as a parent-taxpayer and as an educator. This book is partially an account of my own struggles in the education war, filled with personal stories and observations—a kind of show-and-tell presentation, not of how I spent my summer vacation but how I spent the past fifteen years of my life trying to understand the issues at stake and to effect change in my community. This is far more than a personal memoir, however. It is meant to be a wide-ranging and substantive critique of where American education has gone wrong. To the extent that I indulge in telling my own private horror stories, I do so strictly for the purpose of illustrating the bigger picture of educational theories and practices run amok and exposing the failures of our precollegiate education system.

Others have sought to chronicle the decline of American education and sound the alarm. I owe a huge intellectual debt to such giants as Diane Ravitch, E. D. Hirsch, Chester Finn, Sandra Stotsky, Tom Loveless, Abigail Thernstrom, and the late Albert Shanker. *Class Warfare* is an attempt to offer my own take, to add my smaller, more personalized voice to theirs in the hope that, in combination with similar voices elsewhere, it will somehow get the message through. This book is aimed especially at helping parents caught in the crossfire of school reform better understand the current debate. But I am writing also for professional educators, who I hope will find the discussion thought-provoking, whether they agree or disagree with what I have to say.

Although K-12 educators might well question how a university political scientist can feel competent to comment on precollegiate education, I have always taken a serious interest in not just research but also teaching. During the 1970s, I served as director of the Consortium for International Studies Education, a nationwide network of universities involved in the development and dissemination of innovative undergraduate learning materials, and headed the National Science Foundation's Learning Package Project, which helped to pioneer "learning by doing" pedagogy. I have also spent considerable time in high school classrooms teaching and observing.

I have tried to avoid the standard "left-wing" and "right-wing" charges that are often lobbed back and forth like grenades by those seeking to capture the high ground in discussions of education. The main theme that runs through this book is that it is *ideas,* not interests, that are mainly responsible for our predicament. The ideas I am referring to are really *bad* ideas, yet are admittedly so seductive that they at times manage to gain surprisingly wide currency among parents and scholars alike. I know, since I found myself, as a parent-educator, initially entranced by some of these myself.

I wish to stress that this book is not an attack on public schools. I believe in public schools as the basic provider of education in this country and as a foundation of democracy, or I would not have sent my own children to such schools and would not have invested enormous time and energy in trying to improve these institutions. I also respect the right of families to choose independent schools or homeschooling for their children if they so wish. The problems I discuss may be especially pronounced in public schools, but they are increasingly found in private schools as well. Therefore, the target of my criticism is not public schools but the K-12 culture as a whole. But while I find fault with the dominant K-12 culture, I would be remiss if I did not acknowledge the many brilliant, dedicated individual teachers and administrators I have observed, some of whom my kids were blessed to learn from. This book is not about them but about the system they inhabit, one that they themselves would probably confess is harder to fight than City Hall.

Political scientists refer to the period from 1945 to the present as "the long peace," due to the absence of great-power war. My book manuscript was "the long piece" until Peter Collier improved it with his brilliant editing skills. *Class Warfare* would never have been as readable and, indeed, would never have seen the light of day without his support. I must also thank my wife and co-parent, Ruth, as well as my many friends who have had to endure my frequent sorties over the subject of education. Finally, I want to recognize the Clayton School District for, more often than not, tolerating me as a critic—or as some would put it, a gadfly.

1

How I Became a Soldier in the Great American Education War

"Together, we will reclaim America's schools,
before ignorance and apathy claim more young lives."
—President George W. Bush, Inaugural Address

The math wars, the reading wars, the testing wars, the voucher wars, and all the other schoolyard fights reported in the news today are part of a much wider conflict that is occurring throughout the United States over the meaning of educational excellence and how to achieve world-class schools. Before explaining how I became a combatant in The Great American Education War, allow me to provide a bit of biographical background. I am 56 years old, an early baby boomer, not a late one, having been born on November 24, 1945, one month to the day after the founding of the United Nations that ushered in the post-World War II era. Most of my childhood was spent growing up in a modest area of Baltimore. My father was a pharmacist in those more innocent times when drug stores had soda fountains and the delivery vehicles were bicycles; I doubled as soda jerk and delivery boy. My mother was a schoolteacher, when those same innocent times provided few other career options for women.

My parents sent me and my brother to the public schools. Both the elementary and junior high schools I attended took their name from nearby Pimlico Racetrack, which was only about fifteen minutes from my house if I walked with a fast gait. In contrast, Baltimore City College High School, my next stop, was located several miles across town. I relied on public transportation, which meant my spending an hour each way, as I had to transfer from one bus to another in making the daily trek between home and school. This "busing" was a fact of life for me and my

1

friends. It was the price one had to pay for the quality of the education the high school had to offer. "City" was one of the best schools, public or private, in the entire metropolitan area. For those of us enrolled in the special college preparatory program, the venerable institution—it is the third oldest public high school in the country—rewarded our long commute with masterly teachers and cherished traditions but most of all with a dedication to academic excellence. I graduated in 1962 and went on to earn a bachelor's degree in political science from Loyola College of Baltimore in 1966 and a Ph.D. in political science from Syracuse University in 1972.

Since 1972, I have been a professor of political science at the University of Missouri-St. Louis, a state university with an enrollment of some 12,000 students, making it the third biggest institution of higher education in Missouri. Although the campus address is Natural Bridge Road and the school mascot is the Riverman, the place is several miles from the banks of the Mississippi River, with the only nearby body of water being the local duck pond called Bugg Lake (named for the first chancellor of the college). Owing to its origins as a campus designed to provide a college education for St. Louisans who could not afford to leave home, it is primarily a commuter university, with only a few dormitories and a relatively small percentage of residential students. The university has attracted its share of very bright students, especially after the creation of the Pierre Laclede Honors College in 1989, but the student body as a whole tends to be a working-class clientele consisting mostly of students who work many hours a week to pay their tuition (and hence are necessarily only part-time students), who are often the first in their family to attend college, and who not only come from St. Louis but are likely to remain in St. Louis after graduation.

My professional life has primarily been spent teaching and writing about international relations, including authoring a textbook that has been used at places like Duke, Stanford, and the U.S. Naval Academy as well as community and state colleges. Among my writings is a book on the United Nations calling for improved global institution-building (not world government, but better mechanisms for cooperation among sovereign states). I was recognized in 1995, on the fiftieth anniversary of the UN, by the St. Louis chapter of the United Nations Association of America as one of fifty local "people who have devoted their lives personally and professionally to the values of peace and justice within their own communities and throughout the world." In the pages that follow, I will utter some "politically incorrect" statements, but I can hardly be accused by the PC watchdogs of being insensitive to diversity and not understanding multiculturalism.

As suggested by my scholarly interest in the UN, I have spent much of my adult life as a liberal—participating in the civil rights movement and the anti-war protests of the sixties, delighting in the Republican downfall over Watergate in the seventies, speaking out against some of Ronald Reagan's Cold War policies in the eighties, and even privately wondering whether impeachment was the right punishment for Bill Clinton's sexual dalliances in the nineties. All the while, however, I sensed that, as I was aging, I was becoming more and more alienated from the left. In the circles I travel in, such a confession can raise eyebrows if not hackles, given the overwhelming liberal bent of professors in academia. I have a good explanation for this personal metamorphosis. It is not that I have abandoned liberalism. Rather, liberalism has abandoned me. It is not uncommon to experience such a revelation; the "liberal disillusionment" of the 1920s experienced by John Dos Passos and others, as well as the "neoconservative" conversion of Norman Podhoretz and the New York School in the 1970s, come to mind.

In my case, it was "progressive education," which is closely associated with modern liberalism, that provided the breaking point. Currently in control of the education establishment, progressives have long dreamed of classrooms where children work independently and cooperatively, relatively free of adult direction, grading, and other such "constraints." The more I have seen of progressive pedagogy at work, the more disenchanted I have become. The utter failure of our schools under progressive rule has provoked a backlash, as the public has called for increased standards and accountability. This in turn has produced a backlash against the backlash, mounted by educators on the defensive. If my eclectic ideological history as well as my lifelong commitment to teaching is not enough to convince the reader that I can offer a fair, informed analysis of the contemporary education scene and the war that is now raging, there is one other credential I can furnish—that of a battle-scarred parent.

My Enlistment in the Cause

What perhaps most equips me to comment on the state of precollegiate education, aside from my vantage point as a college professor who annually sees the finished, or not-so-finished, products that are being produced in our schools, is my experiences as a father of two children who recently completed their education. I do not claim to speak for all parents. I can only tell my own story, but there is reason to believe that it is not unique to me. It is a parent's perspective as much as anything else that informs this book.

Certainly, my earliest interest in K-12 educational issues stemmed from my participant observation of what was happening in my kids' elementary school and middle school in the 1980s. I was living then in University City, an established St. Louis suburb that was founded in 1906 by one Edward G. Lewis, a quixotic sort who envisioned creating nothing less than the intellectual capital of the earth. He proceeded to build a number of imposing structures designed to reflect the varied architectures of the world, including a recreation of an Egyptian temple and an ornate, octagonal tower in the Second Renaissance Revival style that became city hall, whose claim to fame until recently was that it had the largest rooftop searchlight on the planet, supposedly having been procured from the Czar of Russia. Lewis' dreams were dashed when he ran out of money, but not before he had laid out a street grid in which most of the avenues were named after colleges and universities. My wife Ruth and I lived with our two children on Vassar, and the neighborhood elementary school was named Delmar–Harvard, since it was situated at the intersection of Harvard Avenue and Delmar Boulevard. The home of Washington University, the municipality was a magnet for academics attracted to the charm of the stately older homes and the bohemian flavor of "the Loop," the downtown row of shops, bars, and eateries. We had bought the house on Vassar from a UM-St. Louis colleague of mine, who had taken a job at the University of Oregon.

U. City at one time had the reputation of being the best school district in the entire state of Missouri. Although long committed to diversity, it had been in actuality a mainly white municipality, with an especially heavy Jewish presence, over many decades. Like so many older suburbs, it started experiencing demographic shifts in housing patterns during the 1960s, which produced greater racial integration of the public schools followed by white flight on the part of many parents concerned about the future of the district. Rightly or wrongly, there was the usual concern whether kids coming from poor households lacking in intellectual sophistication would lower the quality of education. By the time we moved to U. City, black enrollments had already overtaken white enrollments in the district, and the district was in decline at least in terms of the perception of outsiders. Nevertheless, we arrived with the typical idealism and cosmopolitanism that academic families are known for, and that U. City was known for.

These qualities were to be increasingly tested over time, as the enrollment of African-American students was to climb within just a few years to over 85 percent of the district-wide total in a community which remained residentially 50 percent white, yet was not only abandoning the public schools for private schools in droves but was also becoming geographically divided between the predominantly black half living north of Delmar and the predominantly white half living south of Delmar. We lived just north of Delmar, in one of the few truly integrated parts of the city. The St. Louis metropolitan area has always had a strong private school, including parochial school, tradition—it has the highest percentage of school-aged children enrolled in private institutions of any major metro area in the country—but U. Citians, with their liberal, egalitarian personae, were assumed to be above educational privatization. Judging from the rapid abandonment by whites, as well as middle-class blacks, of the U. City public schools, liberalism in U. City went only so far, as parents were unwilling to make their children martyrs to the cause.

Ruth and I gave the U. City public schools our best shot. We became active in the PTO and worked hard with other parents to improve the entire school community. We remained in the system for several years, long after many of our friends had left. By the late 1980s, our older son, Stephen, had made it through Delmar-Harvard Elementary School and was in the seventh grade at Brittany Woods Middle School, while our younger son, Sean, was in the third grade at Delmar-Harvard. On the whole, they had received a very fine education along the way, with many superb teachers who were throwbacks to the days when U. City was known for academic excellence. They, in fact, were performing well in their classes and on standardized tests. I started noticing, however, that, as time went on, the newsletters sent home by the school principals and the curriculum statements endorsed by the school board contained fewer and fewer references to words such as "rigor," "homework," "standards," "merit," and "discipline" and more and more references to "equity," "diversity," "self-esteem," "inclusion," "multiculturalism" and all the other buzzwords that are now recited with rote monotony by K-12 educators. At first, these buzzwords sounded innocent enough. After all, who could possibly be against "equity" and "diversity"? However, I gradually began to realize that these words represented a sea change in K-12 thinking that was moving the U. City schools away from a commitment to academic excellence toward a commitment to academic mediocrity.

When I say sea change, I am referring to the fact that, following the Soviet Union's success at placing Sputnik in outer space orbit in 1957, there was a growing recognition that America's schools needed to be upgraded, particularly through offering more "accelerated," special college prep classes in junior high and high schools for high-achieving students (especially in math and science) if we were to catch up with and surpass the Russians. The K-12 establishment took the advice of the 1959 Conant Report, produced by a committee chaired by the former president of Harvard University, which advocated the practice of grouping students by ability in specific subjects. Although one might rightly question whether these "tracking" policies were excessively exclusive and failed to address the needs of the majority of children who were placed in lower tracks, they produced a level of rigor that was almost unprecedented in U.S. education, even for traditionally strong institutions such as Baltimore City College High and U. City High. I was fortunate to be placed in one of these accelerated programs and to be exposed to a curriculum that was incredibly demanding for a fifteen-year-old high schooler. As just one example, in my senior English course I wrote an eighty-page paper containing over one hundred footnotes on the subject of the sixteenth-century philosopher Erasmus and secular humanism, gleaned from pouring over stacks of books and taking prolific notes in the Baltimore Public Library on weekends. I could not help but laugh when my son's principal tried to convince me that the new direction the district was going in would provide a "richer," "more challenging" curriculum compared with the past. I was to learn that what was meant by this was, among other things, stream-of-consciousness "journal writing" where the student is expected to make a daily entry in a diary based not on reading but "reflections," free of worry about the use of standard English conventions or any of the other strictures associated with good writing.

When I became involved in University City schools as a parent, I found that they were moving 180 degrees from the thinking that prevailed back then in the post-Sputnik era. My suspicions that something was amiss were heightened in 1987, when under a new principal at Delmar-Harvard—a high-minded young man with a freshly minted master's degree in education—there were pressures to do away with ability-based reading groups in favor of "whole-language" instruction whereby all students in a given classroom were to be assigned the same reading and taught with the same exact lesson plan no matter their level of competence. Although grades K-5 had never been tracked like 6-12, it had commonly been understood that within any elementary classroom the teacher had to differentiate instruction to some extent by ability level, especially in heterogeneous classes containing students with wide-ranging competencies. In language arts as well as in math and other areas, the rumor at Delmar-Harvard was that all children were to be put through the curriculum in lock-step fashion at the same pace. No more "bluebird" and "redbird" ability groups—all birds were to be of the same feather. The suspicions and rumors were confirmed when at a PTO meeting later that year the principal stated that the top 20 percent in the past had benefited at the expense of the other 80 percent and that this no longer would be permissible. There was absolutely no evidence that the educational leaps made by high-achievers had been made on the backs of lower-achievers, yet he in effect was saying that, in order to raise the floor, we had to lower the ceiling. In what was to become a commonly repeated rationalization for eliminating ability-grouping, Ruth and I were told by the principal that "research shows that heterogeneous grouping does not hurt bright kids." Does not *hurt*? For me, this was an epiphany—apparently the mission of the public schools was no longer stretching kids' minds; instead they now aimed at damage control. As long as one's child was not harmed by whatever new philosophy the schools had embraced, parents should be content!

This was my first encounter with the social-engineering tendencies of the progressive project and the leveling it sought to foster. It was not the last time I would hear invocations of the "latest research" to justify all manner of experimentation. Shortly thereafter, I learned that Sean, my third-grader, had been accepted into the selective Gifted and Talented Education (GATE) program at Delmar-Harvard. But some other very good students had been excluded, and some students with inferior grades included. It was obvious that, in his rush to fairness, the principal had substituted racial quotas and other counting-by-the-numbers for merit. When Sean's best friend moved out of the neighborhood, because his parents chose to leave the school system rather than stay and fight, it was an especially tough blow, although we could hardly blame them for pulling out. Transferring to another U. City elementary school was not an alternative, since all the schools seemed to be mirroring Delmar-Harvard's changes. I began writing memos to the school board and attending board meetings, questioning the trends but getting little satisfaction.

Meanwhile, our seventh-grader in 1987 was having a decent year at Brittany Woods Middle School. Stephen had just been chosen for the all-county band as a saxophonist and was very much looking forward to the day when he would be able to play in the renowned U. City High Jazz Band. The band always had attracted the best musical talent (both white and black) in the district based on auditions, had gone on concert tours to Europe and other overseas locales, and had produced numerous accomplished musicians (e.g., two horn players who went on to become the chief accompanists to Wynton Marsalis and Harry Connick, Jr.). Then we learned during the year that the powers-that-be in U. City had decided that the jazz band had become too "elitist" and that, in an effort to create a more egalitarian music program, it was being phased out and folded into the high school marching band. The jazz band director chafed at the new plans, resigned in protest, and ended up taking over the band at John Burroughs School, a private school generally regarded as the best school in the St. Louis area.

The demise of the jazz band was the last straw for Ruth and me. I finally telephoned my neighbor, who served on the U. City school board, and asked the following question: "Has U. City abandoned excellence?" I will never forget his answer—a curt "yes." This was a white board member who had been accused of being a racist despite the fact that he and his wife had created a multiracial family which included their own two children and two adopted black children. I, too, would often be accused of racism when I raised concerns about academic excellence at school board meetings. I could live with the race-baiting that unfortunately was becoming an ever more prevalent part of life in U. City, even if it was becoming emotionally draining. What I could not live with was the confession by a school board member whose honesty and integrity I greatly respected telling me that U. City had abandoned academic excellence.

Our choice was either to remain in U. City and switch to private school or to move to another part of St. Louis where the public schools were still strong. There was enough liberalism left in us that we opted for the public schools. Within a week of the phone call, we put our house up for sale; within two months, in March of 1988, we moved to Clayton, a neighboring suburb whose public schools had long since taken over the mantle of excellence that U. City had given up. Clayton was a relatively liberal community since many of its inhabitants, like us, had emigrated there from University City. It was considerably wealthier than U. City and most St. Louis suburbs, so its liberalism was decidedly of the limousine variety. Clayton was the kind of place that, shortly after we arrived, started organizing an annual art fair which drew exhibitors from around the country and where fairgoers could buy anything ranging from full life-sized wax figures costing $40,000 apiece that rivaled Madame Tussaud's museum specimens to jewelry only slightly less pricey than the Hope diamond. Ruth and I had become house-poor to purchase the home in Clayton, but we figured nothing was more important than our children's education. Clayton was ranked third nationally in a survey by a noted business magazine that evaluated the quality of 1,000 public school systems around the country. So we were confident we had made the right decision and had nothing to worry about in terms of education.

Although the City of Clayton was different demographically from U. City, being 90 percent white, the Clayton school district served many African-American children from St. Louis City, who were bused in under a court-mandated "voluntary" city-county desegregation plan. Clayton and other county districts did not participate in this program purely out of humanitarian motives; aside from judicial pressure, there was the incentive of state tax monies that followed each child to their new school. "Deseg" kids constituted approximately 20 percent of the Clayton school district's student body. Although it added valuable diversity to the

Clayton school population, the deseg plan also injected an element of racial politics into educational issues, more subtle and not as volatile as in U. City but nonetheless there beneath the surface. More importantly, there was the element of pack pedagogy, as the same buzzwords I had heard in U. City were quickly making their way across the border into Clayton. Much to my chagrin, I found myself faced with many of the same battles I thought I had left behind.

This was especially so after a new assistant superintendent for curriculum arrived on the Clayton scene in 1990—younger than the Delmar-Harvard principal, armed with a doctorate in education (not just a master's degree), and a woman. I never questioned her brilliant intellect or her good intentions, only her judgment about the definition and determinants of academic excellence. Although she brought some innovative energy to the curriculum development process, she seemed up in the clouds at times. A colleague of hers told me "she thought she was still at the University of Iowa [where she did her doctoral studies]." A new board in the mid-1990s hired a new Clayton superintendent to bring her down to earth, but she remained in a progressive utopia. I would do battle with her and others over the next decade and beyond, even after my children graduated from Clayton High School in 1993 and 1997.

Despite these battles—and maybe because of them—I would have to say that, in retrospect and in fairness, my sons for the most part received a great education in Clayton. Clayton can rightly claim to be called a "world-class school district," if for no other reason than it enjoys state-of-the-art facilities and well over $10,000 per pupil expenditures. It is hard to mess up the education of children under such conditions unless the school district is truly incompetent. Nonetheless, the fact that my kids ended up receiving a great education was due not only to the many competent staff but also to me and other parents maintaining our vigilance and keeping the pressure on against the trendy changes in pedagogy that some of the curriculum gurus were forever contemplating. I found myself getting increasingly involved in K-12 issues, attending virtually every Clayton school board meeting, immersing myself in the education literature, writing op-ed articles for the *St. Louis Post-Dispatch*, giving talks around town to various parent groups, and even testifying before the state legislature. By the time I testified before the Missouri Senate in 1996, I had come to realize fully just how all-pervasive the malaise of K-12 education was. It was not just a U. City problem or a Clayton problem or a Missouri problem but a national problem.

The awful state of urban schools is well-known, that of schools outside the central city less so. If you look beneath the surface, if you get beyond the relative quality of the paint job on the schoolhouse door, you will find that the problem of American education is one that *at its core* differs surprisingly little from one community to the next, whether it is my own upper-middle-class suburban locale or an inner city locale with a large poor and homeless population. Let me try to give a sense of this problem as I discovered it over the years.

What's Nutty About Contemporary K-12 Education, in a Nutshell

M uch has been made of the so-called Stockholm syndrome, that is, the tendency of hostages to gradually take on the attitudes of their captors and to think like them. There appears to be something similar at work in K-12 education insofar as those who spend a great deal of time interacting with kids or studying how they learn seem to start thinking like them. Young children and adolescents are wonderful creatures with lively imaginations and other qualities, but intellectual depth and sophistication is normally not one of them. The history of educational philosophy in the western world is the history of oftentimes bright thinkers producing incredibly sophomoric ideas. There are two clear manifestations of this. One is the tendency to prescribe simplistic solutions to problems. The second is the tendency to revive periodically these same panaceas, usually in repackaged form, forgetting that they never worked to begin with. Almost always leading these reforms are "progressives," with "traditionalists" constantly finding themselves engaged in rear-guard actions.

In *The Anatomy of Revolution*, the historian Crane Brinton observed that political revolutions tend to conform to a pattern. As in the case of the French Revolution in the eighteenth century, they start with a call for incremental reform led by moderates, they then proceed to a stage marked by the domination of radicals, and they conclude finally with a phase marked by a more pragmatic leadership that consolidates the new regime. In the education field, however, the revolution is ongoing. Today, many progressive educators invoke the term "continuous improvement" to characterize the need for ongoing change; the term is borrowed from the successful Total Quality Management (TQM) practices of the business world, ironically a world which educators often disparage. It is odd that the same progressives who claim to be prescribing silver-bullet formulas for classroom success are incessantly seeking to fix things whether they are broken or not, including practices that they themselves have recently proclaimed to be the latest, ultimate salvation of education.

The Education War Between Progressives and Traditionalists: A Neverending Story

The field of dreams where K-12 education lives has been well documented in such recent works as *Tinkering Toward Utopia: A Century of Public School Reform* by David Tyack and Larry Cuban and *Left Back: A Century of Failed School Reforms* by Diane Ravitch, both of which discuss the ongoing, recycled debates that have occurred over the years between progressives claiming to have found the Holy Grail and traditionalists reminding them that there is none to be found. Actually these debates and the wars they have precipitated go back not just years but centuries. It is a neverending story. Some famous and not-so-famous names have been the protagonists. Take, for example, the debate over "discovery learning" vs. direct instruction. At least as far back as Montaigne in the sixteenth century, one can find progressive-sounding statements urging tutors not to "bawl words into [the pupil's] ears as if pouring water into a funnel" since good teaching aims at "a mind well-made rather than well-filled." Through Comenius in the seventeenth century, Rousseau in the eighteenth century, Emerson in the nineteenth century, and Dewey, Freire, and Piaget in the twentieth century, there have been similar railings against "the piggy bank" model of instruction which, according to these thinkers, treats students' minds as empty receptacles to be filled with deposited facts duly memorized and regurgitated on command. Traditionalists such as William Bagley and Arthur Bestor along the way responded by noting that this was a misrepresentation of traditionalist pedagogy, that good teachers since the time of Socrates had recognized the need to offer *both* direct instruction as well as opportunity for student self-learning and not only to transmit facts but also to inspire higher understanding. These thinkers insisted, though, that the essential goal of grade-school teaching remained the delivery of information and insight, that the excesses of progressive philosophy (e.g., substituting the "guide on the side" for the "sage on the stage") resulted in "the equivalent of the Socratic method minus Socrates."

Were these academic debates merely academic—that is, confined to an ivory tower elite with little impact on the average person or the average person's child—the reader would be forgiven for fast-forwarding to the next chapter. But the ideas of these philosophers have often found their way into classrooms around the world, sometimes with highly destructive consequences. The popular classroom practices trumpeted today in school-district PR pamphlets, such as "block scheduling," "multiage classrooms," and the like are not the cutting-edge pedagogical innovations their supporters claim but rather can be traced back decades and centuries to theorists of yesteryear.

The history of precollegiate education can be read as the attempt to institute one round of reform after another, punctuated by efforts to undo reforms, with little cumulative headway made over time as the same questions and concerns resurface. Witness the following "Criticisms of Public Education" articulated in a 1957 publication:

> John Dewey and "progressive education" have taken over the public schools and this philosophy of education is the chief cause of the crisis of education…. The life adjustment movement is replacing intellectual training with soft social programs in most public school systems…. The spirit of competition, an important incentive for learning, has been eliminated by the 100 percent annual promotion policy and the multiple-standard report card…. Lax discipline in the public school is contributing to the increase of juvenile delinquency…. The public schools are neglecting the gifted children because they are geared to teaching the average child…. The public schools are neglecting the training of children in moral and spiritual values…. The academic standards of schools of education are low; their programs of study are of questionable value, and the intellectual qualities of their students are the poorest in the universities.

Sound familiar? These same criticisms are being heard today. Just as the Soviet Sputnik success in the 1950s set off a new wave of reforms in American education, such as "new math," so too did the success of the Japanese economy in the 1980s and the supposed threat it posed to U.S. hegemony spark yet another wave of reforms more recently, such as "new-new math." As Charles Sykes has said, "It's the education disease; they're addicted to it. We're always having these waves of reform, and the only thing they have in common is that there's never any empirical evidence of whether they in fact work. And the worst part is when these things fail, they are repackaged with a different title, presented as innovations and then go on to fail again."

It is curious that, whereas in K-12 education there seems a new flavor of the month every thirty days, and at times every other week, higher education, where I work, suffers somewhat from the opposite problem, that is, an extreme resistance to change. Most college teachers teach in the same lecture style that has been used for the over 1,000 years the academy has been in existence. (College deans are known to share the following joke. "How many college faculty does it take to change a light bulb?" The answer: "Change?") If elementary and secondary educators change pedagogy too often, college educators perhaps do not change often enough, although the latter have tended to enjoy far greater success at what they do. For all the criticism that trendy K-12 reformers heap on stodgy college professors, I would only point out that it is America's higher educational institutions, not its little red schoolhouses, that are the envy of the world.

As a nation we now spend close to a half-trillion dollars annually on elementary and secondary education. The great bulk of this (over 90 percent) are monies spent by states and localities, which traditionally have had the primary responsibility for carrying out the education function in the United States, although the federal government has become a growing source of funding, contributing hundreds of billions of dollars since the U.S. Elementary and Secondary Education Act was passed in 1965. All told, between 1960 and 2000, the cost of education increased more than eightfold; allowing for inflation, there is general agreement that real school spending has roughly tripled since 1960. The U. S. Department of Education estimates that real per pupil expenditures went from an average of $2,235 in 1960 to $7,591 by 2000. Yet there has been relatively little to show for this outlay of money. In 1983, the National Commission on Excellence in Education that had been appointed by U.S. Secretary of Education Terrel Bell released the now famous *A Nation at Risk* report, painting a grim picture of an educational wasteland and issuing a challenge for America's schools to improve their performance. In 1990, at the Charlottesville Summit on Education, which brought together governors, corporate executives, and other leaders, the pledge was made that "by the year 2000, all children in America will start school ready to learn,…students will leave [school] having demonstrated competence in challenging subject matter, including English, mathematics, science, history, and geography,…[and] U.S. students will be the first in the world in science and mathematics." A new millennium is here, and we are still waiting for these goals to be realized or for evidence that we are even on the proper course.

One can find apologists for the K-12 establishment claiming that our schools are much better than critics say. Read, for example, Gerald Bracey's reports "On the Condition of Public Education" that appear regularly in *Phi Delta Kappan*, or the work of David Berliner and Bruce Biddle, whose 1995 *The Manufactured Crisis: The Myths, Fraud, and the Attack on America's Public Schools* manufactured evidence contrary to the conventional wisdom. These individuals seem to be in denial. They are certainly in the minority. The critics have pretty good data on their side that suggest we have been going down a slippery slope for quite some time. Note the following:

- "The [latest] National Assessment of Educational Progress [NAEP, the authoritative standardized test often called "the nation's report card"] reports that 38 percent of fourth-grade students do not even attain 'basic' achievement levels in reading. In math, 38 percent of eighth graders score below basic level, as do 43 percent of twelfth graders in science."

- "As the pupil-teacher ratio has gone down almost 40 percent from 1955 to 1999 and class sizes have shrunk accordingly, student achievement [in many areas] has not only failed to rise, but has dropped, almost in inverse ratio to the size of the educational staff. In science, for instance, where we have NAEP scores going back to 1969, 12th grade achievement has dropped from an average score of 309 to 296 after almost thirty years."

- "[On the NAEP] all three age groups [nine, thirteen, and seventeen] made small gains in reading from 1971 to 1999.… Nine year olds' 1999 scores were below those of 1980.… Thirteen year olds…scored the same in 1999 as they had in 1980.… Seventeen year olds' scores peaked in 1988 and suffered a small decline in the 1990s.… The 1990s do not stand out as a time of great strides forward in academic achievement."

- "In the Third International Math and Science Study (TIMSS) [in 1995], a worldwide competition among twenty-one nations, [the U.S. Department of Education reported that] 'U.S. twelfth graders performed below the international average and among the lowest of the 21 TIMSS countries on the assessment of mathematical general knowledge.'... The American students scored nineteenth out of the twenty-one nations, doing so poorly in math that they only outperformed teenagers from two underdeveloped countries, Cyprus and South Africa." "In December 2000, the Department of Education released findings based on a 1999 repeat of the TIMMS study" that showed a continuing tendency for the United States to be "the only country whose children 'get dumber' the longer they're in school."

- "The annual [bipartisan] Public Agenda poll for 1998... reported that employers and college professors who teach freshmen are disenchanted with the graduates coming out of today's high schools. Almost two-thirds of the employers and 76 percent of the professors surveyed indicated that a high school diploma is no guarantee that a student has learned the basics. Nearly seven in ten employers feel that graduates aren't ready for work, and more than half of the university professors think that those graduates aren't ready for college. High school graduates, according to employers and college professors, rank fair to poor in the following areas: grammar and spelling, essay writing, basic math skills, and work habits like being organized and on time."

- "In 1995, 78 percent of America's colleges offered [remedial] classes, up from 73 percent in 1988.... At [the City University of New York in 1995-96] 46 percent of students entering four-year colleges failed one or more of the placement examinations in reading, writing, and math. At the California State University System, about half the freshmen need such classes to acclimate themselves to the rigors of academia.... Harvard and Yale offer peer tutoring and a writing center. At the University of Chicago, a handful of students are directed each year to a course called essential mathematics that begins with arithmetic, algebra and geometry—comparable to the remedial course at CUNY."

- "From 1967 to 1997, the average composite SAT score fell in the United States. The drop was pronounced between 1967 and 1980, and then shows a partial recovery since. The math scores have risen more than verbal scores, which still languish well below the levels observed in 1967."

As is commonly noted, there are lies, damn lies, and statistics. I do not, however, believe the above statistics are lies or damn lies. I have personally witnessed as parent and professor the reality they describe. And I'm talking about some of the *better* schools; the horror stories I have accumulated cannot begin to compare with those that could be told by the parents of children attending inner-city schools.

It may well be that there has never been any golden era of educational excellence in America, that the neverending story has been one of trial and error which has produced mostly error. But my own sense is that we are even further away from a golden era today than when I was a grade schooler growing up in the 1950s and 1960s. Perhaps I am guilty of a misplaced nostalgia in thinking back fondly about my school experiences compared to my children's. However, today's educational gurus who are reinventing the contemporary school are guilty of something far more dangerous than misplaced nostalgia about the past. They are guilty of misplaced faith about what they see as the future. Mark Twain once said "faith is believin' in what you know ain't true." Today's progressives are true believers who bring a jihad-like fervor to their mission that exceeds even that of John Dewey, their patron saint. They are no closer to finding the Holy Grail than their predecessors, but they are closer to convincing themselves, and others, they have. In what I call The Great American Education War, which is the latest chapter in the neverending story, they have a take-no-prisoners, no-quarter mentality. Why do I say this?

The Core of the Problem

School administrators and school boards are big on mission statements. If I—or, I dare say, most parents—were writing a simple K-12 mission statement, it would go something like this: (1) The primary mission of all schools (public or private) is academic preparation. (2) The primary goal of all schools must be academic excellence. (3) Academic excellence is achieved by giving those individual students who have demonstrated the capacity and willingness to work hard and do advanced work the fullest opportunity to do so. (4) These principles are totally consistent with principles of fairness, ethics, and democracy, i.e., equity. As self-evident as these precepts might seem, they are clearly at odds with current fashion in education.

The basic problem is twofold. First, there is an inadequate focus on academics in our schools—there is a growing "social" mission of schools as they are increasingly assuming functions traditionally performed by family, church, and other institutions, well beyond any previous mission creep. Second, to the extent academics are still the stuff of schooling today, there is systemic collapse of standards occurring—nobody is escaping "the leveller's axe."

Although criticisms of school reformers for promoting academic dumbing-down and distractions are hardly unprecedented, what is different and more worrisome today is that the current reform movement, spearheaded by schools of education, has a sharper edge than in the past. Diane Ravitch, the distinguished educational historian, has documented how throughout the twentieth century our schools assumed that many children could not handle intellectual activity and how progressive educators often were the worst culprits in watering down the academic curriculum. She notes, though, that prior to the 1950s such thinking was limited mainly to the bottom 20 percent or so of the school-age population. What she calls "the great meltdown" occurred after World War II, when the minimal expectations attached to the bottom were extended to the vast middle segment as well—another 60 percent of all students, who were steered away from serious academics toward "life adjustment" course work—provoking an outpouring of Sputnik-era criticisms of public education of the sort I cited. As Ravitch comments, "what had begun as an effort directed at students who were unmotivated and indifferent to academic studies turned into a movement to reconstruct the curriculum for everyone." Only a small, highly selective group of students thought to be of college material were to be spared. In my judgment, a second "great meltdown" is now occurring that extends to the remaining 20 percent—the very top tier of students, including the most gifted. It is occurring as a perverted response to the *Nation at Risk* report and to the century-long failure of American schools to educate the country's children. And it is threatening not only K-12 children but higher education as well.

What is also worrisome is that there is a stronger momentum

behind progressivism today, propelled partly by new technologies and partly by new cultural values.

Two Double-Edged Swords

The main technological developments that are driving the current round of school reform are the Internet and the associated computer applications. Although this technology, with its awesome information-processing power, clearly offers many potential benefits in the education field, it also has a negative side insofar as many reformers have been deluded into seeing it as a quick-fix *deus ex machina* for realizing much of the centuries-old, yet-unfulfilled progressive dream of "every child his or her own Socrates." It is being hyped as giving instant access to resources heretofore denied to masses of students (even though well-stocked public libraries have existed in the poorest neighborhoods in America for decades), as freeing up teachers from teaching mundane subjects and students from learning them (even though spell-check, grammar-check, and other such crutches threaten to create even more of the "dependent learners" that the progressives rail against), and as helping to foster a "community of scholars" (even though one is hard pressed to identify anything more impersonal than on-line chat rooms and more anti-intellectual than relying on the click-click of a mouse to "access" knowledge rather than trying to store some of it in one's head).

Just as technological developments are a double-edged sword in regard to education, so also are recent cultural developments in American society. On the one hand, there is little doubt that the 1960s were a watershed era in moving American democracy forward both in terms of *egalitarianism*—expanding the rights of minorities through the civil rights movement that created greater opportunities for blacks, women, and other historically discriminated groups to participate more fully in the political and economic life of the country—and *individual freedom*—in terms of maximizing opportunities for freedom of expression particularly. On the other hand, we are still living with the excesses of the sixties. In place of the kind of reasoned, balanced commitment to individual liberty and equality that one can find, say, in the writings of Thomas Jefferson and many of the Founding Fathers (slavery aside), today's keepers of the liberal tradition are characterized by a fusion of *radical libertarianism* and *radical egalitarianism* that harkens back to Woodstock. While sixties liberalism has faded somewhat as an ideology, it remains dominant in education circles. In higher education, it has given us postmodernism, which argues that there is no such thing as facts or knowledge, only perceptions based on personal circumstances, all of which are deserving of equal respect. In K-12 education, it has given us the self-indulgent, nonjudgmental classroom, where rigor and merit are now considered four-letter words, for fear of stifling personal creativity or favoring one student over another.

In this sense, the current education war is part of the larger culture war. We have not only dumbed down education, but, as just-retired Senator Daniel Moynihan has said, "we have defined deviancy down" in terms of no longer being capable of shock or shame in our public morality. The new depths to which we have fallen are revealed in the recent lament by the coeditor of *MAD* who, in accounting for the magazine's plunging circulation, commented that "Mad has become mainstream. Either that or society has sunk to our level." It is dangerous to generalize about such things but this much can be said: Whereas previous younger generations eventually outgrew their adolescent behavior, the boomers who now comprise the cultural elite never did; the only thing they are judgmental about is censuring those who say grown-ups should set an example for kids. There is the growing phenomenon of "generational blur," as adults vie with teenagers to see who can be the most hip, whether in the form of casual attire, casual language, or casuistry. What we are left with, then, is the threat posed by intellectual and moral relativism—nihilism—as we now have virtually no standards of either scholarship or ethics. (The horrors perpetrated by Osama bin Laden in 2001 may arouse the nation to a higher, clearer and more coherent purpose, but it is too soon to evaluate the long-range impact of this tragedy on our culture or our educational system.)

The controversial 1999 movie *Pleasantville* satirized the 1950s as an era that overemphasized order, conformity, discipline, routine, deference to authority, and other such traditional values, while it celebrated the 1990s as a post-Woodstock era that was more open to diversity and do-your-own-thing self-expression. As it relates to K-12 education, the movie presented a false dichotomy. It should be obvious that kids need *both* structure (well-defined rules of conduct, good work habits, and the like, however constraining these might be) *and* freedom (opportunity to exercise their imaginations and engage in personal discovery). This should be a no-brainer, but it seems to have escaped today's educators. A colleague of mine once cogently remarked that the main purpose of education is to learn to cope with ambiguity, by which he meant not the absence of truth but its complexity. This point was nicely expressed by F. Scott Fitzgerald's famous statement: "The test of a first-rate intelligence is the ability to hold two opposing ideas in the mind at the same time and still be able to function." Progressives are failing the test badly. They seem incapable of contemplating, in the same breath, rigor and creativity, memorization and understanding, or any other concepts that may seem at odds with each other but in fact are quite compatible and mutually reinforcing. The very folks who preach to the rest of us about diversity and inclusion, it turns out, are themselves often guilty of the worst sort of dogmatic, rigid, black-and-white thinking. In instituting the latest reforms, they seem hell-bent on throwing out the baby with the bath water. It is a shame because they have many good ideas, were they tempered by traditionalist caution and openness to competing beliefs.

The Need for Greater Dialogue

In *1984*, George Orwell warned of a future where authorities would force people to accept as truths certain ideas that were patently and absurdly false, such as slogans that read "war is peace, freedom is slavery, and ignorance is strength." Nowhere is Orwellian thinking more in evidence today than in K-12 education, where absolute nonsense propagated by progressives bent on revolutionizing our schools is the norm. Witness the following examples of commonly articulated slogans in America's classrooms that defy common sense and turn logic on its head, yet are being thrust upon parents, children, and, indeed, rank-and-file teachers by K-12 elites who are now shaping curricula nationwide: "less is more" (i.e., the less coverage of history and other subject matter, and the less drill and practice, the more knowledgeable and skilled one becomes); "teachers should not teach" (i.e., the less direct instruction a child receives, the more profound his or her education); "homework is not necessarily done at home" (i.e., homework can just as well be done in class at school); "all children are gifted" (i.e., all kids are not just above average but exactly to the same degree). Orwell would have a field day in today's classroom because what he called "doublespeak" can be found in schools everywhere.

The ultimate Orwellian turn is that the same K-12 leadership which insists there are no right or wrong answers when it comes to children's work simultaneously claims a monopoly of wisdom for itself any time a parent dares to question the reigning ortho-doxy. As proof, just try asking your local school officials sometime "whatever happened to teaching the basics?" If my own experi-ence is any guide, you will usually get arrogant responses that betray a certain defensiveness. I can recall, for example, when a concerned parent a few years ago tried to organize a support group called "Parents and Teachers for Academic Basics" in response to what was felt to be inadequate attention to spelling, computation, and other basic skills at a Clayton elementary school. The school and district leadership dismissed the com-plaints as the inaccurate perceptions of that individual and a handful of malcontents, despite the fact that several dozen parents packed the meeting room on an icy night in the dead of winter when the PTO took up the matter. The parent organizer was con-demned by at least one member of the school staff as a disruptive force who was trying to further his own career as an education consultant, all because he was engaged in such subversive and self-promoting activity as proposing an open house session on "The Seven Habits of Highly Successful Spellers."

I saw then the divide-and-conquer strategy that administra-tors use to stifle criticism, as they try to make you as a parent think you are the *only* one who has a complaint. If a parent cites a specific example of a questionable classroom practice one's child has been exposed to, that parent is usually told that it is an aber-rant, isolated case, and that few other parents share the concern. If a parent then tries to discuss general educational philosophy, administrators will admonish the parent for engaging in vague atmospherics. This is a game that gets played constantly, one that is always played on the educators' home court, which means that parents have great difficulty winning. Another game that gets played is the tendency for school administrators to respond to parental concerns with glib non-sequiturs. For example, in response to the aforementioned question "whatever happened to teaching the basics?" you likely will hear some gobbledygook about how "we are going forward with basics, not back." In place of the 3 Rs, we get PR.

Just as progressives have challenged longstanding conventional wisdom about what works in education, at times offering useful insights, progressives themselves should be willing to have a wider dialogue that permits questioning of their own favorite bromides. Instead, there is an incredibly closed circle of "experts" today residing in schools of education and other high places from which curriculum fads emanate, who reinforce each other's predispositions as to what constitutes "best practices." The term "best practices," often invoked in defense of progressive pedagogy, has a certain imperious ring to it, calculated to be a conversation-stopper whenever a parent or any outsider, not versed in the *au courant* methodology of the in-crowd, raises issues. Often it takes small children to reveal the obvious and make us aware that the emperor has no clothes, when they come home from school and report in their unsophisticated but nonetheless perceptive way that less is not more, that all children in the class are not equally able, and that other rhetoric in which the latest best practices are clothed does not square with reality. Children should not have to perform this role. We should all be more willing to question and debate the direction schooling in America is going in. More people are asking questions, as the subject of education is becoming increasingly contentious, but the answers remain elusive.

3

For Whom the School Bell Tolls: The Clash Between Excellence and Equity

The debate that underlies and overlaps almost all the other debates in The Great American Education War is the clash between excellence and equity. I have said that a second "great meltdown" in education is now occurring. The first, in the 1950s, brought students of average proficiency down to the level of the least proficient. The subsequent one, which was underway by the 1970s but did not really reach fever until the 1980s, now threatens to cut the best and the brightest down to size as well. The progressive reformers who are now remaking our schools probably count as one of their heroes Roman Hruska, the former U.S. Senator from Nebraska. In 1969, Hruska made one of the most infamous comments in American political history when he tried to make the best case for Senate approval of President Richard Nixon's nomination of an obscure, second-rate jurist named Harold Carswell to the U.S. Supreme Court. Acknowledging that Carswell was not a great legal mind, Hruska nonetheless insisted that "mediocre people are entitled to representation too."

Unfortunately, the Hruska mentality is precisely the dominant ethos now permeating American public schools, in a radical egalitarian ideological agenda that translates into what E.D. Hirsch has aptly called "educational populism." "Class warfare" has taken on new meaning as America's classrooms are literally pitting academic haves vs. academic have-nots. There can be a tension between, on the one hand, seeking to maintain the highest standards and provide academic challenge for gifted students and, on the other hand, seeking to make education more responsive to the needs of slow learners, children with learning disabilities, various minorities, and others who have not always been served well by the ways schools have functioned in the past. We should be trying to resolve this tension in a manner that helps both the more able and less able, but that is not what we are doing.

Today's progressives are not content to insist that society has an obligation to educate all kids, that the school bell tolls for all our children from the least educable to the most educable, and that we must do our best to provide a rich academic experience for each child. They go well beyond this noble principle, maintaining that they can meet the needs of *all* students, ranging from the highest achieving to the lowest achieving, in the same classroom using the exact same pedagogy. When confronted by skeptics, progressives fall back on the cliché that they believe in "individualizing" instruction putting different teaching styles in synch with different learning styles, aiming at "high standards" for everybody. But in a typical classroom of twenty to thirty students, how feasible is this? Inevitably, it is the bottom, not the top, that is driving the curriculum, as schools have moved away from merit-based ability-grouping toward heterogeneous grouping and lowest-common-denominator education.

By ability-grouping, let me be clear that I do not mean differentiating instruction based on the degree to which a student has shown extraordinary potential as measured, say, by I.Q. tests. Rather, I mean differentiation based on the degree to which a student has performed according to some combination of intelligence, motivation, and effort. Progressives like to cite Albert Einstein and Thomas Edison as examples of minds who did not reveal their brilliance in their early school years. They argue that we cannot afford to overlook "late bloomers" and hence should not prematurely label students as belonging to one ability group or another. Although this may be a reasonable position to take in elementary education, the argument carries less water in secondary education, where it would seem far less justified to ignore individual achievement and to build an entire teaching philosophy around the possibility—as opposed to the fact—of late bloomers (or never bloomers). There will always be some late bloomers, including high school dropouts—an example is Leon Uris, the author of *Exodus* and other notable novels, who never made it out of my alma mater, Baltimore City College High School—but our schools should not be obsessed with this population.

A double standard is at work. It is considered unfair to focus resources at the top, on gifted education (indeed, it is considered heresy to even utter the term "gifted" today in some professional education circles), yet it is quite acceptable to shunt resources to the bottom—to have special pull-out programs and resource rooms for students needing remediation or special aides for "full inclusion" students who are placed in regular classrooms despite having severe physical or learning disabilities. It is important to pay attention to students at the bottom. Many children with learning problems for too long were overlooked by our education systems. But why shortchange the top, or for that matter the middle, by insisting on all students going through the curriculum together in lock-step fashion even if some may be bored silly in the process? Why do the apostles of diversity insist on a one-size-fits-all classroom?

The message being sent loudly and clearly by the current generation of educators is that, if a parent is interested in true academic excellence, then the public schools are not for you; for that kind of excellence, you must send your child to a private school. (While many private schools have also bought into educational populism, there are still some that can be found with highly selective admission criteria and extraordinarily demanding curricula.) This message is dangerous for democracy in that it threatens to create a two-tiered education system. Progressives are the worst enemies of the public schools, because, if they have their way, the exodus of the best and the brightest from the nation's public schools will only accelerate, and the widespread public perception that public schools are places of mediocrity rather than excellence will only deepen and we will continue the spectacle of politicians pandering to public schools while sending their own children to private ones. The public schools must stand for excellence no less than private schools, or they are finished. Reformers need to ask themselves how it is that, where once it was understood in many cities that the finest education available for rich and poor alike was to be found not at a private institution but at a public institution (such as City HS in Baltimore or Bronx Science HS in New York), today it is the rare community that can make that claim. There are many explanations for the decline of public schools relative to independent schools, but none is more powerful than the misplaced egalitarianism that altered the image of the former in the public mind.

I have asked the following question over and over again of educators who are leading the "equity" movement: Could you please tell me what is inequitable, unfair, unjust, immoral, anti-democratic, or elitist about giving those students who have demonstrated the capacity and willingness to do advanced work the fullest opportunity to do so? The only answer I ever get is one worthy of kindergarteners: We aim to challenge all children. The bottom line is that each child (white or black, male or female, disabled or not) deserves to be challenged and given the opportunity to *maximize* his or her potential. To do otherwise is to undermine both excellence *and* equity.

One can see the clash between equity and excellence, and how the one often ill serves the other, in the Blue Ribbon Schools Program operated by the U.S. Department of Education since 1982, which has awarded some 4,000 public schools Blue Ribbons as "models of excellence and equity." A recent Brookings Institution report, examining awards given in 1999 to seventy schools in seven states (and adjusting for socioeconomic differences in the school populations), found that "only nineteen of these seventy Blue Ribbon elementary schools score in the top 10 percent of similar schools in their respective states [on state math and reading achievement tests]" while "seventeen schools score in the bottom 50 percent....[In other words,] about one-fourth of these schools can honestly claim that their Blue Ribbon stands for academic excellence." Perhaps we should not be surprised that these schools do not stand for academic excellence, since the application procedures for the award play down not only excellence but also academics. Among the criteria schools must address are "How does the culture of your school support the learning of all its members and foster a caring community?" and "How does your school promote a healthy peer climate among students?" As the author of the Brookings study, a former public school teacher and later Harvard professor, commented, "It's a feel-good program." The distribution of ribbons is becoming something akin to the gold stars or smiley-face decals given out with equal generosity by teachers to kids. Eventually almost every school will qualify, if it is willing to go through the motions of filing the necessary paperwork and documenting its political correctness. That the Blue Ribbon Schools Program is supposed to help identify and reward "exemplary" schools is a glowing commentary on how standards of excellence have fallen.

An Assistant Superintendent's Support for "Mass Excellence" (and Other Memories)

All schools in our Clayton school district have won the Blue Ribbon issued by the U.S. Department of Education. And all students are considered blue ribbon students. I say this because I actually heard the assistant superintendent for curriculum in Clayton, the ardent progressive thinker I mentioned earlier, once comment at a public meeting that she disagreed with my argument that "mass excellence" is an oxymoron and that you cannot have a school district of distinction without *some* distinctions. That meeting, which occurred on December 7, 1992, was called by the district leadership in response to complaints from a number of parents who were concerned about the recent anti-ability grouping trends in the district, including the creation of an "enrichment" program that made no differentiation between gifted students and learning-disabled students. The timing of the meeting, on the anniversary of Pearl Harbor, was purely coincidental, although I did use the occasion to offer as an example of how some students have a greater grasp of history than others the fact that one of my son's fifth grade classmates, when the teacher mentioned the bombing of Pearl Harbor, asked "Was she hurt?" The assistant superintendent, with her endorsement of the concept of mass excellence, essentially took the view that you can put kids whose I.Q.s range from 70 to 130 in the same classroom and not miss a beat in terms of the level of education going on.

Some of those in our parents group took to calling ourselves Parents Against Average Schools (PAAS). (When African-American parents later began a support group called Parents of African-American Students [PAAS], our group was accused of being racially insensitive, even though we had prior claim to the acronym.) I guess we were what the educational theorist Alfie Kohn has called "Volvo Vigilantes." Kohn, an exemplar of progressive education, used that term derisively to describe pushy parents in an article entitled "Only For My Kid: How Privileged Parents Undermine School Reform," published in the April 1998 issue of *Phi Delta Kappan*, a widely read professional K-12 journal. In the article, Kohn spoke out strongly against honors courses, ability-grouping, grading, standardized testing, and anything else that reflected a commitment to standards. Any parent who demanded such things was presumed to be by definition either a racist or plutocrat or, more disastrously, in some kind of coalition with the "Christian right." Kohn is not a wild-eyed radical on the extreme fringe of K-12 education; he is considered a mainstream thinker in contemporary education circles, reflected by the fact that a year after the article appeared he was invited to be a featured keynote speaker at such major K-12 gatherings as the annual conventions of the National Council of Teachers of English and the National Association of School Superintendents.

Kohn and the K-12 intelligentsia believe that folks like me and the other parents who showed up at the December 1992 meeting are responsible for the plight of the public schools, since we resist many of the latest progressive reforms. (Those parents in attendance included the dean of the school of engineering, the head of the drama department, the chair of the neurology department in the medical school, and other respected educators at Washington University, as well as educators at other local universities, physicians, lawyers, and other "privileged" types.) *We* are the problem—the parents who read to our kids regularly, who show up faithfully at parent-teacher conferences, and who dare to take the word "education" seriously. I found out about the Kohn piece when a Clayton social studies teacher, knowing of my role in PAAS, called to tell me jokingly, "Marty, I saw a reference to you in a *Kappan* publication." To me, it was no laughing matter. I was so enraged by Kohn's argument that I wrote a rebuttal entitled "What's It All About, Alfie?: A Parent-Educator's Response to Alfie Kohn," which *Phi Delta Kappan*, much to my surprise and delight, agreed to publish. In my article, I stated the following:

> I am one of those "privileged" parents, to use Kohn's term, one of the "robber barons" of the school system. According to Kohn, I didn't work for anything I have—not my 13-year-old auto with 150,000 miles on the odometer [it is not even a Volvo], my $200,000 home mortgage (a debt owed because my wife and I thought our children's education was important enough to justify the move to Clayton no matter how broke it left us), or any other earthly belongings Kohn feels are immoral.

> My kids are "privileged," too. My older son, as a debater at Clayton High, got up at the crack of dawn almost every Saturday morning (while most kids were still sleeping, in preparation for a tough day at the mall), lugged crates of research evidence he had meticulously gathered at university libraries during the week, and boarded a bus to take him and his intellectually curious peers to such well-known haunts of the rich and famous as Festus, Missouri....

> The concept of *earning* through hard *work* the right to be in an honors class is foreign to Kohn. If "Volvo vigilante" parents are pressuring school administrators to accept into honors courses

[their] kids who would not otherwise qualify, the solution is not to eliminate all honors courses, as Kohn proposes, but rather to summon the courage and integrity to enforce standards. If you give every student the *same* exam and apply the *same* standard to each in order to determine admission to an honors course, how is that discrimination? How is that a "privilege" or a "perk"?...

Kohn, the self-appointed voice of the people, ignores the bipartisan Public Agenda surveys that report year after year that an overwhelming majority of Americans support ability grouping. Any 10-year-old can understand the logic, wisdom, and *justice* of merit-based education, but it seems to have escaped Kohn. It makes about as much sense to put an intellectually gifted child into the same math or English or science class with a low-to-average student as it would be to put Kohn or most human beings on the same basketball court with Michael Jordan. Would we expect Michael's game to improve as a result of playing against Alfie? Do we really think Michael would gain leadership, sensitivity, and team-building skills as a result of working with Alfie?

Indeed, it was so nonsensical that Kohn was selected in 1998 for the annual "Goofy" award given each year by PAAS for the most bizarre idea or practice appearing in the K-12 field in the previous twelve months. When I started the awards in the early 1990s, little did I realize just how difficult our job as judges would prove to be, given the dozens of kooky things that were to become a regular feature of the K-12 scene. The Goofys were every bit as competitive as the Grammys, Emmys, Oscars, and other contests.

A local Goofy winner in Clayton was a Clayton High English teacher who, in 1996, had her class write condensations of a literary work which were then sent to *Cliff Notes*, complete with the famed yellow covers that adorn the cheatsheets for lazy students, oblivious to the fact that she effectively was encouraging her charges to associate themselves with perhaps the single greatest symbol of the dumbing-down of higher education in recent American history. Around that same time, Villanova University was taking the lead among institutions of higher learning in banning *Cliff Notes* from the campus book store, noting that students needed to do "serious critical and original thinking, rather than working with simplistic study aids" and that "anything we can do to...discourage a notion that you can capture truth in 20 pages is very important." Not to worry. Villanova students could obtain the notes from either the national publisher or, in a pinch, by contacting Clayton High School. I was not sure what was worse, that Clayton High was encouraging students to use *Cliff Notes* or perpetrating the production of them. I expressed outrage at a school board meeting that our high school would be an accomplice to academic fraud and, moreover, would go so far as to publicize the project in the local newspaper, where it was praised by the editor of Cliff Notes, Inc. I was told by the superintendent that my comments were in bad taste, but apparently not the school district's legitimization of a publishing enterprise whose "sole purpose," as admitted by the National Education Association, "is to help a kid get through a course and fake it."

What was odd was that Clayton High School justly enjoyed a reputation as an outstanding academic institution, known for strong honors and advanced placement (AP) courses. In some years, over 10 percent of the senior class were recognized as National Merit Scholars based on their performance on the Scholastic Aptitude Test (SAT) exams, a remarkable achievement. In my younger son's graduating class of only 160 students, six students gained admission to Stanford, and many others were accepted by other Ivy League-quality schools. The *Cliff Notes* episode was, however, symptomatic of the changing mores of the K-12 culture that were beginning to infect even Clayton and that had occasioned the formation of PAAS and had led numerous parents to start raising concerns about the direction in which the district was going. That the *Cliff Notes* project was done in a non-honors class was a sad commentary on the lowered expectations for those students; that such a mentality might take hold in honors classes as well was all the more alarming.

Our assistant superintendent was a kindred spirit of Alfie Kohn. As she put it to me once, there should be as little "institutional sorting" as possible. This was certainly the pot calling the kettle black. Apparently, institutional sorting was okay when progressives engaged in bean-counting to engineer diversity in classrooms—assuring the same distribution of students by race, gender, and other ascribed characteristics in each room—but it was not okay when traditionalists engaged in merit-based ability grouping to create a fast track for the academically more able. Telling me in a letter that "we must consider side effects of ability grouping which limit its usefulness," she made it sound as if the honors program was some kind of caste system that assigned kids to different levels of education based on birth or which side of the tracks they lived on, rather than being achievement-oriented. I always felt that had she had been able to dictate the curriculum of the district, that would have meant the end of the honors courses at the high school. She and like-minded Clayton staff knew, however, that many parents of high-achieving children had drawn a line in the sand over this issue and that any attempt to eliminate the honors program risked a blood bath in the community. If the demise of the honors program were to occur, it would not be through outright termination, which nobody had the guts to try, but through death by a thousand cuts in the form of a gradual attrition of standards.

As time went on, I witnessed, if not a thousand cuts, at least several dozen. I and others in Clayton had to resign ourselves to the virtual elimination of ability-grouping in the three elementary schools and Wydown Middle School except for token efforts. The "enrichment" program that Clayton created in 1992 signaled the lack of commitment of the school district to gifted education. The program called for a skeleton staff to serve the highest and lowest performing students alike through supplemental instruction a few hours during the week. When some parents on the committee asked why Clayton was not choosing to apply for and take advantage of state funds allocated specifically for gifted education, district officials responded that it would be difficult to distinguish gifted from non-gifted students and that, in any event, the identical teaching strategies that worked for accelerated learners could also be used for those needing remediation. One parent, a respected lawyer, did his best to point out the absurdity of this viewpoint but was rebuffed and ultimately lodged his protest by refusing to sign the final committee report. Other parents on the committee, thrown a bone of having two persons per building added as support staff rather than the one-and-a-half originally proposed, decided to cave in. Any parent who has seen "enrichment" in action knows that it normally amounts to little more than extra busywork "activities" done either alone or with peers, billed in sugarcoated fashion as "independent study." Given the scarce resources directly targeted at gifted education in Clayton, this is what we had to settle for.

The principal of Clayton's Captain Elementary School in the 1990s was also an Alfie Kohn clone, signified by her comments in her "Captain's Log" newsletter of February 1991, which heralded a new philosophy she had just been exposed to at a conference she had attended with our assistant superintendent: "All students will need to develop the high-level math and communications skills we now make available to only those students we consider the most able. This will require a major shift in the way we think about ability and we approach instruction....Major components of the instructional program [will] include heterogeneous rather than homogeneous grouping." She was denigrating not only rigid *tracking* (that is, segregation of students by steering them into wholly distinct career or curricular paths), something Clayton and most school districts had long since done away with, but also flexible subject-by-subject *ability-grouping*. Note her implied assumption that raising the bar for the bottom, certainly a worthwhile goal, was mutually exclusive with continuing to raise the bar for the top. I had heard the same exact premise articulated at Delmar-Harvard Elementary School in U. City a few years earlier. The education "gap" had to be closed, even if it was by holding the top students down.

A similar assumption seemed to be at work when Clayton recently implemented a new math curriculum in K-8 that was gaining popularity nationally. Called "fuzzy math" by critics because the curriculum played down the importance of computation skills and getting the right answer, its original developers explicitly acknowledged it was aimed particularly at students with math phobias who needed to be shown how math could be made fun and interesting. But instead of being used exclusively with this group, it became the standard math program for all Clayton students in the early grades, math whizzes and math phobes alike. Although the curriculum did encourage some higher-order skills, its main appeal was its promise to relieve the pain and suffering of those at the low end of the academic spectrum (for example, by allowing kids to use calculators instead of having to learn their multiplication tables or perform long division). One of my sons' math teachers at Clayton High School—he taught the most advanced math courses there and was considered one of the intellectual giants of the school—confessed to me that "the pervasive spirit of egalitarianism at our elementary and middle schools make for many genuinely frustrated (sometimes angry) parents whose high school children are unable to compete successfully 'as before.'" What he meant was that kids were being stroked so much in K-8 that parents were misled into believing that all their offspring were honors students and hence were frequently upset upon learning they had not been recommended for the more advanced offerings at the high school which had certain admissions criteria.

The quality of the high school honors program itself was being threatened by a number of other developments. When Clayton High School eliminated the lowest, remedial set of courses in many fields of study in the early 1990s, leaving the honors/AP courses and a somewhat less demanding but still rigorous college prep set of courses, this put increased pressure on the honors/AP program since many parents of average children understandably did not wish to see their children placed in what used to be middle-level courses but which were suddenly now the bottom rung that included the most severely learning-disabled and behavior-disordered children. Parents increasingly were tempted to use the district's "override" policy whereby you could insist that your child be placed in an honors course no matter how questionable the child's grades or teacher recommendation or capacity to do the work. The question remained whether the honors courses could maintain their integrity as demanding academic challenges when growing numbers of students were entering who seemed likely to water down expectations and standards. The district could claim it was adding more honors courses at the high school, but what good were these if the standards were being compromised? Even worse, there was talk of possibly eliminating at least a few of the honors courses altogether.

The high school social studies department actually did eliminate a couple of advanced courses in favor of heterogeneously grouped courses. In 1992, the decision was made to convert a select "college credit" American Government course to a mixed-ability course where the teacher had students using different textbooks and doing differing assignments of varying degrees of difficulty depending on whether they were pursuing the college credit option or not. It was like a three-ring circus, as the teacher was somehow expected to do a juggling act and teach to the top, middle, and bottom all at once! A year earlier, Sophomore Honors Western Civilization fell victim to a new two-year U.S. and World History sequence, designed to enable students to learn simultaneously about happenings in North America, Europe, Africa, and other continents circa 1700, 1848, and other time periods. The move away from Western Civilization to World History was motivated by a convergence of political-correctness factors—bowing to equity concerns relating to slow learners as well as to multicultural concerns relating to the "Eurocentric" bias of the traditional curriculum.

Because the high school had decided to cram the history of the entire world into a single course package, it meant they had to shift some of the most important "stuff" of Western Civilization—the study of Ancient Greece and Rome—down to Wydown Middle School. This raised the prospect of Clayton kids having "experiential learning" units in which they dressed up in toga costumes and wrote journals on what a day in the life of Plato must have been like. Progressive efforts at reforming the middle school in Clayton, like most places, drew on the latest research showing that most kids, especially slower learners who could not handle abstract concepts, benefited from "situational learning" and "hands-on" activities which brought the ideas home to them through personal experience. I saw this pedagogy at work at the high school as well, in the heterogeneously grouped U.S. and World History course, where my son was asked to do a "Building Assignment" calling for him to "choose a building you consider a special place in your neighborhood or community," "produce a photograph or sketch of that building," and answer such deep questions as "where is the building? how does this building fit into your community or neighborhood? why is this building a special place for you?"

I criticize these teachers reluctantly since, in truth, most of them (including, for that matter, the authors of the "Cliff Notes" and "Building Assignment" lesson plans) were outstanding educators who found themselves sucked into the dumbed-down currents of the day. I do not want to leave the impression that the Clayton school district has fallen off a precipice and plunged into the abyss, only—as is the case with so many districts—that it has been sliding down a slippery slope. Some parts of the school system, like Sisyphus of Greek legend, gamely keep trying to push the rock back up the mountain. Clayton High School, in particular, thanks to its recent principals, has been trying very hard against the odds to resist the pressures of educational populism and to hold the line on standards, with some success. For example, there are still placement procedures for entering freshmen in first-year honors English, math, and science, although there is a new "Pathfinders" program at the middle school that has introduced race as opposed to achievement into the equation insofar as it is designed to steer

African-American students toward honors courses as "they transition to CHS." In order to deal with the parental override problem, the English department even adopted a policy of requiring all students in honors English courses to maintain at least a B- grade if they wanted to continue in those courses, although what was at first an "ironclad" policy has since been softened by an "elastic clause" that permits waivers under certain circumstances.

The forces of mediocrity remain powerful. The problem became clear to me when a Clayton school board member told me of a conversation that he had recently with the head of the math department. He asked whether the high school still "tracked" in math, that is, placed students in courses of varying difficulty levels based on ability. The math chair responded, "Yes, Marty Rochester won." While I found it gratifying that apparently my battles had paid off, I had to ask myself why it was parents had to *fight* to sustain opportunities for excellence. I did not delude myself into thinking I had achieved any final victory, for I knew there would be an ongoing struggle.

A Spreading Conflict

I have cited numerous examples of the confused state of affairs in Missouri cities where I've lived. But The Great American Education War is not confined to any one theater. It is being fought throughout the United States.

Close to home, in the larger St. Louis metropolitan area, the progressive principal of a high school in Parkway, one of the most respected school districts in the state, called for an "end to honors classes" early in the 1990s, a proposal that failed only due to the strong opposition of outraged parents. In response to an op-ed commentary on the subject I wrote around that time, on "The Dumbing Down of American Education," I heard from many local parents. One of them, in the Pattonville district, a middle-tier school system, described a recent principal's coffee she had attended at her daughter's school: "Most of the time the principal waxed poetic about how all students can achieve equally and how there was no need for any ability-grouping. I was so frustrated I was near tears." In nearby Ladue school district, comparable in reputation to Clayton, one board member was so upset over the relaxation of admission standards for the gifted program that she lamented in the local media "We're trying to be politically correct. Why don't we just let the gifted be gifted?" In at least two other nearby districts, Rockwood and Mehlville, concerned parents have formed gifted and talented student advocacy groups like PAAS which have invited speakers to provide some balance to the anti-ability-grouping drumbeat they hear from their school administrators. I was invited by the Rockwood group to participate on a panel in which I had hoped to debate school district officials, who at the last minute didn't show, obviously unwilling to defend their ideas.

The same leveling trends could be seen statewide, well beyond the St. Louis area. For example, a chief consultant to Missouri's Department of Elementary and Secondary Education proclaimed in 1993 that "the following are non-negotiable: eliminate tracking and ability grouping. All kids should be taught the same thing." Similarly, the Dean of the School of Education at the University of Missouri-Columbia urged that "we must cast aside old notions that there is a trade-off between excellence and equity that must be resolved in favor of excellence.... [We need] uniform expectations for all students." Sounds wonderful, but how do we manage to enforce uniform expectations that are not uniformly low?

The very same day that my "Dumbing Down" article appeared in the local paper, another article appeared entitled "Science Academy: Excellence Need Not Apply," which reported on the decision taken by the Illinois Junior Academy of Science to ban Avery Coonley School from the annual state science fair because "the demanding academic expectations of the school [a private elementary school in Downers Grove that offered a strong traditional program] resulted in the unheard of string of [four consecutive] victories. What is astonishing was the decision...to banish the school from team competition for the next year, on the grounds that their students were 'just too good,' and therefore put the other schools at a distinct and unfair disadvantage." The author of the article noted the absurdity of it all: "Should we limit the University of Chicago professors from receiving any additional Nobel prizes since they have such an unbelievable string of them? ... Should we take the *Chicago Tribune*, the *New York Times*, and other flagship newspapers who continually win all those Pulitzer prizes for journalism out of the competition for awhile so the *Downers Grove Reporter* has a shot at glory?" The headmaster of

Avery Coonley School later moved on to a similar school in Canton, Ohio, the home of the Pro Football Hall of Fame, which, sadly, is more selective in rewarding performance than the Illinois Junior Science Academy.

At the same time the science academy fiasco was occurring, elsewhere in Illinois another strange drama was unfolding, reported in the *Washington Times*: "New Trier Township High School in Winnetka, Ill., with a per-pupil expenditure of $16,500, has been a superb school for 50 years, relying on traditional academic rigor. But...New Trier is on the brink of major change and parents of the school's brightest students are upset. The new school superintendent abolished class rankings and tried to get rid of ability-grouping, which [according to a board member] 'parents fought off.'" I first got wind of this when I met an ex-New Trier parent who had just moved to St. Louis and who had hoped to find refuge from the equity disease in Missouri but instead ended up homeschooling his children. In a subsequent phone interview, another New Trier parent told me that "it took twenty people spending 100 percent of their time to prevent the end of ability-grouping, but the administration was still chipping away at it."

As evidence of how educational populism knows no geographical bounds, witness the recent events in another well regarded school system, the Montgomery County, Maryland school district on the east coast. (This happens to be the school district in which my brother lives. No part of a family is untouched by the education war.) Like New Trier, a number of high schools in this district have abolished class rank, including valedictorian honors for the top student, although not without protest. At the elementary and middle school level, there has been a continuing fight waged by the Montgomery Gifted and Talented Association (GTA) against the adoption of fuzzy math curricula aimed at accommodating low-achieving students. This fight reached a crescendo that touched the high schools in 2000, when a report prepared by consultants hired by the district blamed the district's achievement gap in mathematics between whites and Asians vs. blacks and Hispanics on tracking arrangements that amounted to "racial segregation." One reputable critic denounced the audit for its "fiction in concluding that tracking has caused these gaps" and urged as a solution to the problem that the district target more resources at insuring solid early preparation in math fundamentals for all students—the opposite of the fuzzy math reforms the trendy consultants were proposing in K-8. The consultants ultimately recommended abolishing the high schools' three-tiered placement system, with the parents left to do battle with the administration over what course of action to take. As one GTA parent remarked, "Once again, we are faced with the notion that we cannot let some kids move ahead, even if their ability dictates that, because then we are destroying the egalitarian nature of public education."

On the opposite coast, in California, there are "math wars" going on between some school districts adopting fuzzy math and others retaining a more traditional curriculum that continues to stress strong computation skills. California is the home of Mathematically Correct, a group of parents and educators based in San Diego who for many years have been spearheading the nationwide battle against trendy math. A former UM-St. Louis colleague of mine, Deborah Haimo (Ph.D. in Mathematics from Harvard), a past president of the Mathematics Association of America and currently a professor at the University of California-San Diego, has joined with that parent-educator group to help write state standards in math which reaffirm the traditional curriculum, but this has drawn fire, of course, from self-described reformers. The chair of the state's Math Framework Committee, Haimo e-mailed me in March 2000 that "the reformers are so eager for students to like mathematics that they have distorted the subject completely." Even within districts, different schools are in conflict. For example, in the Santa Monica-Malibu district, Lincoln Middle School uses the traditional approach while John Adams Middle School has switched to the new math. According to one report, the explanation for this is that "John Adams students [representing more Latino and lower-income families] overall have historically scored below Lincoln students on standardized exams, including math, prompting John Adams administrators to embrace new teaching methods considered by some to be more inclusive and fair." As the district math coordinator commented, "the traditional way of teaching math doesn't get to all of those kids at the bottom end." But there is no reason to assume that fuzzy math does either. In fact, what it primarily does, in that time-honored California tradition, is make them "feel good about themselves" and feel also that they shouldn't try hard to make up the ground on the good students.

If present trends continue, there soon will be no refuge left for the high achiever. Take, for example, what is supposed to be the pinnacle of K-12 academic excellence in many school systems—the hallowed "AP" (Advanced Placement) program, which allows mostly seniors to enroll in courses that can carry subsequent college credit if students pass exams administered by the College Board. Where once it was understood that AP courses were reserved for only the very top students, now K-12 leaders, unwilling to leave even one stone unturned in the quest to abolish merit-based ability-grouping, want to open up AP courses eventually to the entire student body. The desire of progressives to do good, and also not to have to worry about making distinctions between academic performers and nonperformers, has been reciprocated by the College Board's catching the equity fever and, also, its desire to collect more test-taking fees. In the rush to see who can outdo whom in destroying standards, the College Board now advertises, on the one hand, that "through AP courses, high school students engage in college-level study and participate in classes that are invariably more rigorous than most high school offerings," yet, on the other hand, that the objective is "to promote access to AP for *all* students [italics mine]." I guess this is supposed to be the culmination of "mass excellence" at work in our schools. I will leave to the reader to ponder how it is possible for a course to be at once the most challenging academic experience a school has to offer, yet at the same time is doable by every last kid in the school.

A Jeffersonian Aristocracy of Merit, or A Democracy of Dunces?

Thomas Jefferson was very much the visionary when he proposed to the Virginia legislature in 1787 that all children be given free elementary education in the 3 Rs at public expense. The best of these students, based on performance, would receive scholarship support to pursue further study all the way to William and Mary College. Through this modest proposal, Jefferson noted wryly, "the best twenty geniuses will be raked from the rubble annually." Jefferson sought to begin to create an "aristocracy of merit" dependent not on heredity and class but smarts and effort. Wealth and privilege admittedly still counted for much in Jefferson's America, and continue to. But he at least had the good sense to understand the concept of meritocracy in a way that today's K-12 leaders, committed to lowest-common-denominator education, do not.

Although higher education in many ways suffers even more from outbreaks of political correctness than K-12, nonetheless public universities increasingly have created special "honors colleges" to serve highly motivated and talented high school graduates. They have recognized the appropriateness of establishing centers of excellence to challenge students who have demonstrated the ability and willingness to do advanced academic work. For example, at my own university the Pierre Laclede Honors College was established in 1989 to "bring together a highly select group of intellectually curious and gifted students." Similar colleges within a college have been started at the University of Michigan, the University of Georgia, and other large state universities. Commenting on "the new honors programs," one magazine notes that "large public universities are the megamalls of higher education. Long aware that they were not adequately serving the needs of the best and the brightest of their students, an increasing number...are attempting to remedy this deficiency by launching honors programs that are the equivalents of educational boutiques. The result: public universities are attracting more and more high-achieving students." One should add that within many multi-campus state university systems, certain campuses have been designated as "*the* premier undergraduate liberal arts college" for the system as a whole, exemplified by little St. Mary's College on Maryland's bucolic eastern shore, which even has its own yacht as part of its special mission. (One wonders whether students can take courses Pass-Sail instead of Pass-Fail!) Then, too, there has been a long tradition of the "public Ivys"—highly selective public institutions. Virginia's College of William and Mary, which became a state school in 1906, is where the Phi Delta Kappa honor society was founded, and (as would do Jefferson proud) by the 1990s had become "the most selective public college in America."

What characterizes all these schools is not a set of perks. If all they offered were lessons in yachting, they could be easily dismissed as elitist. They are distinguished from other public institutions by the *demands* they place on their students. I certainly try to challenge all my students in all my courses, but I know from my own experiences as a faculty member at UM-St. Louis that the level of effort I can expect out of my honors classes is far superior to that which I could extract from my regular classes. It would be hard to find a professor anywhere in America who, if pressed, would not agree with this.

Meanwhile, precollegiate education is moving in exactly the opposite direction, with public schools replacing ability-grouping with heterogeneous grouping. The U.S. Department of Education, in its 1993 study entitled "National Excellence: A Case for Developing America's Talent," confirmed that "the United States is squandering one of its most precious resources—the gifts, talents, and high interests of many of its students." This has been called "the quiet crisis" in K-12 education. The "dirty little secret" might be a more direct way of phrasing it. It is bad enough that gifted programs are being gutted and honor courses are under attack in many school districts. What aggravates the situation is that most districts now promote "full inclusion" classrooms, which are supposed to accommodate the most severely learning-disabled and behavior-disordered alongside the most academically proficient. As Sandra Stotsky, a respected scholar in the language arts field, has said: "The post-Sputnik concerns about the intellectual limitations of the [K-12] curriculum and the needs of the academically motivated student did not have a long shelf life.... Americans rapidly resolved a long-standing ambivalence about educational efforts aimed at academically able students by turning their attention to the other end of the educational spectrum altogether."

What accounts for these opposite philosophies operating in public sector education? There are at least two explanations.

The Power of the Disabilities Movement: A Flawed IDEA

K-12 education is subject to a growing body of federal and state statutes that require a "free appropriate public education" for all children regardless of mental or physical capacity. In 1975, Congress passed the Individuals with Disabilities Education Act (IDEA), requiring states wishing to receive federal assistance not only to demonstrate that they offered free appropriate education for children with disabilities but that they taught these children "in the least restrictive environment," placing them with their non-disabled peers "to the maximum extent appropriate." A 1988 Supreme Court ruling went so far as to bar schools from expelling or removing a disruptive or emotionally disturbed student from class for more than ten days, even to protect others from physical assault, without parental or court permission. This has given parents of disabled children a powerful political and legal lever to use in pursuing their agenda, which has often meant insisting on full inclusion of even the most seriously impaired in a regular classroom for the entire day.

Charles Sykes describes the way in which IDEA has impacted public schools: "Educationists now find themselves in a system in which teachers with little or no training must somehow handle classrooms with students still wearing diapers or fed through tubes. In some cases, math and English teachers have to be prepared to stop their lessons and suction mucus from a child's lungs or deal with a child who kicks, bites, and pummels other students. High schools are forced to cope with students who may urinate on the floor and shred their clothes when frustrated." He cites specific cases: "Nothing prepared Debbie Masnik for the day an emotionally disturbed youngster defecated on his seat and set off a 'near riot' among the class's twelve-year-olds. Other teachers in her school in Fairfax, Virginia were told that they must be prepared to catheterize a paralyzed girl who has also been administratively mainstreamed. In Eden Prairie, Minnesota, a seventh-grade social studies teacher must teach a class of thirty-two children that includes eight low-IQ children, a deaf child with cerebral palsy who can read at only a third grade level, and several gifted children."

Another commentator notes: "Jimmy...is described as 'communicatively handicapped.' In his kindergarten class in Huntington Beach, California, teachers say, he threw chairs, toppled desks, and disrupted class by throwing tantrums. The Ocean View School District wanted to transfer Jimmy to a special-education class. His father said no. The district sued to remove the boy. A county judge temporarily barred Jimmy from class, but a federal judge ordered him readmitted." Still another reports on a high school freshman algebra class in Whittier, California, in which the teacher must cope with an autistic child and a child with Down syndrome; during a class session, one "repeatedly jingles a set of keys" while the other "says he wants to eat and starts crying." The same reporter quotes a special education teacher as lamenting, "It's like saying 'I want my five-foot-two son to play varsity basketball.'"

Just as one can find the occasional 5'3" athlete who can compete with taller hoopsters (e.g., Muggsy Bogues of pro basketball fame), some full inclusion classrooms work. But even with "shadows" (itinerant helpers who accompany inclusion children from class to class), it is difficult for most such classrooms to function with any degree of normality.

I have heard these stories on a daily basis from a reliable source. My wife Ruth has worked for over two decades in the St. Louis County Special School District (SSD), which is virtually the only such system in the country that pools taxpayer monies across all districts countywide in order to serve the disabled student population in a targeted fashion. When it was created in 1957, it was considered a highly innovative measure resulting from the most humane, enlightened motives imaginable—insuring that concentrated attention would be paid to kids who were truly "special," who had serious physical or other problems that interfered with learning, no matter whether they lived in a rich district or poor district. The assumption then was that you could not place slow learners with crippling ailments in a regular classroom without jeopardizing the education of the other students and, just as importantly, without jeopardizing the education of the slow learners themselves, since the latter would not be given the extra help they needed. Today, SSD is under siege and threatened with extinction, because it violates the current PC dictum that *all* kids are "special" and that we should avoid branding and stigmatizing disabled children. Even though SSD has not yet been dismantled (only because the county districts are afraid they would lose the substantial funds that now are attached to SSD), the main responsibility for delivery of special education is being shifted more and more to the home district and the regular classroom teacher.

Clearly, there is a moral dilemma. Disabled kids, many who are tragically dysfunctional and who heroically attempt to overcome obstacles, deserve not only our sympathy but also every possible educational opportunity. Forcing these children into the regular classroom setting, however, does them a disservice in denying them the maximum use of specialists trained to instruct the handicapped (one of those out of fashion words), undermines the education of the non-disabled student majority, and also makes it harder to recruit to the teaching profession a new, higher quality corps of K-12 educators (given the work conditions Sykes and others have described). The dilemma would seem resolvable by developing more flexible arrangements whereby mildly disabled students could be mainstreamed in regular classrooms with support services while severe cases would remain in special education classrooms. But this goes against the current thinking of the K-12 establishment, which is responding partly to pressure from the disabled lobby and partly to its own "progressive" impulses.

Just as social security has been called the "third rail" of American politics, inclusion is the "third rail" of American education. Leaders discuss it candidly at great peril. How many of them are willing to say "no" to young cerebral palsy victims paraded by their parents before Congress and state legislatures in front of TV evening news cameras? The second, self-imposed pressure may be even stronger. Rather than being dragged into accepting full inclusion, many school districts have enthusiastically embraced it, in keeping with their utopian vision. Typical is the following passage from a newspaper op-ed by a local school superintendent in rebuttal to an article I had authored criticizing attacks on ability-grouping: "I don't apologize for our high expectations for all children. Every child can learn. Every child has a right to be in a public school as long as he or she is not a threat or danger to others. All of us should agree to a collective obligation to our democracy, our culture and to our country's future. And that obligation is to support and educate every student well."

The antipathy toward merit is more forcefully expressed in the following report on special education prepared by the National Association of State Boards of Education (NASBE): "The [NASBE study group] has looked to a new way to organize special and general education—namely, an inclusive system of education that strives to produce better outcomes for all students.... Creating an inclusive system begins with state board goals that apply to all students, as well as with creation of a total policy environment that supports systemic unity.... Schools in an inclusive, restructured system must look very different from the typical school that exists today.... Students do not move through the traditional... age-grade progression, but rather are grouped heterogeneously."

If one cuts through the bureaucratese, the term "systemic unity" says it all. As one gifted education teacher who was complaining about full inclusion once told me, what progressive educationists are calling for here is, in fact, tracking—*one* track! To hear these progressives tell it, of course, they are doing quite the opposite—urging several hundred tracks, with each student in the school building, disabled or not, having his or her own individualized education plan (what special educators call IEPs). The

NASBE study states that "several leading education reformers have proposed that to truly meet the needs of today's student population, nothing short of an IEP for *every* student is needed [italics mine]." One cannot begin to understand the inanity of this proposal until you talk to teachers who now teach disabled children and who are increasingly inundated with IEP forms they must fill out that subtract from their teaching time. The thought of inflicting this sort of paperwork on all teachers, in the education of all students, defies belief.

One last point about inclusion: what are the implications of the Individuals with Disabilities Act if former president Bill Clinton's dream of a K-16 system becomes a reality, that is, if every student is expected not only to graduate from high school but also from college? Will honors colleges be disbanded because they are too "exclusive"? As a college professor, will I, too, be faced with several hours a week spent filling out IEPs? This scenario is not as improbable as it sounds. Already at the beginning of each semester I usually receive a memo from the head of the UM-St. Louis office that serves disabled students telling me that I have at least one student in my class who "cannot concentrate" or "has trouble staying awake" and who needs special accommodations for taking exams, including not only extended time but also his or her own private isolation chamber to avoid distractions. Other students have "writing disorders," "math disorders," or other sorts of problems that used to be grounds for our denying them admission to the university but which now must be accommodated. What is now a trickle of such students promises to become in the future a flood. Will a college diploma become worth about the same as a high school diploma when we cannot certify that higher education graduates are capable of demonstrating even the most minimal skills, such as staying awake?

On the subject of slumber, Jon Westling, the former president of Boston University, recently told the "tale of dozy Samantha," an undergraduate who presented her professor with a letter from the BU Office of Disability Services indicating that she might fall asleep in class and that the instructor was expected to fill her in on any material she missed while dozing. Westling concluded that "inappropriate diagnoses of 'learning disabilities' wreak educational havoc from kindergarten to the university. Students who have genuine learning disabilities, lumped together with sufferers of imaginary complaints, are denied the education they deserve.

Students who could overcome their problems with concentrated effort are soothed into complacency. The genuinely talented are left to fend for themselves in classes that orbit around the dwarf and dwindling star of equality of outcomes." Robert Sternberg of Yale University adds: "The basket of benefits some of these students are offered rewards them not for achievement based on their abilities but for embracing their deficiencies—or, in some cases, the appearance of deficiencies that may actually have been misdiagnosed.... Though some students who receive generous accommodations for learning disabilities may gain in the short run, with improved grades and test scores, the long-term implications can be disturbing. Such students may simply not be able to handle the careers they have been able to enter with the extra assistance they have received."

It remains to be seen whether universities will be able to counter radical egalitarian pressures, and continue to promote honors colleges as they have been doing lately, in a world of full inclusion.

From "All Kids Can Learn" to "All Kids Are Gifted"

The divergent paths so far taken by higher education and precollegiate education as regards ability-grouping cannot be blamed solely on the disabilities movement. There is a second explanation. While the tracking policies supported by the Conant Report a generation ago had the salutary effect of providing added academic challenge for top students in junior high and high school, another effect was the reinforcement of the unfortunate practice of denying a rich academic program to average students, particularly those coming from working-class backgrounds. As Diane Ravitch documents, low expectations for masses of students in K-12 did not begin with the Conant Report. As she also notes, the Conant Report did nothing to improve the inferior education the majority of students were getting.

Modern progressives were right to address this problem. They have overcorrected, however. In the 1980s, they invented the slogan "every child can learn." In the 1990s, this sound principle became stretched to the point of absurdity, to where the reformers now claim, as one local St. Louis elementary school recently trumpeted, "all kids are gifted—some just open their packages up later." Such syrupy sayings flow freely in K-12 education, where it seems many practitioners have read *The Little Engine That Could* one time too many. Most educators know this rhetoric is at odds with reality, but they have gotten caught up in it nonetheless. Having become consumed by a fantasy, they have compounded the problem by advancing a number of specious arguments in order to rationalize to themselves and to others the virtues of heterogeneous grouping. What parent of a high-achieving child has not heard the following hype uttered by administrators, calculated to make one accepting of and even thankful for such grouping?

First, they constantly repeat the mantra that all students benefit from exposure to diversity. No doubt there are potential benefits, but there are also obvious potential drawbacks when students in the same classroom are on completely different academic wavelengths. There is no attempt made to engage in a serious discussion of the tradeoffs. All manner of differences are now to be understood, empathized with, tolerated, accommodated, and ultimately celebrated. I have even seen schools rotate schedules from week to week in order to insure that "morning people" are not given an unfair advantage over "night owls" who have trouble getting up early and making it to first-period class on time. One has to hope that employers will be equally sensitive to the temporally challenged.

Second, administrators have the gall to contend that, rather than dumbing down, heterogeneous grouping actually represents smarting up, since the new pedagogy associated with such grouping aims at developing higher-order skills *for all*. The reality is that reformers will not endorse any new pedagogy that is not compatible with the low end of the education spectrum. As suggested by fuzzy math, most of the instructional innovations are aimed at the bottom rather than the top, that is, at alleviating the supposed boredom of the traditional academic routine and substituting thrills and frills for drill and kill. As Ravitch notes, in their role as champions of disadvantaged students, progressives over the years have been patronizing toward these students in trying to make classrooms as student-friendly and easy as possible. What is frightening today is that this condescending attitude now extends to the highest achievers as well, who, like other members of the MTV generation, are thought to be incapable of sitting still for any length of time to read or listen to what a more learned mind has to say. It is curious that the same anti-lecture, anti-textbook pedagogy that is the recommended mode of instruction for alternative schools and vocational schools, which serve many children with attention deficit and other learning problems, is increasingly becoming the dominant model for the best college prep schools. There is little difference between the pedagogy now being prescribed for Clayton and that prescribed for the St. Louis Career Academy, a "voc-tech" school. In both cases, the heavy use of computers, the emphasis on hands-on learning, and the exposure of all students to practical "school to work" curricula are of the same one-size-fits-all cloth. Indeed, as I will discuss more fully later, the delivery of academics is increasingly being crowded out everywhere by the teaching of conflict resolution and anger management skills and other nonacademic concerns heretofore confined mainly to reform schools.

As dubious as the "diversity" and "smarting up" arguments are, the most intellectually dishonest argument used by K-12 administrators is the claim that science is on their side. Principals are forever reassuring us that "all the research" supports heterogeneous grouping. They base this not so much on hard empirical evidence as on the theories of Alfie Kohn and other radical-left ideologues or social critics masquerading as behavioral scientists. A particularly influential work was Jeannie Oakes' 1985 book *Keeping Track*, in which the UCLA education professor examined a national sample of twenty-five schools and concluded that "no group of students [high or low achievers] has been found to benefit consistently from being in a homogeneous [tracked] group." Given Oakes' penchant for quoting from Marxist writings such as *Schooling in Capitalist America*, and given her not-so-hidden agenda to reduce social inequalities between minority and non-minority children, one would be shocked if her "scientific" study had reached a different conclusion. Another scholar whose research has been cited to support heterogeneous grouping is Robert Slavin, an education professor at Johns Hopkins University and director of the Success For All Foundation, whose 1990 review of the literature on tracking led him to conclude that neither high-achieving students nor middle- or low-achieving students did any better in tracked classes than in mixed-ability settings. Slavin's ideological leanings can be seen in his stated view that "[ability] grouping is by its nature an elitist strategy, an anti-democratic strategy."

Even if research can be found supporting heterogeneous grouping, educators conveniently overlook the substantial body of research that supports ability-grouping. Biased, selective reporting of research findings can be found in any discipline, but perhaps nowhere is it more commonplace than in the K-12 education field. Many K-12 educators pretend that scientifically sound alternative points of view to progressive orthodoxy do not exist. Slavin's own colleague at Johns Hopkins, William Durden, is a supporter of ability-grouping; he laments the fact that "we have arrived at a moment in our cultural history in which we're inspired by the excellence of athletes, but we're resistant to the accomplishments of our intellectually aspiring students." A 1996 study of 3,400 students found that "detracking boosts the test scores of students in the bottom tracks, but it hurts average and high-achieving students." One of the authors of the study put it bluntly: "Somebody's going to pay for the choice to go to detracking." Similarly, James Gallagher of the University of North Carolina has argued that "the homogeneous grouping of slow-learning children does not appear to be profitable, but the homogeneous grouping of bright students is a very different matter, and [is] often ignored." Other scholars also have concluded that heterogeneous grouping *does* hurt bright kids. Karen Rogers, based on a 1991 survey of scientific studies, urged that "students who are academically or intellectually gifted and talented should spend the majority of their school day with others of similar abilities and interests." James Kulik of the University of Michigan, based on a similar "meta-analysis" of the scientific literature, concluded that Oakes' call for the elimination of ability-grouping "could greatly damage American education." Tom Loveless of Harvard and the Brookings Institution, after visiting twenty-nine schools and interviewing some 250 teachers and principals, found that the "gospel [among progressives] that tracking is a bad thing" is open to question and that "generally speaking, research fails to support the indictment," as there is at least as much evidence supporting tracking as there is opposing it.

Suffice it to say, as Kulik warns, "our children will be the losers if reviewers continue to twist research findings to fit their personal and political philosophies" and "political and social agendas." One wishes that K-12 educators would be more forthcoming about how their belief systems often color their professional judgment and how they often mix normative analysis with empirical analysis. That there is an ideological agenda which informs the current K-12 reform movement is hard to dispute. In one sense, it is inevitable, and appropriate, that our schools be guided by certain values. A century ago, John Dewey, the godfather of progressive education, was quite open about his commitment to using schools to inculcate democratic values. The key question is whether social engineering should be the overriding mission and, if so, whose values should be "privileged." Dewey and some of his comrades went much further than simply preaching good citizenship. George Counts of Columbia University, in 1932, urged that "teachers should deliberately reach for power and then make the most of their conquest," in order to "influence the social attitudes and behavior of the coming generation.... Our major concern consequently should be...to make certain that every Progressive school will use...its power in opposing and checking the process of social conservatism.... Ignorance must be replaced by knowledge, competition by cooperation,...and private capitalism by some form of socialized economy."

If one attends K-12 "professional development" workshops or reads the K-12 professional literature—written not just by Alfie Kohn and Jeannie Oakes and a handful of proselytizers but by K-12 scholars generally—one often gets the impression that the goal of our schools is to become collective farms. One cannot attend one of these workshops or pick up a journal in the education field without seeing an attack against the very idea of *competition* upon which the free enterprise system is based. In my own school district of Clayton, virtually every curriculum report that has been presented over the past decade did not stop at encouraging "cooperative learning" and "collaboration" but felt it necessary to condemn competition. It is usually only once a year that I hear the district leadership speak of competition in a different context—during staff salary discussions before the school board, when we are told that Clayton must pay "competitive" salaries to keep our teachers happy.

Typical is the language that appeared in a handout distributed at a recent professional development workshop in St. Louis: "Where is the active contestation of the destructive cultural values embedded in American education? Where is the contestation of the popular cultural values of *competition* (as opposed to unity and collaborative work), *meritocracy* (smart is something you are, not what you become), *maximizing personal wealth* (as opposed to collective responsibility), etc." A commentary in *Education Week* stated that "the [K-12] paradigm needs to shift from competition and excellence to cooperation and equity." Charles Willie of the Harvard Graduate School of Education has declared that the objective of education should not be excellence but "adequacy." Perhaps the weirdest rationale used to attack "competition" and "excellence" is the feminist contention that these are "male" values which patriarchally dominated societies have forced upon their citizens. One of the grand dames of this perspective is Peggy McIntosh of Wellesley College, whose extremist tirades against "white males" and against a "win/lose" culture have led some to call her "the Pol Pot of education."

One might ask why it is that, if higher education has been touched by many of the same sixties cultural forces as K-12 and is inhabited by many ideological soul-mates of Peggy McIntosh in schools of education and other academic departments, universities like mine nonetheless are creating selective honors colleges. I suspect it is because, unlike K-12 schools, public universities do not enjoy a monopoly. They know they must compete with private institutions to attract the best students and hence cannot take them for granted, since parents interested in academic excellence have a "voucher" system available in higher education in the form of publicly funded scholarship and loan money (e.g., Pell grants) which can be used even at religious schools such as the Jesuit-run St. Louis University.

The Standardless Society

One could accept educational populism if it could be demonstrated that excellence has not been sacrificed at the altar of equity, but no such case can be made. In fairness to K-12 education, the decline of standards is a society-wide problem. At the college level itself, grade inflation is rampant. According to one study, which examined a cross-section of institutions from community colleges to research universities, "in 1969, 7 percent of all students received grades of A- or higher. By 1993, this proportion had risen to 26 percent. In contrast, grades of C or less moved from 25 percent in 1969 to 9 percent in 1993." The *Boston Globe* reported that "Harvard's dirty little secret" is that "since the Vietnam era, rampant grade inflation has made its top prize for students—graduating with honors—virtually meaningless.... Last June [2001], a record 91 percent of Harvard students graduated summa, magna, or cum laude." At Princeton, 83 percent of the grades between 1992 and 1995 were A's or B's, compared with 60 percent between 1973 and 1975. *The New York Times* noted in 1994 that "at Stanford, an astonishing 93 percent of all letter grades are A's and B's, a huge increase over 20 years ago." The *Times* observed "this has been an odd way to prepare students for an ever more competitive world."

Grade inflation in higher education has been accompanied by a deflation of expectations, particularly at state universities, where, except for honors colleges, the workload has been reduced. Students are being rewarded more for doing less. Where at my university we used to assign twenty-page research papers in many undergraduate courses, most professors are now reluctant to ask for fifteen pages. Where we might previously have assigned four required books, we are now down to two in many cases. My alma mater, Syracuse University, has gone so far as to offer "popular television" as a new field of study; in the words of one critic, "imagine four years of studying 'Gunsmoke.'" Perhaps, to get students to come to class and stay awake, we can install laugh tracks in the classrooms.

K-12 educators are not alone, then, in fostering a decline of standards. They have a valid point that universities, in particular, are part of the problem insofar as, given the lax admissions standards at many universities, high school students have few incentives to perform well prior to entering college. It is a chicken-and-egg problem. Since most students know they can find a Slippery Rock or some other university somewhere willing to admit them and confer a college degree upon them, many do not work hard in K-12, so that precollegiate educators have trouble enforcing high standards; since high standards are not enforced in K-12, many students enter college without basic skills, necessitating colleges lowering their own expectations of and demands on students. (It could be argued that, if state universities were not so permissive in admitting masses of students needing remediation, there would be less need to establish honors colleges to separate the skilled from the unskilled in college classrooms.)

Although higher education and K-12 education are accomplices in this race to the bottom, it is the latter which arguably bears the heavier blame since its leaders have most vociferously spoken out of late against meritocracy. Theodore Sizer, a leading educationist, echoes Alfie Kohn when he criticizes "our absolutely myopic concern about assessment, grading, and evaluation. We have this mania for rating people....It's really kind of sick." But what is "sicker"—a society that "rates" people based on performance, or one that hands you an A for simply showing up? How equitable is it to give two students the same grade, when one spent hours devouring a Shakepeare play and writing a paper on the subject while the other spent hours munching away at Shakey's pizza parlor?

The Attack on Grades

It is bad enough that many school districts have eliminated class rankings and valedictorian honors. But the attack on merit extends to efforts to eliminate grades altogether. Indeed, why not eliminate them, if in many school districts they have become meaningless? In some schools, merely "being there" entitles a student to the "gentleman's C" or higher; if you did not get an A on a paper, no problem—visit the local art museum for thirty minutes of "extra credit" work and you earn the A retroactively. Gradations in student performance are becoming more and more difficult to discern. The late Albert Shanker, head of the American Federation of Teachers and an eloquent critic of progressive education, wrote the following in one of his many *New York Times* Sunday columns:

> The school board in Clark County, Nevada, has decided that its students deserve a new grading system.... Here's how the system goes, according to the most recent issue of *The Quarterly Review of Doublespeak*: "[S]tudents who earn D's or below will be characterized not as borderline passing or failing but as *emerging*. Those earning A's will no longer be commended for excellent work but will be told merely they are *extending*, and those in between will not be described as doing adequate or mediocre work but [that] they are *developing*."...Grades [once]...distinguished between levels of performance, showing who was doing well and who was not cutting it. The nearly indistinguishable present participles that the Clark County board plans to substitute for A's, B's, and the rest imply that, if there is any difference, it's not important. The new "grades" are the educational equivalent of the familiar smiley face. Their message: "You are all terrific!"

One does not have to go to Nevada to find this kind of nonsense. Pack pedagogy has brought the gradeless report card to communities all across the country. Most school districts limit the practice to K-8, since universities ordinarily want to see high school grades on admissions applications, inflated or not. In my own home district of Clayton, parents of K-4 children receive report cards with categories labeled "developing," "expected," and "exceeds expectations." (We were using the Clark County "emerging" category until we abandoned it for the "developing" category, apparently because the "emerging" one was thought not to be euphemistic enough in terms of disguising failure. A "U" for unsatisfactory or "F" for failing is simply too scarlet a letter to allow on a report card.) Clayton parents are not treated like adults when it comes to report cards until their student is in fifth grade, when they can opt for the standard graded report card or for one that continues the obfuscated categories. The latest rage in Clayton and elsewhere is to have students assess *themselves* by presenting "portfolios" (collections of their best papers and other work) at parent-teacher conferences. Taxpayers watch a dog-and-pony show staged by their youngsters while the paid professional in the room sits in the audience. If a lawyer who represents himself has a fool for a client, what does that say about a student who evaluates his or her own work?

I have found that when I complain about dumbing down, I am told by my progressive friends that standards have never been higher and that I have some naively nostalgic notion about tough grading "in the old days." No amount of hard data on grade inflation will persuade these folks that there has been a decline in standards. Hence, I decided to do a bit of oral history and interview some retired teachers from University City and Clayton to get the benefit of their personal experience. (Progressive educators are very big on kids doing these sorts of oral histories as a basis for improving their understanding, so I thought I would give it a try too.) Speaking to a retired social studies teacher who taught at University City High School in the 1950s, I learned that the school had a system where high-performing students were placed in a high ability-grouped history class that had numerous written assignments, while low-performing students were placed in a different class with fewer such assignments. If you were placed in the latter group, the best grade you could earn was a C+, since it was assumed that those students did not have nearly as onerous a set of demands made on them and, hence, did not deserve to receive an A grade no matter how well they scored on assignments. One might question whether this policy was a bit draconian, but one cannot question the fact that this represented a reverence for work ethic and a sanctity surrounding the A and B grade which does not exist anymore. Try adopting a policy like that today, and you risk child abuse litigation.

The Attack on Standardized Tests

Although individual school districts have always been tempted to curry favor with parents by fudging grades, the public could always be comforted in the past in knowing that there were certain standardized tests administered nationally which could be relied on to indicate where the achievement level of their child and their child's school stood relative to other children and other schools. One such test has been the Scholastic Aptitude Test (SAT) administered to high school seniors. One of the ominous trends it has revealed is that between 1963 and 1994, there was a nationwide drop in verbal and math scores on the SAT exam. On the math test, the score declined from a postwar high of 502 in 1963 to a low of 466 in 1980, with a partial rebound in the 1990s. On the verbal test, the score declined from 478 in 1963 to 424 in 1980, with virtually no rebound thereafter. Although K-12 educators argued that the decline could be explained by the simple fact that more students, including minorities, were taking the SAT (by the 1990s, some 40 percent of high school seniors were taking the exam, compared to far fewer in previous decades), critics attributed the drop to weaker curricula. Whatever the explanation, the College Board, under pressure from various constituencies, decided in 1995 to "recenter" the test so that the then current average scores (424 for the verbal section and 478 for the math) were artificially raised to 500, the midpoint on the 200-800 scale. The result of this, as one commentator noted at the time, was that in the future "it means every child in America will get something like 100 free points added to his score.... By decree, every 424 turns into a cool 500.... Anyone getting 730 in verbal will now get 800." Another commentator summed it up, "This is nationalized grade inflation; the solution to low test scores is to jack them up."

The assault on the word "standard" in standardized testing did not stop there. Also starting in 1995, SAT test-takers were given thirty more minutes to answer fewer questions. They were permitted to use calculators on the math section. By 2002, the notoriously difficult analogies section of the verbal test had been eliminated. This is in addition to special accommodations for "disabilities" sufferers. It has reached the point where it may no longer even be possible to monitor trends in achievement levels and compare scores from one decade or year to the next, whether on the SAT or other national exams, because the growth of special accommodations may well be inflating and distorting the recent scores. *Education Week* recently reported that "trends in state results from the National Assessment of Educational Progress could be 'significantly threatened' by the rising number of students who require accommodations for their disabilities, federal officials told the independent board that governs the assessment.... States with high proportions of children needing the accommodations may be reaping artificial increases." State-level exams are suffering from the same monitoring problems. One can find stories of middle and high school students suing state testing agencies to allow the use of spellcheck rather than insisting that students demonstrate spelling competence on writing exams. In Missouri, one state senator was so alarmed about the relaxation of state testing requirements that he wrote an op-ed piece in the *St. Louis Post-Dispatch* calling attention to the fact that

> in 1900, the...procedure set [forth by the state] for the students to take the written examination [said], "No aid whatsoever should be given, no questions should be answered and no suggestions made that would in anyway hint at information required in the examination. The teacher should not let kindheartedness nor desire for high marks for pupils betray him into wronging them, or their parents, by assisting them to tell that which they do not know. Do not deceive by false grades."...Contrast this approach with the language contained in [DESE's current publication relating to assessment of mathematics].... The instructions to the teacher state that "the pre-test activities of the exercise enable teachers to work with students with diverse languages and backgrounds to overcome some of the linguistic and cultural differences that might arise between the student and the testing exercise. Scoring can allow for contextual differences created by students from diverse backgrounds."

The whole idea behind standardized testing is that it is an effort to use an objective, fair measure in assessing a student's performance and ultimately rewarding merit-based achievement. With the concessions now being made to learning disabilities, cultural differences, and other assorted extenuating circumstances, standardized tests are losing their credibility as objective measures. Indeed, the SAT has been attacked as culturally biased against African-American and Hispanic students, because it produces "disparate impacts" whereby blacks and Hispanics tend to score lower than whites. The possibility that these disparate impacts might be due to poor educational preparation and other variables rather than cultural bias apparently has not crossed the minds of the SAT critics. Under pressure from these minority groups, the U.S. Department of Education in 1999 issued the following order: "The use of any educational test which has a significant disparate impact on members of any particular race, national origin, or sex is discriminatory, and a violation of [the civil rights laws]...unless it is educationally necessary and there is no practicable alternative form of assessment which...would have a less disparate impact." The practicable result of this edict is that "educators have been put on notice that if minority applicants are admitted to their universities in smaller numbers because their SAT scores are too low, colleges must get rid of the SAT or, at best, minimize the weight it carries. If they don't, they can expect litigation and a loss of federal funding." Several universities, in fact, have decided to eliminate the SAT (or its sister exam, the ACT) as an entrance requirement, choosing to rely instead on more impressionistic, less comparable "data"—grades (which at some schools are more inflated than at others), teacher recommendations (which with some teachers are more inflated than with others), and essays (which can be written in undetectable fashion by a parent or hired hand rather than by the applicant).

Such attacks on standardized tests make it almost impossible to sustain merit-based academics. They also make it almost impossible to hold schools accountable for the various pedagogical reforms they are constantly instituting and for the resulting products, since they leave us only with soft, subjective assessment measures that are open to fudging, which may be why the K-12 establishment is so supportive of these trends.

The Attack on Homework

Yesteryear progressives could be found at times railing against homework. Take Edward Bok, for example, who, according to Diane Ravitch, "mounted a campaign in 1900 alleging that the mental health of American children was being destroyed. Bok charged that there was 'A National Crime at the Feet of American Parents.' What was this terrible national crime? Homework. Homework was ruining American childhood." Still, such anti-homework fulminations were relatively rare, and in any event were aimed at relieving anxiety for low-performing children more so than high-performing ones. A hundred years later, these noises are being heard again, in support of all stressed-out kids.

American students spend fewer hours doing homework than students in many other countries, yet there is a movement afoot in America's schools to assign even less. In the previous chapter, I noted the strange Orwellian logic that produces such K-12 pronouncements as "homework is not necessarily done at home." If all this referred to was the use of study hall time to catch up on schoolwork, there would be nothing wrong with it. But the meaning most educators attach to this statement is that it is entirely appropriate to use regular class time for homework rather than it being an add-on which students are expected to complete after the bell rings. The above quotation actually appeared in the policy manual of the Clayton school district until recently. Only after I and other parents called attention to the absurdity of the wording did the school board and administration agree to remove this language from the manual. That the language ever found its way into the district's official policy guidelines, which as far as I can tell occurred some time in the 1980s, is testimony to the capacity for silliness in K-12 education.

The reaffirmation of homework as something, by definition, that kids do at home, or in a library, after 3:00 p.m. was one of those small victories I will always cherish in my battles with the Clayton school district. In the education war, success is usually measured by such small victories, because those are the only ones you can usually hope to achieve against a more powerful foe.

My hunch is that there are policy manuals in many school districts around the country that contain similar wording as Clayton had. Check out what your own school district has to say about homework, and you will probably find an assault on homework no less than on grades and other traditional practices that used to be considered an axiomatic part of schooling. In fact, there is a concerted campaign in schools of education and other elements of the K-12 establishment to throw into question and discredit homework. What to most normal human beings is self-evident—that is, the proposition that practice makes perfect, and that homework at *home* is a useful supplement to in-school learning in helping to develop good study habits and to reinforce lessons—has been subjected to deep rumination by K-12 gurus, who, like Bok, now argue that the benefits attributed to homework have been exaggerated, that they can just as readily be gained by having students do the work during the school day, and that homework can harm children and families by adding stress to their lives.

Typical of the attack on homework is a flyer recently sent to the teaching staff by a middle school principal in the Parkway school district that borders Clayton; the principal approvingly quoted a National Middle School Association publication: "Research really does not demonstrate that homework makes a difference in achievement. Only when certain conditions are met does homework actually impact positively students' achievement, and those conditions rarely prevail. The advantages and disadvantages of homework in the middle school grades seem to cancel one another out. So where do we go from here?" I can tell you where I as a parent would go—as far away from this school as possible, although it can be hard to find another these days that is not sending the same message. Let's assume that this "research" is even to be taken seriously and that, somehow, having students practice their math or other skills at home has no appreciable effect on their learning; let's also assume that we could be assured that, in lieu of homework, Johnny and Shirley are spending quality time with mom and dad as opposed to cruising the mall or playing Mortal Kombat. Even given these dubious assumptions, how can one arrive at the conclusion that doing or not doing homework is a wash in middle school, when you are trying to prepare students for the rigors of high school and ultimately college?

The real rationale behind the movement to abolish homework as we know it is not grounded in scientific research but in a hidden ideological agenda having to do with equity. Some K-12 progressives are more honest than others in openly admitting why they are against homework. Take for example, William Glasser, whose 1969 *Schools Without Failure* lamented that "realizing that poor students rarely do homework...teachers gear the assignments to the A and B students who do the homework, thus widening the gap between the successes and failures in school." He called for shorter and fewer assignments so that more students could complete the work. (Glasser also argued that grades were "an unpremeditated plot to destroy the students.") Of course, one could tailor homework to the capabilities of the individual student if one were willing to allow ability-grouping, but Glasser prefers lowest-common-denominator education, while insisting this is not dumbing-down. A recent work that disparages homework because it widens the education gap between economically advantaged and disadvantaged students is *The End of Homework: How Homework Disrupts Families, Overburdens Children, and Limits Learning* by Etta Kralovec and John Buell. The authors posit that homework does "much to widen the educational gap between the nation's 'haves' and 'have-nots.'...Few inner-city children...have quiet, well-lit places to study or well-educated parents to help them with their homework [or, one might add, computers at home]." Reading such materials, we begin to understand, then, the origins of the phrase "homework is not necessarily done at home." In order to accommodate intellectually and economically impoverished students, we are told that the entire regime of homework must be overhauled so that the schoolhouse rather than the house becomes the site for the bulk of such activity.

Reconciling Excellence and Equity

John Gardner, who once headed the U.S. Department of Health, Education and Welfare before there was a separate cabinet-level education department, years ago wrote a book entitled *Can We Be Equal and Excellent, Too?* One certainly would hope so, since both these values are worthy, important ones we should aspire to. The question is what is the proper balance, and which of these values is most at risk today in American schools? The president of the University City, Mo. school board, sounding very much like Alfie Kohn, recently expressed concern over the "creeping idolatry of the ideology of elitism and meritocracy, which increasingly finds acceptance in the highest circles of government and academia." One might find it amazing that a school board president would attack the idea of meritocracy, but such is the culture we now live in. What is odd is that, contrary to this board member and many other progressive types who decry elitism in our schools, the United States has been more egalitarian than most countries. Michael Kirst, writing in 1984, noted that "the egalitarianism of the American system distinguishes it from the school systems of the European democracies. About 75 percent of our students graduate from high school, and some 44 percent go on to higher education. In most other Western nations, students are diverted into vocational and technical programs at age fourteen or fifteen, and only 15 to 30 percent are graduated from a secondary school." By 2001, 70 percent of American high school graduates were enrolling in some form of postsecondary education, although many of them were unprepared. Japan is sometimes cited as having a more egalitarian system than the United States, since ability-grouping is rare in K-8, but this ignores the fact that Japanese high schools are highly tracked and that relatively few Japanese students receive postsecondary education. It would seem that what should be most worrisome today in K-12 education in America is not "creeping elitism" but just the opposite—creeping populism that is jeopardizing academic excellence.

Precollegiate education should take its cue from higher education and recognize the need for offering greater, not fewer, challenging educational opportunities aimed at those students who have demonstrated the ability and willingness to do advanced academic work. This need not take the form of the highly exclusive tracking systems that used to predominate in some public schools, where one set of students never saw another set of students in any courses. Rather, what seems reasonable is to allow students with special talents in art to have access to advanced art classes together, for gifted writers to take writers' workshops together, for math whizzes to take math together, and so forth. But the "idolatry" of radical egalitarianism that now prevails in our schools is working against this, since such practices would entail "segregating" students by ability, something that is anathema to progressives. Instead, progressives today prefer to engage *all* students in unison in writing, drawing, dancing, singing, and performing every other imaginable skill across the curriculum in the search for a germ of genius in *every* child. Not only do we now have "schools without failure." We now have schools, as in Garrison Keillor's mythical community of Lake Wobegon, where every child is above average. No, make that brilliant or, better yet, gifted.

Crazy as it sounds, this crackpot idea has been given credence by a body of theory that has caught on as gospel in K-12 education because it fits so well with the times. Indeed, the theory has proven to be a godsend to progressive reformers, since it gave them the perfect rationalization and legitimization for abandoning ability-grouping in favor of heterogeneous grouping. There is so much infatuation with this theory, called *multiple intelligences*, and it enjoys such visibility, that it deserves a more detailed discussion.

4

Are the Three Stooges Really Geniuses in Disguise?

When I say that multiple intelligences (MI) theory has caught on as gospel in K-12 education, I mean just that. We are told that religion is not permitted in our public schools, but exceptions are made for certain forms of worship of which MI theory is one. Its high priest is Howard Gardner, a highly regarded professor of education at Harvard University and a recipient of a MacArthur Fellowship "genius" award, whose 1983 *Frames of Mind* is the bible of the movement. His disciples and followers can be found throughout the K-12 world, in not only public institutions but also private ones, with whole schools in some cases devoted to his preachings. In fact, it is hard to read a K-12 journal or a school district "statement of philosophy" anywhere in the country today without seeing some reference to MI thinking. MI could well stand for mission impossible, since multiple intelligence adherents have attempted to do nothing less than change our very conception of what the life of the mind is all about. Yet Gardner and his band of devotees have been remarkably successful. Just as the Lubavitcher sect of orthodox Judaism has "emissaries" or "messengers" who spread the teaching of torah through the establishment of *chabad* houses, and the Hare Krishna faith sends pamphleteers into airport terminals in search of converts, the MI church has its own system of proselytizing, which has proven far more effective in its evangelical outreach. Based in schools of education and the professional development workshop circuit, it has created a vast network of believers. And, like any secular religion, it seeks affirmation by wrapping itself in the garb of science, undeterred by the fact that leading experts in cognitive learning have questioned its validity.

In fairness to Gardner, he probably never intended to be the cult leader of a movement that propagates robotically his dictates about the human mind. As one commentator describes Gardner's reluctant celebrity: "Multiple intelligences is not the name of a theory about learning...[so much as it is] the extremely catchy phrase that Howard Gardner...devised to describe a broad conception of human gifts which he propounded in a 1983 book, *Frames of Mind*. Gardner had virtually nothing to say in his book about schooling or school reform, but many educators were enthralled by the sense of possibility latent in his theory. They passed the book among themselves like samizdat, and very quickly 'MI' schools, exercises, symposia, manuals, and so on sprang to life." Gardner offered a dissenting view about the brain's functioning that has since become dogma in education circles. Where he can be criticized is not so much for his theory, which contains some interesting insights, but for his failure to articulate the limits of the theory, thereby encouraging a good deal of nonsense to be uttered and a good number of abuses to be practiced in the classroom in his name. In criticizing him here, my objective is not to perform a wrecking operation. I do not wish to savage the theory so much as salvage it. The theory may well have utility if it can be ridden of some of its more dubious applications.

What exactly is MI theory, and why is it so seductive? Gardner argues that educators should take a broader view of mental capacity—of intelligence—than the traditional one that is embodied in IQ tests, SAT college entrance exams, and other such standardized measures, which tend to focus on a combination of verbal, linguistic ability and mathematical, analytical ability. Instead of thinking in terms of a single general intelligence, according to Gardner we should think in terms of intelligences. In his 1983 seminal work, he identified seven distinct, independent intelligences, or seven "kinds of smart." He argued that all people possess all seven of these capabilities to varying degrees and that these often work together in concert. In addition to *linguistic* intelligence and *logical-mathematical* intelligence which schools have always valued and tried to develop (as the three Rs), he urged attention also to *spatial* intelligence, *bodily-kinesthetic* intelligence, *musical* intelligence, *interpersonal* intelligence, and *intrapersonal* intelligence. These seven intelligences are defined as follows in a publication of the Association for Supervision and Curriculum Development, which is a key professional gatekeeping body that influences K-12 curricula nationwide:

Linguistic: The capacity to use words effectively, either orally or in writing. Highly developed in story-tellers, orators, politicians, poets, playwrights, editors, and journalists.

Logical-Mathematical: The capacity to use numbers effectively and to reason well. Highly developed in mathematicians, tax accountants, statisticians, scientists, computer progammers, and logicians.

Spatial: The ability to perceive the visual-spatial world accurately and to perform transformations upon one's perceptions. This intelligence is highly developed in hunters, scouts, guides, interior designers, architects, artists, and inventors.

Bodily-Kinesthetic: Expertise in using one's whole body to express ideas and feelings and facility in using one's hands to produce or transform things. Highly developed in actors, mimes, athletes, dancers, craftspersons, sculptors, mechanics, and surgeons.

Musical: The capacity to perceive, discriminate, transform, and express musical forms. Highly developed in musical performers, aficionados, and critics.

Interpersonal: The ability to perceive and make distinctions in the moods, intentions, motivations, and feelings of other people. This intelligence can include sensitivity to facial expressions, voice, and gestures, as well as the ability to respond effectively to such cues—to influence other people, for example.

Intrapersonal: Self-knowledge and the ability to act adaptively on the basis of that knowledge. This intelligence includes having an accurate picture of one's strengths and limitations, awareness of one's moods and motivations, and the capacity for self-discipline.

Gardner more recently has added an eighth intelligence—"the naturalist's intelligence," which has to do with having an appreciation for nature—and has hinted at the possibility of several others, such as "existential" or "spiritual" intelligence.

The theory is seductive because it feeds nicely into the modern educationist's belief in "mass excellence" and the modern parent's hope that his or her child is gifted or is at least a cut above the neighbor's kid. With Gardner's theory, the reformers can make it look like the students at the bottom are not driving the curriculum, because suddenly there is no bottom! There is no hierarchy of abilities. All abilities are equal. Even if a child cannot read or write or count or analyze very well, he or she *must* have one of the expanding menu of skills that falls within Gardner's growing smorgasbord of intelligences.

When I first heard about the applications of multiple intelligences theory, I jokingly warned the Clayton school board to watch for barber shop quartets in history classes, plays presenting the discoveries of lab scientists in physics classes, and other avant-garde experiments in pedagogy. Little did I know that what I thought of as a joke was soon to be common practice. Especially frightening are educators taking seriously bodily-kinesthetic ability as an "intelligence," in effect equating slam-dunking or finger-rolling a basketball with performing open-heart surgery as a mode of brainpower. Move over Dr. DeBakey and make room for Dennis Rodman, since both the famed AMA cardiologist and the infamous NBA rebounding specialist, we are told by MI gurus, draw on the same tactile talents. One wonders what other bodily functions represent intelligence at work.

Play-Doh, Cut-and-Paste, and Other Diversions for Talented Teens

I have already described the Clayton High School English teacher who had students produce bright yellow *Cliff Notes* covers and the CHS history teacher who had students draw a picture of any structure in their neighborhood that had meaning for them. Although on the surface there is nothing wrong with art assignments in English or history classes, the problem here was that artistic expression was not considered an optional or peripheral task but was an integral part of the assignment, distracting from what should have been a focus on developing writing skills in the first instance and historical knowledge in the second instance. In the case of the building assignment that my younger son Sean was asked to do, all students were required to demonstrate their drawing ability, no doubt because the teacher had been exposed to Gardner's theory and was looking for artistic intelligence. I could accept the pedagogical legitimacy of this if the teacher was seriously trying to produce well-rounded students and had graded the students rigorously on the art they submitted. But, of course, that was not the case. After all, the teacher knew nothing about art, and the students knew he knew nothing. He should have stuck to being the first-rate historian he was. Sean ended up producing something that looked like the "etch-a-sketch" doodling my wife and I used to have him do as a small child in the back of our car to preoccupy himself during long cross-country trips. My strong hunch is that the teacher gave his sketch about the same level of scrutiny I did as I was driving.

I should have been prepared for this assignment, since just a year earlier, while in middle school, Sean's social studies teacher had each member of the class draw a poster on "what the 1950s mean to me." My son produced a series of incredibly juvenile drawings (a smiley-faced figure that was supposed to be President Truman proclaiming the Truman Doctrine, a large object that looked like a tree but purported to be a mushroom cloud signaling the atomic age, a box that represented a TV set with the words "Howdy Doody" scribbled inside, a large circle that was supposed to be a hula hoop, a picture of Sputnik that was indistinguishable from the hula hoop, and assorted other doodlings).

This, too, was MI theory in action. Sean received an A for the assignment, again suggesting the level of expectations to which students were being held. In encouraging superficial treatment rather than mastery of skills, and making a mockery of standards, such applications of MI theory diminish respect not only for the core competencies traditionally emphasized in schooling, but also for the very spatial and other intelligences the theory aims to promote.

If these examples of MI theory at work were isolated ones, perhaps they could be forgiven. But they were not isolated. Inane as these assignments were, they paled in comparison to others I witnessed.

First, there was the "Play-Doh" episode. Sean was in an eighth grade English class at Wydown Middle School in which the teacher, known for her strong progressive leanings, required her students to do a project expressing their feelings about prejudice, using any "communication" medium they wanted. This was classic progressive education—note the emphasis on personal, affective, emotive learning; the social, ideological agenda of combating prejudice; and the child-centered license to express oneself through whatever "language" one wishes to utilize even if it is not really using language as such. Students approached the eighth grade English project in a variety of ways, the teacher being careful not to "privilege" verbal, linguistic intelligence. Some painted, some pasted, and some engaged in other activities. My son, recognizing the fatuous nature of the project, decided to mount a personal protest. Taking the teacher up on her invitation for him to express his feelings through *any* medium, he chose to communicate via Play-Doh. He went to a toy store and bought a container of this stuff he had played with in early childhood and proceeded to mash together red Play-Doh, green Play-Doh, and other colors into a large multi-hued round mound that he entitled "unity amidst diversity." He did this in tandem with another classmate (easily among the brightest students in the class), who was equally determined to communicate to the teacher just how stupid he felt the whole exercise was.

The teacher did not appreciate the contempt that these two boys displayed toward her teaching, and she scolded them for not taking the assignment more seriously. My wife and I, in turn, did not appreciate the contempt that she showed these and other children, in failing to provide much in the way of a challenging, rigorous language arts secondary education. When we first heard about the assignment Sean was doing, we were quite excited, mistaking his reference to Play-Doh as Plato. Our excitement was short-lived, but, fortunately, so was the teacher, as she was gone by the following year, sparing future generations of Clayton kids the burden of being taught by someone who failed to understand the distinction between a college prep course instructor and an arts and crafts summer camp counselor.

Another notable encounter I had with MI theory occurred in Sean's freshman year at Clayton High School, where he was enrolled in an Honors English course. The teacher, who was very bright and well-read, had the students do a unit on Greek mythology. They didn't read Plato but did read Homer and other Hellenic writers. The Greeks certainly believed in the virtue of being a well-rounded person—Aristotle's "golden mean" suggested that one cultivate a balanced set of interests—but they never could have imagined how far some educators two millennia later were willing to go to promote this ideal. For the capstone project in Sean's Greek mythology unit, he and his classmates were asked to produce a cut-and-paste collage that consisted of pictures, newspaper clippings, or any other items they could cull from contemporary sources that contained references to ancient Greek culture and showed the relevance of that culture to today's society. My son resorted to xeroxing or tearing out several ads from the yellow pages phone book and magazines and then gluing them onto pieces of construction paper, bound together in a scrapbook whose exterior was a Kinko-produced plasterboard reproduction of a *Sports Illustrated* cover featuring the 1960 Olympic Games. Among the items included in the scrapbook were ads for Ajax cleanser, Atlas Foundation Repair Systems, Apollo Hair Systems, and Olympus cameras, a *Newsweek* photo showing tennis star Andre Agassi and his Nike shoes, and a cartoon depicting the Greek god Hermes in flight. Aside from questions about copyright infringement, there was a more basic question to be asked: what was this assignment doing as the *capstone* project in a *high school* class whose subject was *English* and which was an *honors* course no less?

A parent of another student in the class told me that she put that very question to the instructor, who, according to the parent, responded: "Haven't you heard of Howard Gardner's multiple intelligences theory?"

Although Gardner cannot be held responsible for everything that goes on in his name in America's classrooms, he cannot completely escape blame for inspiring the Play-Doh and cut-and-paste extravaganzas that go on every day in schools around the country. He has attempted to speak out against the simple-minded misuses of his work. In his 1999 book *The Disciplined Mind*, Gardner staunchly defended the traditional academic disciplines and insisted, "I am a demon for high standards and demanding expectations." Perhaps he needs to speak out more loudly and offer more public disclaimers or cautionary advice about the dos and don'ts of MI theory, because his ideas have been invoked as justification for some of the most amazing pedagogical practices imaginable. It has spawned an entire industry of professional development experts engaging hordes of teachers in MI workshops, where their unquestioning acceptance of what is presented as scripture makes Rush Limbaugh's so-called dittoheads look like cynics.

A Spreading Conflict

All over the St. Louis metropolitan area, parents are witnessing their kids doing projects like the ones my son Sean had to endure. In the elementary grades, parents are increasingly finding themselves having to supervise them as well as endure them. "Project learning," of course, has always been an important part of K-12 education, as kids have always been expected to do science projects, research projects, term papers, and other assignments that went beyond mere homework. What distinguishes today's project learning from yesterday's, however, is its heavy MI flavor.

New City School is an independent school located in the city's Central West End that serves preschoolers through sixth grade. It bills itself in its advertising as a school "founded on the premise that the opportunity to learn should be shared by children of diverse racial and socio-economic backgrounds, as well as varied academic abilities. The approach to education used by New City School is that of Multiple Intelligences Theory. This approach emphasizes the variety of talents each child possesses, and recognizes the array of these talents." It adds "we teach the feelings along with the concept." Indeed, a recent article in the *St. Louis Post-Dispatch* had the headline "West End School Is Mecca for Intelligence Theory." Mecca was an appropriate term, since the headmaster of the school views Gardner as something of a deity and views himself as a mullah, having organized MI conferences drawing educators from half the fifty states and having collaborated with his faculty in producing a 273-page *Celebrating Multiple Intelligences* guide for teachers that is in its fifth printing and has itself sold more than 22,000 copies.

Another *Post-Dispatch* article described some of the things that go on at New City: "Sixth-graders in small groups use multicolored blocks to build a design. The group then writes four clues to help other classmates figure out and re-create the design [which is supposed to tap spatial intelligence, linguistic intelligence, and interpersonal intelligence].... A variety of sculptures by sixth-graders about 'The Cay,' a book about the Caribbean, line up on cafeteria tables on the second floor. Students have chosen materials from plaster of Paris and cookie dough to Styrofoam to create island scenes.... Teachers [ask] third-grade students to draw three pictures of what happens to a character in 'Sign of the Beaver,' as he tries to get honey from a beehive.... [One teacher's] classroom features a life-size teepee, arrowheads and other Indian artifacts, including ceremonial rattles, a drum and a gourd.... Incorporating music skills into the [curriculum] has proved to be the hardest.... [The teacher is quoted as saying] if you encourage students to beat a drum to develop their musical intelligence, 'you can't complain about the noise.'" Busy as bees and beating the drum for MI theory—that's New City School.

To be sure, New City School graduates do fine on standardized tests and go on to excellent secondary schools and colleges. That is not surprising, since, its advertisement notwithstanding, it tends to draw students from mostly high-income households or at least from families with strong educational support systems. It is testimony to the power of MI theory that well-educated consumers will pay tuition to have their children attend a private school like New City; whether driven by noble egalitarian impulses or by the hope that their child will test out as "gifted" based on the gamut of intelligences surveyed, many parents are attracted to what such schools offer. (The problem is that MI theory is now everywhere, in almost every school building, whether a parent wants it or not. Magnet schools that focus on specialized interests and aptitudes are an exception, but even they often stretch their mission to incorporate elements of MI theory.) While there is no doubt that serious education occurs at New City, the activities described above suggest there is also considerable fluff. In fact, when a *New York Times* education writer showed Gardner copies of some of the exercises in *Celebrating Multiple Intelligences*, Gardner himself, apparently unaware he was putting down one of his chief disciples, "frowned and said, 'the only answer I can give to this is: I would certainly not want to be in a school where a lot of time was spent doing these things.'"

The same writer observed that Gardner had an "explicitly political agenda of democratizing human gifts." It should not be surprising that his theory has resonated with advocates for minorities, who have long claimed that traditional definitions of giftedness tend to privilege whites and help account for underrepresentation of certain ethnic groups in gifted programs (to the extent such programs still exist). Why traditional measures should be biased against minorities is uncertain, unless one adopts the racist view that blacks and other minorities are somehow inherently inferior when it comes to using the written word or mathematical algorithms. Despite the large numbers of Asian and other minority children who defy such stereotypes, progressive educators continue to turn to MI theory—rather than to doing a better job of teaching critical language and analytical skills—as a solution to racial disparities in gifted programs. As a recent *St. Louis Post-Dispatch* front-page story stated, pointing to developments in metro area schools: "Blacks and other groups are underrepresented in programs for schools' brightest students. Now teachers are working to change that.... Schools are developing new ways to find and nurture their brightest students."

It would be surprising if there was a school district anywhere within several hundred miles of St. Louis that had not yet introduced its teachers to MI theory. The Cooperating School Districts, a St. Louis-based umbrella organization that acts as an information clearinghouse and professional development center for some fifty school districts in a six-county area serving nearly one-third of Missouri students, has held workshops devoted to Gardner. A 1996 workshop sponsored by CSD's Staff Development Division featured an MI guru named Thomas Armstrong, who brought his one-man show "Seven Kinds of Smarts" to town as part of his cross-country tour. In one of his handouts, he first listed Gardner's seven intelligences, using an "MI pizza" pie chart divided into equal slices labeled "self smart," "people smart," "music smart," "body smart," "picture smart," "number/logic smart," and "word smart" and then, under each of the seven categories, presented an inventory of statements which, if checked off as applying to oneself, indicated that you might well possess a high degree of that particular intelligence. For example, "I find it difficult to sit still for long periods of time" was a likely indicator of bodily kinesthetic intelligence, although it can equally get a student a diagnosis of ADD (attention deficit disorder) and a prescription for Ritalin. "I have at least three close friends" and "I would rather spend my evenings at a lively party than stay at home alone" are manifestations of interpersonal intelligence. "I regularly spend time alone meditating or thinking about important life questions" and "I would prefer to spend a weekend alone in a cabin in the woods" hint at intrapersonal intelligence. "I have vivid dreams at night" suggests spatial intelligence. It is reassuring to know, however, that "books are important to me" is a telltale sign of linguistic intelligence, even if something as integral to schooling as reading rates no more than one line out of sixty-seven items in the inventory!

In addition to these local workshops sponsored by CSD, the Missouri Department of Elementary and Secondary Education (DESE) has been disseminating MI theory statewide, insuring that all districts have equal access to such daffy pedagogy. I once attended a DESE summer workshop, as part of an effort to involve university arts and sciences faculty in discussions of the new K-12 state assessments. It was a real eye-opener. These workshops are like revival meetings. Throngs come from far and wide to hear The Word. Based, I guess, on the premise that those most recently converted tend to be the purest and most zealous in their belief, DESE relies heavily on a teacher-trainer delivery model whereby select school district faculty are bused in for a few days to learn the latest theological revelations and are then systematically dispersed to spread the message to the flock back home. There may be multiple intelligences on display at these meetings, but not a lot of multiple perspectives, at least not any that question MI theory and other progressive dogma. My hosts did not know they had an agnostic in their midst. I distinctly recall a three-hour session that the conference program billed as a math assessment discussion but which, to my bewilderment, was spent almost entirely on communication skills. When I dared to suggest that a math session should focus on math, I was told by one of the apostles in charge to get with the program.

A beneficiary of such training was a high school history teacher described as "the senior leader in the Pacific School District's program to weave the philosophy of the Missouri Assessment Program into the district's classrooms," who after attending DESE professional development institutes was expected to transfer his new-found knowledge to his fellow district teachers. A newspaper article revealed the heavy MI flavor of the "philosophy" behind the new state assessment procedures, particularly the devaluing of books and the written word; the teacher was quoted as saying that "the only resistance we have had [to the new assessments] has been from the very bright students who had a history of high success by reading and performing on written tests. Sometimes they are shaken up a bit when they have to put the pencil down, get up from their desk and complete a project that illustrates what they've learned. A student who can write a beautiful essay on the history of jazz might not be prepared to get up in front of class and perform a song. But both demonstrate learning." Yes, I would be shaken up also if, in a U.S. history class, I was told that not only was I expected to give my best imitation of Kate Smith belting out a chorus of "God Bless America," but also that such an activity was considered intellectually equal to writing an analysis of Alexis de Tocqueville's *Democracy in America*.

Speaking of jazzing up the classroom, some teachers at Red Bridge Elementary School in Kansas City, Mo. must have also attended the DESE workshops or consulted with "senior leaders," judging from recent news reports on how they were combining dance and math lessons, "using twists, turns, and pirouettes to help students learn the basics of math." Citing Gardner as the inspiration for such pedagogy, the school principal stated that "this kind of activity challenges teachers to find different teaching styles." A professor of math education at the University of Missouri-Kansas City added that "what it does is allow the student to learn through his or her strength, and that is better than trying to make them struggle through their weakness." This might even make sense were it not for the fact that all students are put through these paces, whether numerically challenged or not, whether more at ease in the classroom or the ballroom. According to this logic, should we not also be bringing set theory exercises into the gym to nurture the physical education of those nerdy students averse to playing tennis, volleyball, and other sports? Who knows, maybe there is a future Olympic decathlon or pentathlon athlete among them waiting to be discovered?

Around the same time as this Kansas City story appeared, there was another, perhaps even stranger story that appeared in the Philadelphia area, which focused on intrapersonal intelligence as an underutilized strategy in math education. Posted on an e-mail listserve, it is worth quoting at length:

> I am a student at Villanova University in an independent study project.... I am studying Howard Gardner's Theory of Multiple Intelligences and how this theory has affected the teaching of mathematics in elementary education. Studying the NCTM [National Council of Teachers of Mathematics] standards for grades Pre K-2 that are posted on this web page, I was unable to identify standards that involved the intrapersonal intelligence.... I found many points throughout the standards that spoke to the logical mathematical, linguistic, visual/spatial, kinesthetic, interpersonal and even the musical intelligence. However, I was very surprised that I was unable to find any direct reference to the intrapersonal intelligence. The standards seem up to date and progressive.... But I feel that it is extremely important that teachers incorporate the intrapersonal intelligence into math learning by giving students the opportunity to determine and express the way they think and feel about the subject matter.... One technique to integrate the intrapersonal intelligence into the teaching of mathematics is to ask students to keep a math journal. This way students can express any problems or frustrations they may be having....

It seems never to have occurred to this e-mailer to wonder what expressing one's *feelings* about 2+2 has to do with learning math. It is truly amazing that, at a time when progressive educators are constantly questioning the value of children learning their multiplication tables, they are quite open to kids spending time lying on a couch and reflecting about whether they are mathphiles or mathphobes.

Hard as it might seem to top such psychobabble, there is no shortage of examples of similar thinking. One of my favorites is an advertisement that appeared in an education publication that read as follows: "*Adventure Tales of America: An Illustrated History of the United States, 1492–1877* fully integrates recent learning research in a U.S. history textbook.... Through its multicultural emphasis, strong role models and dramatic style, students experience U.S. history as a personal adventure. The key to this textbook is its left brain/right brain format.... It presents U.S. history to both sides of the brain simultaneously through: words and analysis for the logical, sequential left brain, and pictures, humor, emotion, and drama for the creative, global right brain." We have here not only rewriting history but rethinking, refeeling, reenacting, and redrawing history. Again, we have a case of progressive educators often arguing that getting kids to know dates, names, and other information is unimportant and, to the extent that they should bother reading about historical figures and events, it is no more critical than emoting about them. I will wait until later in the chapter to discuss the "brain research" upon which this history text claims to be based, but I think I can safely say here that most college professors who teach history would take one look at this and conclude it is brainless.

More silly pedagogy: "Michele Zuckerman's fifth-grade son brought home this science assignment from his northern Virginia school: 'Choose a chemical element and write two paragraphs telling why it is your favorite. Be creative.' Only weeks earlier he brought home another winner: 'Find a rock. Decorate your rock and make it special. Write a story about your rock.'" According to another account, closely paralleling my son's experience, "Andrea was an eighth grader at Chinook [Middle School in the Seattle area].... For homework in the science class, students created collages and drew pictures of scientists.... One month-long project had Andrea copying a picture of a town in a textbook and drawing in several new buildings. 'That's stupid,' she later told a local newspaper. 'You can't tell if the structures are well built.... And especially the way I draw, you can't tell.' She received an A."

One would hope that K-12 educators would more carefully examine the application of MI theory in the classroom. Yet there is little criticism coming from the profession. The September 1997 issue of *Educational Leadership*, the official journal of the Association for Supervision and Curriculum, is one long ode to Howard

Gardner, with virtually no objective assessment of the subject. The pages teem with personal testimonies, as opposed to conclusive data, on the healing power of MI theory. A perusal of the volume finds the editor questioning the value that universities place on "logic and language" and "academic studies" compared to K-12's more enlightened, broader view of intellectual activity that refuses to differentiate between the smarts of "programmers and polo players." A contributor lauds a high school math teacher who has her students "physically pretend to be graphs" and an elementary school teacher who equates "singing about photosynthesis" with reading about it, as an intellectually demanding and rewarding task in a science unit.

Elementary school, middle school, high school—no matter the level of education, no matter the geographical location of the school, MI theory is omnipresent in K-12. Not surprisingly, pre-school educators have also discovered MI theory, including the producers of the nationally televised "Sesame Street," who, noting that "children have difficulties recalling the letter and number of the day" and thinking "how we might teach them in a different way," have recently turned to Gardner for advice. In order to convey an understanding of rain, for example, "first, Ernie and the Twiddlebugs go out in the rain, then there is a rain dance in clay animation, and finally rain and wind are rendered in Chinese calligraphy." Some would argue that "Sesame Street" and MI theory were made for each other, that many uses of the theory exhibit the level of sophistication one would expect of a typical Big Bird watcher.

Who Is More Intelligent, Shortstops or Surgeons?

Let's do a thought experiment for a moment. If we were to ask Howard Gardner and his disciples to rate George W. Bush's intelligence against that of his predecessor, what would be the likely result? When George W. Bush was elected president in 2000, many liberals in the media and in other circles, including many of my progressive education friends, argued that he was not very intelligent. Just as Dan Quayle, the former vice-president under Bush's father, was the butt of many jokes about his mental capacities, so also was George W. (although few barbs aimed at him were as brutal as the one that claimed "Roe v. Wade are the two ways

Quayle thinks you can get across the Potomac River"). What these critics meant was that George W. was lacking in terms of historical knowledge, verbal skills, analytical reasoning prowess, and other such assets—in other words, he supposedly came up short in the traditional linguistic and mathematical/logical intelligences that have always been associated with smarts and have always been valued in school in the past. However, even if it were true that he seemed not very "intelligent" in the latter terms, he did seem to be very "intelligent" at other things, at making friends, at charming people, at being at peace with himself and with others, at using body language, and so forth—in other words, even his enemies would have to admit that he deserved high marks for those overlooked "intelligences," such as interpersonal and intrapersonal intelligences, that Gardnerites trumpet constantly today. Yet, would Gardner and his followers really concede, then, that Bush was just as intelligent as a Bill Clinton or an Albert Gore, which is the logical implication derived from MI theory? I do not recall seeing any op-ed pieces in the *New York Times* or anywhere else written by Gardner or other progressives in schools of education coming to George W.'s defense, and I certainly did not hear any MI supporters in my own circle of acquaintances willing to make such a statement. Perhaps it was an oversight on their part, perhaps they could not bring themselves to say something nice about a Republican, or perhaps they knew better than to seriously contend that an ability to make friends is the intellectual equal of being a high-achieving "policy wonk" like Clinton and Gore.

Deep down inside, MI supporters are smart enough to know that the theory of relativity that Einstein gave us did not include the notion that all intelligence is relative. Nonetheless, they persist in taking a good idea—that we should take a somewhat broader view of intelligence than the one commonly held—and carrying it to the point of absurdity. And when critics such as myself point out the absurdity, we are often accused of misrepresenting the theory. Fortunately there is a paper trail that validates what the critics have to say. For example, in an op-ed in the *St. Louis Post-Dispatch* entitled "Different Strokes for Different Folks," the headmaster of the New City School that bills itself as an MI school plainly stated that "bodily kinesthetic intelligence [refers to] using one's body, or part of it, to solve problems and communicate. Children with strong bodily kinesthetic intelligence are highly coordinated and often tactile.... Surgeons and shortstops have

highly developed bodily kinesthetic intelligence." Here was someone trying to convince readers like me that baseball shortstops
evidence, and owe their success to, the same type of intelligence as
surgeons, which is not necessarily traced to one's head but to other
body parts. I'm sorry, but I do not believe for a moment that even
as brilliant a shortstop as the St. Louis Cardinals' Ozzie "The Wiz-
ard" Smith was, his intelligence could compare to that of one
Charles Mannis, the orthopedic surgeon who miraculously managed to put my son's knee back together in a three-hour operation
after Sean had destroyed his anterior cruciate ligament and every
other ligament he could tear in a high school soccer injury. Likewise, as good a soccer player as Sean was (he made all-conference
following the surgery, thanks to Dr. Mannis), even a father's pride
does not allow me to say that Sean was as intelligent as his physician just because he could kick a ball fifty yards.

Few people get their backs up so quickly as a let-a-hundred-
flowers-bloom progressive educator whose ideas are questioned
by others. No sooner did I write my own op-ed commentary in the
Post-Dispatch in rebuttal to the "Different Strokes" commentary
than the author of the latter piece, the New City School director,
got his guru—Howard Gardner himself—to contact the newspaper and publish a rebuttal to my rebuttal. Re-rebuttals are rarely
allowed in a newspaper, but when someone of Gardner's stature
insists on being heard, it is hard for an editor to say no. Gardner
accused me of not having studied his works and of "sheer fraud"
(because I took literally the analogy explicitly made between
shortstops and surgeons).

I was flattered when I sent him a letter complaining of his
accusations and he bothered to respond, which initiated a brief
flurry of very civil correspondence between us. I must confess that
he was very gracious in his willingness to engage me in a conversation about MI theory. Harvard professors and winners of
MacArthur "genius" awards are not known for their accessibility,
but here Gardner was quite cordial and quite generous with his
time. I genuinely appreciated it. He attempted to clarify a number
of misconceptions about MI theory, defending himself against the
charge that his theory had had the effect of debasing traditional
academics and inviting dumbing down. He made many reasonable, persuasive arguments, as one would expect from a respected
world-class scholar. But in the end he stood by the published comments of his New City School colleague, contending that he was

not as confident as I was that shortstops and surgeons could be readily rank-ordered in intelligence, leaving me with the nagging feeling that it was not just the misapplications of his theory that were worthy of criticism but the theory itself.

Gardner deserves to be taken seriously, but so do the following criticisms.

MI Theory Lacks Much Scientific Support

Science, by its very nature, is characterized by constant doubts about the empirical certainty of any propositions and constant probing to examine and reexamine whatever truths are thought to exist at any given moment. There are relatively few proven, observable, well-established generalizations in the physical world that deserve to be called scientific "laws," and still fewer that can be found in the social order. In medical research and most other areas of scientific research, findings are usually reported in a very tentative fashion and used very carefully. In contrast, there is an air of casual confidence and certainty that attends almost every pronouncement of findings from "research-based" studies in the field of K-12 education. I have noted how K-12 administrators, fresh from professional development seminars that promote the latest fads, regularly assure parents that "all the research" supports the reforms they are instituting, whether it is the movement away from ability-grouping or away from time-consuming homework or whatever. It is the rare administrator who will cite any research that directly contradicts the espoused reform or will instruct curriculum coordinators to include such contrary evidence in curriculum proposals. Certainly that has been my experience over the years listening to discussions of "best practices" in my own school district. The entire K-12 profession, with few exceptions, tends to close ranks behind the theory of the day. So it is with school reform based on MI theory, which is said in journal after journal to be supported by *all* the latest "brain science."

Brain scientists themselves—biologists, neurologists, cognitive psychologists, and the like—are not the ones making this claim. It usually emanates from professors of education and those who study under them, whose standards of proof are generally not as exacting as those found in the hard sciences. Gardner himself, perhaps because of his grounding as a psychologist, has been much more guarded about the scientific evidence for his theory than are many of his ardent followers. (He even confessed in a radio interview once, when asked why he chose the term "multiple intelligences," "If I had called them talents, no one would have paid any attention.") Typical of the educationists who overstate the science is Susan Kovalik, who offers annual summer institutes on such subjects as "brain-compatible learning," advertised in brochures that contain the obligatory reference to multiple intelligences, in declaring that "brain research has given us a window on learning never before realized in the history of civilization."

Although it is true that there have been many advances lately in brain research, Kurt Fischer, the director of the Mind, Brain, and Education program at Harvard University's Graduate School of Education (Gardner's home institution) has said that "you can't go from neuroscience to the classroom, because we don't know enough about neuroscience." John Bruer, author of a recent book on brain research, is more emphatic that "educators are making a very big mistake by wasting their time on 'brain-based' curricula." The jury still remains out about MI theory in particular. As one writer notes:

> MI theory has received an extremely mixed reception among Gardner's own peers. Psychometricians point out that Gardner has not done the testing needed to show that these are, indeed, autonomous faculties, rather than aspects of the traditional intelligences. And most neuroscientists, even those sympathetic to Gardner's model, continue to believe in a central processing capacity, which has traditionally been called "general intelligence," or g [captured by IQ tests].

The same writer adds: "Most people who study intelligence view MI theory as rhetoric rather than science, and they're divided on the virtues of the rhetoric." George Miller, a Princeton University scholar considered to be one of the founders of cognitive psychology, has said that Gardner's classification scheme of seven or more intelligences "is almost certainly wrong." He elaborates:

> Since none of the work has been done that would have to be done before a single-value assessment of intelligence could be replaced by a seven-value assessment, the discussion is all hunch and opinion. It is true that, if such profiles were available, an educator might be better able to match the materials and modes of instruction to an individual student. But since nobody knows whether the educator should play to the student's strengths or bolster the student's

weaknesses (or both), the new psychometrics does not seem to advance practical matters much beyond present psychometrics.

Other well-known skeptics include psychologists Jerome Bruner of Harvard and Robert Sternberg of Yale, who are sympathetic to progressive ideas about education but question the basis for the theory. Bruner notes that the cases made for the kinesthetic and personal intelligences, in particular, "stumble badly" and concludes that Gardner's intelligences are "at best useful fictions," while Sternberg has observed that "there is not even one empirical test of the theory."

The point here is not that Gardner is necessarily wrong but that there is no clear scientific basis for believing he is right, certainly not enough to justify the near universal adoration he has received among K-12 educators, where one never hears about "the extremely mixed reception" he has received in the scientific community. Even if science were to support his theory, there is reason for concern over possible fallout in the classroom. As one article states, "evidence for the specifics of Gardner's theory is weak, and there is no firm research showing that its practical applications have been effective. No one says that using MI in schools is directly injurious. The danger is that it leads to wasted time, to an emphasis on less important skills, and to a false sense that learning has taken place when it has not."

MI Theory Invites Fluff

Certainly, one can cite examples of intellectually serious work that draws its inspiration from MI theory. As a case in point, one teacher "gives her fifth-graders extremely complex architectural assignments which draw on spatial rather than linguistic skills. The children had to build a robot at least forty inches high, with one limb that rotates through 360 degrees; an ant colony that could withstand flood, hurricane, and enemy attack; and a Mouse House with a site plan and proper draftsmanship." But one has to wonder about a theory that inspires at least as much fluff as seriousness—Play-Doh and Elmer's glue exercises in English class, doodling in science class, and left-brain/right brain textbooks that aim for laughter and dramatization as much as factual knowledge and understanding. Will we next see limbo contests in classrooms to determine whose bodies—not minds—are most nimble? How *low* can we go in the name of equity?

What is especially worrisome is the impact of MI theory on literacy. The nonliterate culture has been gradually driving out the literate culture in K-12 education, as teachers try to accommodate those children who come from homes where reading is not a regular pastime, now estimated to be at least 70 percent of the U.S. population. Hence the growing emphasis on "visual arts," which MI theory feeds into. The latest national English standards produced by the progressive-minded National Council of Teachers of English "elevate media-viewing and visual representation to the same status as the more traditional language arts of reading and writing." The notion of "Great Books" is being supplemented with "Great Flicks" as television and films are now considered coequal with literature as intellectually taxing and rewarding learning media.

Imagine walking into a K-12 classroom and asking the students, "Class, what would you rather do today, watch a movie or read a book?" Gee, what do you think the average student would prefer? Who among us can ever forget in our own education the sheer glee that would accompany the teacher's announcement that there would be no teaching that day but audio-visual instead? Visual images can convey very sophisticated meaning, but by their nature they tend to be easier on the eyes and the brain of most people, which is precisely why they are being used increasingly as we continue to lower our expectations for kids and place fewer demands on them while claiming otherwise. In a word, visuals as objects of study are less labor-intensive, and more *fun*, than books. To borrow the title from Neil Postman's book, we are "amusing ourselves to death." Witness the following solicitation letter I got in the mail, addressed "Dear Educator":

> *Cartoon News* will serve as your Trojan Horse into the minds of your students, who most likely, raised by the television set and comic strips, may not always be enthusiastic about reading. *Cartoon News* adapts the subject of current events studies to the young person's habits. If you can't open their mind through the door of long gray text—then enter it through the window of great political cartooning.... In each issue there's a fascinating "Connect-the-Dots" draw-it-yourself caricature of a newsworthy world leader, a regular "Who Are These World Leaders?" caricature puzzle, and a "What's Wrong With This Cartoon?" visual quiz.

Books are fast disappearing in public school libraries, which are themselves now called media centers. In the Clayton High

School library in my school district, most books have been shoved out of view to make room for computers. Schools are not alone in devaluing reading—even the Library of Congress, amazingly, recently proposed shelving its books according to size and shape rather than subject matter in order to relieve space problems.

What reading that *is* done in our schools today seems to be of the truncated variety. There are increasing reports of schools offering condensed versions of classic literary works to their students, such as a 133-page version of Louisa May Alcott's original 500-page *Little Women* that Columbia Pictures requested accompany its 1995 film by that name. Even *Harry Potter* comes with a *Cliff Notes* edition! The *Cliff Notes*-meets-video culture that is now pervasive in K-12 is inevitably affecting higher education. I noted in the previous chapter that professors everywhere are cutting back on reading assignments. Take my own field of study, for example. The leading international relations college textbook in the United States for many years in the 1950s and 1960s was Hans Morgenthau's *Politics Among Nations*, a 700-page pictureless tome that was assigned as an introductory text to undergraduates yet was so erudite that it was also considered the single most respected treatise in the discipline. Today, the leading undergraduate international relations text is also roughly 700 pages, but reads almost like a comic book, given the profuse number of cartoons, photos, and other visuals that dot virtually every page. And, for those students who have reading "disorders" of some sort, there is even a "Brief" version available! When I recently attended a college textbook authors meeting, where publishers were urging even more pictures, I heard one professor lament, "What's next—pop-ups? a box of crayons in the back of the book?"

It is not just a matter of dumbing down. Benjamin Barber suggests some profound implications for society as we move from print to pictures:

> As survivors of aging print technologies, books are relics of a slowly vanishing culture of the word—democracy's indispensable currency and a faltering bulwark against the new world of images and pictures flashed across screens at a speed that thwarts all deliberation. Democracy, like a good book, takes time.... Imagine a debate conducted in the flash-card imagery of MTV; can there be deliberation? Imagine imagination without words: does it ennoble or debase? Or simply cease to exist?

The electronic media are so powerful as communication

tools, whether in their potential for harm or for good, that there may be no turning back. The MTV culture is probably here to stay. But surely our schools should, at least for a few hours each day, provide a refuge from that culture and a countervailing force.

MI theory clearly can be linked to the devaluation of literacy. In a recent *Harper's* article, one teacher brutally tells it like it is: "If they [students] still have not passed [an exam on *Hamlet*], allow them to do an art project. They could make a model of the Globe Theatre with Popsicle sticks or draw a picture of a Danish prince, or Prince Charles, or even the Artist Formerly Known as Prince. Those not artistically inclined could make copies of Shakespearean sonnets with macaroni letters on construction paper. If all else fails, try group projects. That way you can give passing grades to all the students, even if only one in five produces anything."

Curriculum a Mile Wide and an Inch Deep

I teach a global ecology course aimed at education majors. Out of curiosity, I frequently ask them what they are learning in the school of education. Recently, one of the students told me that their professor said "today gym, art, and music are considered just as important as the three Rs." I fully recognize that playing the violin, playing shortstop, and performing in a play require extraordinary talent to be done right. That is not at issue here. At issue is whether we can realistically expect teachers to hone, much less perfect, these and all Gardner's other intelligences in an eight-hour school day and 180-day school year. We are forever expanding the mandate of schools without expanding the time at their disposal. In an ideal world, all seven intelligences and more should be cultivated. But only progressive educators live in that sort of utopia. The rest of us have to function in the real world, where there are tough choices and tradeoffs, and the need to prioritize.

Our schools already find it difficult to get students to master one skill, like writing a complete sentence. Leo Botstein, the president of Bard College, notes that "in the last four years of American schooling, high school pupils study the core subjects of mathematics, science, history, the national language and literature for less than half the time French and Japanese students do. Only 41 percent of the American high school day is spent this way." We are told we need a longer school year if American children are to match the math skills demonstrated by Korean kids, who go to school 220 days a year. Before extending the school year, however, we should be making better use of the existing time.

The Gardnerites are stretching the schools still thinner with their pursuit of seven or eight or more intelligences which are rapidly becoming part of the "core" academic curriculum in K-12. The simple fact is that the more time spent on artwork and song and dance, the less time spent on English, math, and those subjects long viewed as the mainstays of education. I have already indicated how literacy has suffered. So, too, are the other traditional academic areas threatened by MI theory. We now have a curriculum that is a mile wide and an inch deep. School is no longer about mastery. It is about dabbling. It is no longer about "time on task," the slogan that enjoyed a brief revival in the 1980s, but time on tasks—so many tasks as to make a charade of serious learning and serious preparation for college.

K-12 educators love to talk today about "critical thinking." Okay, let's do some. How realistic is it to think that (1) you can have an English teacher in middle or high school address, in addition to language arts training, non-language arts training and not lose precious time teaching composition and literature skills; and (2) you can expect that same English teacher to seriously teach and grade non-language arts work?

I am not even sure how an instructor begins to tap and assess intrapersonal and interpersonal intelligence, which can easily degenerate into musing and schmoozing. Do you flunk someone for not "knowing thyself," for not "going along and getting along"? One can assess spatial and musical intelligence more easily. Still, children with artistic talent should ordinarily demonstrate that ability in art or music class, not in English or French or science or math or history class. If art and dance and other such "intelligences" are so important as to now be considered part of the core academic mission of schools, then let's get serious about teaching these skills. Either teach these skills rigorously and assess them properly or toss them out of the classroom. At present, we are not promoting art and arias but doodles and ditties. Gardner and his minions do not address these practical issues associated with MI theory, probably because there is no ready answer. Even if we did away with instruction in grammar, punctuation, computation, factual knowledge, and all the other things that progressives consider expendable, thereby opening up time and space for other activities, it is still unclear how drawing, etc. "across the curriculum" produces anything but superficial proficiency. What is missing from discussions of multiple intelligences theory is any *logical* intelligence.

I would only add that MI theory is a dead end—it stops in twelfth grade. I'm not about to allow pirouetting in a political science classroom. Even with the relaxation of standards that increasingly marks the undergraduate experience, most professors share the view expressed by a chemistry department colleague of mine who, upon seeing my op-ed on MI theory, e-mailed, "I was very happy to see a rebuttal to the dumbing-down of public schools under the guise of this multiple intelligences nonsense."

Concluding Thoughts

If I have sounded sarcastic about MI theory, I am not alone. One can find many spoofs of the theory. For example, Will Fitzhugh, editor of the newsletter of the New England History Teachers Association, suggests that we add to Gardner's laundry list of intelligences the following ones that progressives seem to over-look: "Paying Attention Intelligence," "Memorization Intelligence," "Punctuation and Spelling Intelligence," "Hard Work and Diligence Intelligence," and "Turning in Homework Intelligence." Steve Kirsh, a psychologist at the State University of New York at Geneseo, goes further; his candidates include "spousal intelligence" ("the ability to manipulate your significant other without him/her knowing it"), "uvula intelligence" ("knowing what that little thing that hangs down in the back of your throat is called, possessed especially by ear, nose and throat physicians as well as bulimics"), "remote control intelligence" ("the ability to watch two or more TV shows at the same time"), "intra-bodily function intelligence" ("the ability to recognize when one has to urinate or defecate, and can judge how long they can 'hold it'"), "other-bodily function intelligence" ("the ability to tell when somebody else has to go to the bathroom"), and "unique intelligence" ("that intelligence which is unique to each individual, guaranteeing that we are all geniuses, at least in our own way").

I do not wish to make light of the subject. Of course, we need to respect diverse abilities and give all children the support they need to succeed in school. These irreverences actually point to a fundamental issue, however. Is there anything that goes on in school, and in life, that is *not* an "intelligence"?

Closely related to Gardner's work is Daniel Goleman's *Emotional Intelligence*, which states that "academic intelligence offers virtually no preparation for the turmoil—or opportunity—life's vicissitudes bring.... Our schools...fixate on academic abilities, ignoring *emotional* intelligence, a set of traits...that also matters immensely for our personal destiny. Emotional life is a domain that, as surely as math or reading, can be handled with greater or lesser skill.... Much evidence testifies that people who are emotionally adept—who know and manage their own feelings well, and who read and deal effectively with other people's feelings—are at an advantage in any domain of life."

Goleman should be happy. Thanks to him, Gardner and others, our schools no longer are "fixated" on academics but are becoming increasingly anti-academic and anti-intellectual. The increased emphasis being placed on *feelings* (and the decreased emphasis placed on scientific or any other kind of literacy) can be seen in the following example cited by Charles Sykes, in a writing entitled "How Did Einstein *Feel*?," which vividly shows MI theory at work:

> In May 1994, the *New York Times* published three eighth graders' answers to this question on [California's outcome-based] reading test: "Think about Einstein as a person and a scientist. In the split profile and below it, use symbols, images, drawings, *and/or words* to give your ideas about Einstein the person and Einstein the scientist" [emphasis added]. Students worked with two pictures of Einstein's head in profile (one head was labeled "scientist," the other "the person"), like a drawing in a coloring book. . . . One student who described Einstein "the scientist" as "smart, hopful [sic], commonsents [sic], and easy going," and Einstein "the person" as "sad, lonely, happy, postive [sic], loving," was awarded two points for his analysis. Another student who described Einstein as "smart" (next to a picture of a light bulb) was awarded five out of a possible six points. Another student drew pictures to illustrate Einstein "the scientist" [including]...a sheet of music illustrating "a masterpiece such as a syphony [sic]." The student also describes the scientist as "determined." Einstein "the person" is depicted as "peaceful" (accompanied by a hand-drawn peace sign), "open-minded" (illustrated by open windows), "beautiful inside" (a

butterfly).... The student was awarded the highest possible score—a perfect six out of six—in spite of the misspellings and the absence of any reference to Einstein's scientific contributions.

The Therapeutic Classroom

Thus far, much of the discussion in this book has been about the decline of academic standards. But that is putting the cart before the horse, since a dumbing down of academics presumes that our schools are at least focusing on academics. What is especially distressing today is the threatened disappearance of academics altogether. I don't believe the disclaimers one hears from the educational establishment that schools have a renewed commitment to the academic mission. There is too much evidence to the contrary.

There has always been the temptation to use schools for purposes other than schooling, for proselytizing or other ends, since children are the ultimate captive audience. The history of American education is littered with examples of K-12 educators of various stripes, progressive and otherwise, succumbing to the temptation. Michael Kirst, commenting on nineteenth century schools, notes that "the *McGuffey Readers*, first published in 1836,...were frankly moralistic [preaching the Protestant ethic in stressing honesty and industry as the leading values].... Courses in bookkeeping, surveying, industrial drawing, and commercial skills, at first taught in proprietary schools [private vocational schools], moved into the public schools in the decades from 1845 to 1865.... Henry Barnard, a nineteenth century leader of education, believed...that the school should inculcate positive rules of healthful living, among these the dangers of tobacco and liquor. Catharine Beecher [another leader] urged that the school teach the importance of fresh air, loose clothing, simple diet, and exercise." By 1890, there was sufficient concern over the seeming drift and lack of focus in the mission of public schools that the National Education Association created the Committee of Ten chaired by Charles Eliot, president of Harvard University, which urged a

rigorous academic curriculum for high school students as preparation for college. In her lengthy critique of progressivism's
preoccupation with nonacademic concerns throughout the twentieth century, Diane Ravitch starts with the progressives' rejection
of the Committee of Ten's recommendations as a premonition of
what was to follow.

Ravitch devotes considerable space to a leading critic of progressive education and a kindred spirit of the Committee of
Ten—Robert Hutchins, the boy-wonder of the University of
Chicago who became president of that institution in 1929 at the
age of thirty. At the same moment as the Great Depression was
descending upon America and as educators in the Teacher's College of Columbia University were advocating using K-12
classrooms for vocational training and social engineering to cure
the problems of industrial society, Hutchins reaffirmed the importance of intellectual pursuits and the role of academics as the core
function of schools:

> Hutchins disapproved of the objectives of progressive education. It
> was wrong, he asserted, to "adjust" students to their environ-
> ment.... Nor did he approve of preparing youngsters for a
> collectivist social order. No one, he noted, could say with any cer-
> tainty what the social order of the future should be, and it was mere
> conceit to design a course of study based on one's own political and
> economic opinions. Nor did he agree that the shaping of personal-
> ity or character should be the object of education. . . . Character, he
> said,...was a by-product of "hard work well done." Worse, the
> resources that ought to go into intellectual training would be "lav-
> ished on athletics, social life, and student guidance, a kind of
> coddling, nursing, and pampering of students that is quite
> unknown anywhere in the world." Hutchins insisted that the object
> of general education should be "the training of the mind."...Only
> the school and college could supply intellectual discipline, and if
> they abandoned this responsibility, no other agency would do it.

Over time we have moved further and further away from the
Hutchins ideal. By 1950, when "life adjustment" curricula
abounded in many American schools, the Harvard scholar David
Riesman was observing that "teachers were now being told to pay
more attention to their students' social and psychological development than to their intellectual prowess." What was observable in
1950 has only become more prevalent since, fed by the radical libertarian and radical egalitarian cultural aftershocks of the 1960s.

The pampering and nursing Hutchins worried about has reached new highs in the growth of the self-esteem movement and the conversion of schools into mini-hospitals, as school boards spend as much time debating mental health delivery services as they do the delivery of academics. The shaping of personality and character is now formally enshrined in the curriculum in the form of anger management/violence prevention programs and character education. Social engineering is provided through cooperative learning and multiculturalism/diversity sensitivity training as well as coerced volunteerism (service learning). Vocational education has morphed into school-to-work programs. And more energies are now devoted in many schools to improving school "climate" through enhancing participation in sports and other extracurricular activities than are devoted to strengthening academic coursework. The title of a recent *American School Board Journal* article, echoing Hutchins' concerns, sums up the problem posed by recent trends: "Nurturing the Life of the Mind: If Schools Don't Value Intellect, Who Will?"

Current K-12 educational research and practice is being driven primarily by a clear set of biases in support of the psychological well-being of the child and the social harmony of the classroom, school, and community rather than by the search for academic excellence. Teachers increasingly play the role of psychologists and sociologists, for which they are untrained. When our schools are not engaged in personal self-esteem-building, hormonal development, and other extracurricular matters, they are so preoccupied with promoting an ideological agenda that includes equity, diversity, multiculturalism, gender-neutral instruction, abilities awareness, inclusion, and assorted other commitments that it is remarkable they have any time left over for what used to be defined as education. We have been so busy turning our schools into social science laboratories, social work agencies, churches, psychiatry wards, wellness clinics, parenting surrogates, and day-care centers that we have completely lost sight of what is uniquely their mission—giving students a solid foundation of knowledge and understanding, a love of learning, and the tools for pursuing that learning.

Commenting on the increasingly overcrowded school day, a veteran teacher told me "we are trying to pour 60 gallons of education into a 10 gallon hat. It can't be done." Yet we continue to delude ourselves into thinking we can keep adding to the hats teachers wear. Typical is the following statement calling for "an inclusive system for the education of *all* children" published by the National Association of State Boards of Education: "[There is a] need for education that encompasses the many facets of the 'whole' child. That is,...his or her schooling must encompass a holistic view that is attuned to the student's non-academic needs. Incorporated within this model...[are] at least three spheres of development: (1) the academic...; (2) the social and emotional...; and (3) personal and collective responsibility and citizenship." Note there is no hierarchy of functions, just a mandate to do it all. Actually, this is a fairly tame statement compared to many other such pronouncements one hears today that even more blaringly trumpet the importance of the nonacademic over the academic mission.

Who is responsible for the added burdens being placed on our schools? There are many sources of the problem. First, there are those liberal-minded progressives, concentrated especially in schools of education, who see the schools as agents for saving the planet. This includes getting students to develop greater empathy for the oppressed, for the less fortunate, for the spotted owl and snail darter, and for various other victims of an often harsh world. Rita Kramer, after observing school of education classrooms over a substantial period of time, concluded:

> Everywhere, I found idealistic people eager to do good. And every-where, I found them being told that the way to do good was to prepare themselves to cure a sick society. To become therapists, as it were, specializing in the pathology of education. Almost nowhere did I find teachers of teachers whose emphasis was on the measur-able learning of real knowledge....The school is to be remade into a republic of feelings—as distinct from a republic of learning—where everyone can feel he deserves an A. In order to create a more just society, future teachers are being told they must focus on the handi-capped of all kinds—those who have the greatest difficulties in learning, whether because of physical problems or emotional ones, congenital conditions or those caused by lack of stimulation in the family...—in order to have everyone come out equal in the end.

Self-esteem-building and community-building are seen here as part of the same project, not so much a dumbing down as a substitute for academics. Although schools often complain about being saddled with too many peripheral demands that reduce time on task, the fact is that they often invite their expanded mission, possibly because it can be more exhilarating to engage in the atmospherics of transforming individual lives and society at large than getting one's hands dirty in the nitty-gritty of diagramming sentences or teaching multiplication tables. It can also be easier to cover up incompetence, when the main competency teachers are supposed to demonstrate is being a nice person and getting their students to be nice people, as opposed to becoming more intellectually competent. While many serious teachers resent the nonacademic expectations imposed on them, the less able view these as welcome distractions.

The touchy-feelies and social engineers on the left are not solely to blame for the movement away from academics. The bottom-line business sector along with the family-values folks on the right bear some responsibility as well. Conservative corporate interests are often behind school-to-work programs, while conservative religious groups support character education programs, both of which can consume substantial parts of the school day no less than sensitivity training and can be just as anti-intellectual. Although the advocates for these programs argue that they are needed to impart firmer values than our schools are now producing, their rationale seems as flimsy as that invoked by the more mushy-headed progressives.

Parents themselves are part of the problem. With so many households now dependent on two wage-earners, many parents have been derelict in assuming responsibility for tending to their children's emotional needs and character building and instead have looked to the schools to help perform this function. Although the many bipartisan "Public Agenda" surveys reported in recent years show parents much more focused on academics, especially on a back-to-basics agenda, than are education professors and teachers, parents often send schools a mixed message. In one survey, for example, done by John Goodlad, it was found that only about half of all parents interviewed selected "intellectual" development as the single most preferred goal of schooling, with the other half supporting personal, social or vocational development as a higher priority.

Both liberals and conservatives are guilty today of deprecating academics. But it is the progressives who must bear primary responsibility. They are in charge of the national educational bureaucracies as well as most local school systems that are now trying to juggle independent and cooperative learning and other conflicting ideas. In fact, although ideas such as cooperative learning are being heralded as cutting-edge pedagogy, they are better understood as repackaged nostrums having a long pedigree in the history of American education going at least as far back as Dewey. What *is* new and different today is that *all* students, from the most able and well-adjusted to the least, are to be subjected to the *same* regimen in the modern therapeutic classroom under the watchful eye of a teacher/facilitator whose job it is to insure that all kids end up in the same place in terms of attitudes if not academics, "discovering" those values and beliefs which are mandated from on high. Today's therapeutic classroom might be best described as "manipulated empowerment."

Cissy Lacks, the Tale of the Tape, and Other Recollections

Our schools have become "empowerment zones." If one did a content analysis of speeches made at professional development meetings, the word "empowerment" would probably pop up as the most frequently uttered. Educational reformers have essentially given up on producing an informed, knowledgeable citizenry. Instead, what counts the most is "empowering" students to construct their own meanings out of life and to express their personal opinions and feelings. The Oprahization of American education is actually far from spontaneous, however. It is fairly tightly scripted, with some opinions (the politically correct ones) being tolerated more than others. I have seen manipulated empowerment at work first-hand, as schools embarked on the contradictory quest, with my kids and others, to liberate and indoctrinate at the same time.

The St. Louis-area school district of Ferguson-Florissant found itself embroiled in an "empowerment" controversy relating to both students and teachers in which I became indirectly involved. It concerned one Cecilia (Cissy) Lacks, a white English teacher at the predominantly black Berkeley High School, who was fired in 1995 for permitting her students to use profanity in a creative writing assignment. She took her case all the way to the U.S. Supreme Court, which ultimately rejected her argument that the school district's policy regarding acceptable classroom language was unclear. Although the legal issues centered on the technicalities of the circumstances under which she was fired—she claimed not only that the policy was unclear but that there was racial discrimination on the part of a black principal toward a white staff member—the larger issues involved free speech and academic freedom. Lacks used the empowerment defense, defending her teaching techniques as "student centered and designed to unleash students' creativity." This position—that students should be given carte blanche to express themselves any way they wanted while teachers should be given carte blanche to promote such expression—was supported by the National Education Association, the National Council of Teachers of English, and the PEN American Center (a writers' association led by the actor Paul Newman and others who protect First Amendment rights and who eventually awarded her a medal for her efforts).

What exactly was it that Lacks and her supporters were defending? I cannot fully describe here the nature of her teaching technique since many of the words she approved of fifteen-year-olds using are not fit to print even for adults. She had her students, who were mostly black, write and perform plays that contained assorted obscenities, including multiple uses of the f-word, and violent physical action. She videotaped the plays for all to see, although she probably did not anticipate that parents and Supreme Court judges would view them. It was not just a case of allowing the language; the teacher also appeared to be signaling to the students that she encouraged their "authentic" voice and that she did not want them to hold back anything. (It is a testimony to how lewd the language was that the *St. Louis Post-Dispatch* ran an editorial supporting Lacks but could not publish the actual contents of student writing for fear of offending its readers.)

I wrote a memo to some members of the Clayton school board who I knew were "child-centered" types and who I suspected were closet Lacks supporters, in which I used the f-word and said "lest I offend you, I feel free to use this language here since it has the blessing of the NEA, which has helped pay for Lacks' legal fees, and if it is OK for fifteen-year-olds to use such 'voice,' why can't I?" I told the board I was not making the case for preventing students from reading *Huckleberry Finn* and other literary works that contain colorful language, only not actively eliciting and condoning such language from them. I was not advocating prudishness, only prudence, not censorship but censureship of mindless vulgarities. I got no response, as usual.

The Lacks case smacked of political correctness. A hidden

agenda that seemed to be at work was the need to respect diversity, in this instance the presumed native dialect of the "hood." In turning her classroom into a Snoop Doggy Dogg jam session, Lacks seemed to be engaging in the most banal sort of "situational learning." No matter how well-intentioned, she was patronizing black children and insulting black parents, who, like all parents, presumed that school was the place where kids learned to move beyond the confines of their circumstances to become more educated individuals. Such a display of "language arts" would never have been contemplated in a private or parochial school, which is precisely why such schools are becoming increasingly attractive to black parents. Although some parents of Berkeley High students supported Lacks, most were understandably infuriated at a white teacher trying to "cure" black students of their pathological behavior with a misguided dose of multiculturalism.

Around the same time that the *Post-Dispatch* was printing a pro-Lacks editorial, the newspaper also published my op-ed piece in which I suggested that Lacks was essentially applying the model of the therapeutic classroom that had become widely accepted among progressive educators, even if she had perhaps taken it to such an extreme that most progressive educators in town, though no doubt sympathetic to her, could not publicly defend her. I noted that her methods were a logical extension of contemporary progressive thinking:

> It is not so much Cissy Lacks who has been on trial in this case as the entire public school reform movement she is a creature of.... Almost anything goes.... [This approach] has become a pervasive part of educational practice even in rich suburban districts.... In the worst sort of way, we are pandering to the MTV generation when we constantly encourage students to speak from "their" experience, to tell us "their" stories, to use "their" language (or if they cannot write, to draw or act out or use any other means "they" are comfortable with) and to approach all of education from where—in Lacks' words—"they are at."

I received a mixed bag of responses, including some rather scathing letters from some of my ACLU friends and some more supportive letters from parents, such as one who wrote that "I think most people with school-aged children would find Cissy Lacks' methods of teaching offensive and self-defeating. I know I do, and if my children were in such a class, I would have them removed pronto. Most people I know with children in public schools are moderates with a lot of good, common sense. Unfortunately, some of the people running our schools and some of the people teaching in our schools have the common sense God gave a goose." I also received a nice call from Easy Ed McCauley, the St. Louis Hawks basketball star of the 1950s and now a local radio personality, whose station cited me for a "best commentary" that month.

When I said in my op-ed piece that even rich suburban school districts had adopted an "anything goes" view of education, I meant that these districts were often among those most wedded to a "situational learning" pedagogy that was an offshoot of the progressive child-centered philosophy focused on where students "are at." Although our own Clayton school district certainly could claim to be teaching some high-powered academics, such as advanced calculus and AP history courses, and could point to "teaching and learning" as the first principles that appeared in its districtwide curriculum development plan, I saw nonacademic stuff increasingly creeping into the curriculum. For example, a news release issued in November 2000 entitled "Educating the Whole Child" stated that "developing a student's mind is no longer the sole focus of education. We look to educate the total student. That is, educating both a student's mind and a student's body. This approach promotes development of the 'whole' person and helps establish life-long habits of learning and wellness." If all that was being alluded to here was the normal role of the school in supplementing schoolwork with physical education, there would be little to complain about. Not only, however, was Clayton elevating the body to the same status as the mind as the subject of schooling; it was also dedicating itself to servicing the psyche, the soul, the heart, and all other parts of the human anatomy.

In February of 2001, the Clayton Language Literacy Committee submitted its five-year report to the Citizens Curriculum Council, a parents group that had been formed to provide added input to the school board and administration. The committee continued to embrace trendy "whole language" as an approach to reading despite mounting evidence against that approach. And also, on its very first page, the report stated, "We felt it was time to eliminate the long term, homogeneous grouping of children for instruction and move to more flexible grouping strategies that better met individual needs and *preserved children's self-esteem as learners* [italics mine]." Here was as explicit a statement as one could imagine calling for building the entire language arts curriculum, including a ban on ability-grouping, around the fear of damaging somebody's self-esteem. If one reads between the lines, what was at work here was the desire to serve not only "individual needs" of students but also the needs of staff and administrators who did not want to make the hard decisions of who were "bluebirds" as opposed to "redbirds," something that could threaten what they define as school harmony and the development of "community."

The twin goals of self-esteem-building and community-building in fact have been a constant theme in the Clayton school district in recent years. I distinctly recall a flyer that went out to parents in 1994 announcing the appearance at a Clayton High all-school assembly of Mark Scharenbroich, "a nationally recognized motivational speaker" whose "style combines the art of a stand-up comic with...issues of respect for self and others." My immediate reaction was one of stupefaction, wondering how it was that, even though parents such as me were being told that schools simply did not have time to teach multiplication tables and other basics, we apparently did have time to bring in a combination Rosie O'Donnell and Jerry Seinfeld. Mr. Scharenbroich might well have been a good speaker, but I would rather supply jokes and pep-talks to my kids myself after hours. If the kids' self-esteem needed to be pumped up, it could be done through programs like the one started by a former Clayton High principal named Al Burr, who initiated an annual "trump card" award given to the student who showed the most progress academically in the face of obstacles that had to be overcome.

It is a toss-up what is more important in K-12 schools today—self-esteem or cooperative learning. Cooperation and collaboration is everywhere in the air. It makes for a difficult target of criticism, since one does not wish to be seen as promoting Social Darwinism, especially among kindergarteners. Indeed, cooperative learning has much to commend it, if it were balanced by an equally healthy respect for the virtues of competition. But "competition" is not a favored word in today's curriculum materials. Nowhere is the mantra of cooperative learning more in evidence than in the case of the multiage classroom, which is the latest rage in America's elementary schools and which two Clayton schools have implemented. Clayton describes the multiage classroom as "a learning-centered heterogeneous classroom which contains children of varying ages who remain together for two or more years." The idea is to mix kids of different ages together in, say, a combined first grade-second grade class, on the assumption that the younger students will learn from the older students by utilizing them as role models while the older students will deepen their own learning by mentoring the younger ones. The people who invented this practice apparently forgot that we once had one-room schoolhouses which were abandoned for various reasons, one of which was that they did not work as well as having age-specific, grade-specific classrooms. They also apparently have not questioned the propriety of having seven-year-olds serve as appropriate "elder" role models for six-year-olds or expecting those same seven-year-olds to tend to their own learning at the same time that they are being pressed into service as free labor to help the $50,000 a year professional teach classmates who need help.

Although proponents of the multiage classroom offer various arguments to justify this innovation, it is clear that nonacademic concerns are at least as important to them as academic ones. Clayton's own Multiage Curriculum Study Group issued a report in 1997, stating that "children in multiage classrooms do better than their peers in traditionally grouped classrooms on measures of self-esteem and social development; [they] exhibit less aggressive and competitive behavior than children in traditionally grouped classrooms; [they] exhibit more altruistic and nurturing behavior." We have what amounts to a controlled experiment in Clayton that provides a ready empirical test of these claims of the multiage classroom advocates, since one elementary school (Meramec) follows a traditional philosophy while the other two (Captain and Glenridge) have adopted the multiage innovation, yet there is no evidence whatsoever that the non-multiage school has more school yard fights or a poorer school climate. Indeed, it is silly to expect otherwise, notwithstanding the research studies cited by progressives. (The 1997 report said little about real, non-therapeutic learning. It no doubt must be a source of great annoyance to the two trendier Clayton elementary schools that neither one is able to top Meramec in the annual statewide academic assessments and school rankings despite the constant hype that attends all the latest progressive reforms adopted by staff in those buildings.)

When I asked the Glenridge principal why she supported multiage classrooms, she said, "I want our schools to mirror the real world, and where else other than in schools do we segregate six-year-olds from seven-year-olds and so forth? I want our schools to be like family." When I then noted that competition is also part of the real world, she replied "I don't believe competition is healthy for kids." Progressives love to invoke the real world as the justification for their reforms, but in fact they are only interested in those aspects of the real world that fit their ideological predispositions. Aside from promoting collectivist values, the multiage classroom helps get around the problems of social promotion and ability grouping, and is aimed especially at the low-achievers and kids from unstable homes (lacking "family"), who it is felt need the extra security of having the same teacher from one year to the next rather than being thrown annually into a new environment, even if the latter can provide a strong growing experience and foster self-reliance and an ability to meet new challenges.

The principal of Captain school was an even more ardent progressive than her Glenridge counterpart. She was intent on eliminating the multiage vs. traditional options that the school board had mandated be available to parents, wanting to see all children placed in the former setting, partly because she believed in the educational superiority of that approach and partly (I surmised) because a uniform system would be easier to administer. As so often happens in school districts, there was a carefully orchestrated effort at Captain to co-opt parents into accepting the changes desired by the building administration. In 1998, the principal brought in a "facilitator," an education professor from a local university, ostensibly to engage parents in a dialogue about the relative merits of multiage and traditional classrooms and elicit their views but who in fact was there to make a sales pitch for the new model. The professor in question was a known devotee of every progressive educational fad imaginable. As is often the case at such events, instead of balanced argument, full debate, presentation of hard empirical data, and other such things one might wish in a decision-making process, the deck was stacked. Parents were presented with a handout that stated "key reasons for breaking with traditional classroom structure" (a list of ten reasons supporting multiage grouping, which took up almost the entire page) and "some of the perceived negatives" (two items questioning the practice, which were buried at the very bottom of the page). Not only was there disparate space devoted to the two sides of the question, but note how the positives were characterized as "reasons" while the negatives rated only the word "perceived." The real kicker was the admission that "there are not huge differences between gains in these types of [multiage] classrooms and traditional classrooms," but "the anecdotal evidence *strongly* favors the multiage classrooms [italics mine]."

I dwell on this episode because it is as an example of how "facilitators" often operate as hired guns rather than as neutral peacemaking agents in K-12 education, how most progressive claims ultimately rest on anecdotal rather than scientific evidence, and how the anecdotes almost invariably happen to confirm the progressive position. It was a great illustration of "manipulated empowerment," in this case applied to parents. I should note that, in one of those too infrequent victories for parents, the principal failed to get the school board and administration to endorse multiage-only classrooms. One key to victory was my enlistment of a Captain parent in the traditionalist cause who happened to be a Harvard Law School graduate and was more than able to punch holes in the facilitator's argument. Other parent groups haven't been so fortunate. I heard from a parent in the Lake Oswego, NY School District who said that despite forming a "Citizens Against Blends" committee and publishing a brochure publicizing the negative features of multiage classrooms, they were unable to overcome the steamroller tactics of the district administration.

For those students whose "aggressive" tendencies are not adequately cured by the multiage classroom, Clayton has adopted a "violence prevention" curriculum which "must be integrated into the curriculum experienced daily by our students," which "is rooted in the context of all coursework," and which focuses on "personal development, building community, and conflict resolution." Upon learning of the adoption of this curriculum in 1996, I wrote to the school board as follows: "I can understand your being concerned with school safety, and I can even understand your having periodic student assemblies or programs on conflict resolution, but to expend energy on a violence prevention *curriculum* strikes me as overkill."

Like all school districts around the country, Clayton is awash in anti-prejudice as well as anti-violence projects. The centerpiece of this agenda is the "voluntary desegregation plan" whereby hundreds of African-American children from the city of St. Louis are bused to Clayton schools. Our district superintendent has called this "the largest school choice plan in the United States," even though there was never a vote (it was imposed by a federal judge) and even though choice is limited to only some city residents (wealthy blacks can participate but not poor Central European immigrants). Notwithstanding a recent court settlement permitting Clayton to end the program, the school district has continued this arrangement, for some noble motives (the desire to promote integration) and some less so (the desire to maintain access to state funds that support the plan and that augment district budgetary resources). The official justification usually offered to Clayton taxpayers by our district leadership is that kids who live in an almost all-white suburb must be exposed to diversity through the desegregation program if they are to be cleansed of their inborn racist tendencies, although it is curious that the leaders who most vociferously voice this social analysis generally attended segregated schools themselves but, miraculously I guess, managed to overcome their cloistered education.

If the deseg program and related multiculturalism efforts in Clayton could be proven to promote integration, then they might well be worthwhile. But these efforts often appear to be more likely to produce a boiling cauldron of racial and ethnic hypersensitivity à la Yugoslavia rather than the melting pot of the recent American past. In Clayton, as in much of the country, we seem to be turning our national motto "E Pluribus Unum" on its head, just as Al Gore inadvertently did in the 2000 presidential campaign when he erroneously translated our national calling as "out of the one, many."

We obsess over race in the Clayton school district, looking at children through their group skin color rather than treating them as individuals. Let me offer a few quick illustrations. The Pathfinders Project at Wydown Middle School aims to "increase enrollment of African American students in the Clayton High School Honors English program." The meaning of the boilerplate is obvious: honors selection will be based on group characteristics rather than personal performance. As an example of how invidious this is, I recall that, as my son Sean was about to graduate from Wydown and was being considered along with other children for the honors program at Clayton High, he told me that he saw a black friend of his brought to tears when her English teacher told her it did not really matter how well she did on the screening criteria since the district wanted to see more blacks in the honors courses. Until recently, Clayton also had a program which provided cash incentives for "deseg kids" to improve their grades, leading me to ask the school board whether we could expect to see newspaper headlines like "Deseg Kids Flock to Clayton, Where the Money Is." We seemed to be giving new meaning to the phrase "it pays to learn," one we would never consider applying to white students, for whom payola is considered a tacky substitute for gold stars and self-motivation. Since 1993, when Clayton convened an African-American Student Achievement Task Force, there have been dozens of programs targeted at blacks which, based on the premise that they needed special help, have had the effect of stigmatizing an entire group of students. "The soft bigotry of low expectations" may not be as virulent in Clayton as elsewhere, but it is present nonetheless.

In 1995, the all-white school board, elected by Clayton residents, voted 4-3 to appoint a liaison to the board from the black community to represent the city transfer students. I commented in the local paper at the time that "we are giving special treatment to one group of kids, based on the most odious of distinctions—skin color. [Appointing a special liaison for blacks indicates] that white members of the board, by virtue of their skin color, are incapable of representing African-American kids." The board majority seemed to take the view that there was a "black" perspective on math, English, professional development, building design, playground equipment, and other district business and, hence, a black had to have a seat at the table. Although the majority wrapped this decision in the rhetoric of democracy, there was no intention to put such a fundamental district governance change to a vote of the people, nor was it clear how one person, selected to fill the "black" seat, could purport to speak for the entire black community. As it turned out, the issue became so controversial that the liaison position ultimately was redefined so that the occupant did not participate in board meetings but merely periodically reported to the board about concerns raised by black parents.

Although African-Americans were the only group given a special liaison to the board, balkanization was not confined to race. At the same time that Clayton during the 1990s initiated a new organization called Parents of African American Students to share "issues especially relevant to the African American experience," it started up another group called Clayton Advocates for

Abilities Awareness to provide a voice for parents of disabled children and developed an "abilities awareness curriculum" to sensitize students to learning differences. There were efforts to organize girl support groups; I distinctly remember a candidate for school board one year making a big campaign issue out of fighting presumed discrimination against girls in the classroom, at a time when the president of the Clayton High School student body and the recipient of the senior scholar-athlete award were females along with over half the inductees into the CHS chapter of the National Honor Society.

I organized Parents Against Average Schools as an advocacy voice for the high-achievers, whether they were white or black, male or female, or belonged to any other category. The only qualification for "membership" in this group was that you had to be among the truly academic-minded. I never actually tried to get any official district endorsement of PAAS—in truth, it wasn't so much an organization as a mailing list of citizens with similar views—but it surely would have tested how fully committed the district was to diversity had I done so. My hunch is that the district would have sooner recognized a transgender group than a gifted association.

Clayton is also big on character education. All over the country, the *McGuffey Readers* have been reincarnated in the form of programs designed to instill "respect" and other "word of the day" values in today's student. Although I realize that most traditionalists (following William Bennett's lead) support character education, I nonetheless have raised several basic objections before the Clayton school board about the special curriculum that we adopted. First, there is the matter of it being a further distraction from academics; teachers are getting professional development training in character education when they should not be hired in the first place if they need this training, and when they should instead be getting professional development in upgrading their knowledge of history or math or other subject matter they teach. Secondly, I don't trust many of today's teachers to teach my kids values, given the politically correct mindset that currently dominates schools. Third, although I agree some children may well need character education to remedy the failure of their parents, other kids do in fact get it through home and church and do not need to have their school day taken up with this.

The minefield that is moral education today can be seen in

the travails experienced by Lee Turner, who, upon taking over as principal of Clayton High School in 2000, lasted exactly one semester. He brought sterling academic credentials to the job—the private Florida high school he had headed produced many National Merit Scholars and, as a forensics coach, his debate students had won a national championship. But today academic leaders must first and foremost be good therapists, and Turner was old-school. He believed in a kind of Boy Scout code of honor that stressed duty, obedience, patriotism, decorum, discipline, and other such values that the flower-children generation of parents had long since repudiated. Even though Claytonians talked a good game about "personal responsibility," there was an air of extreme permissiveness at the high school, reflected not only in a rampant drug and alcohol culture but also in a library where the noise level and unruliness gave the appearance more of a cafeteria or gym than of a place of learning.

Turner saw his job as changing the school culture, restoring some civility (which in itself is "character education" *avant la lettre*). Although his authoritarian style certainly contributed to his downfall, he may well have failed even had he exhibited better, shall we say, interpersonal intelligence, given the mismatch between his values and the values of the school community. His first mistake was demanding that one student sporting a garish Mohawk hairdo see his barber; it was probably the wrong battle at the wrong time at the wrong place, since the principal instantly attracted the ire of the "free expression" police who admonished him for violating the first amendment right of students to parade in outlandish costumes. He also arranged a Veterans' Day assembly that engaged students in old-fashioned flag-waving, instituted new rules in the library calling for quiet, strengthened policies against student absences and tardiness, and took other measures which produced considerable snickering and ridicule in the community. In the end, he was forced to resign.

A Spreading Conflict

Clayton is not alone in its embrace of the therapeutic classroom. I recounted the Cissy Lacks' "tale of the tape." Although the Ferguson-Florissant school district sanctioned her for carrying the therapeutic classroom too far, many local educators consider

Lacks a role model for the modern teacher and a martyr to the cause of progressive education. The growth of the nonacademic mission can be found increasingly throughout the St. Louis metropolitan area and the nation. Indeed, the trend is even making its way around the world. The Clayton High flyer that announced the appearance of Mark Scharenbroich noted that he "has personally spoken in over 2,000 high schools from above the Arctic Circle to below the Panama Canal," suggesting the international reach of his comedy act. As further evidence of how such practices as cooperative learning have spilled across borders, I remember reading a newspaper at breakfast a couple of years ago while attending a conference in Toronto and seeing a teacher quoted as saying (about the new standardized tests used in Ontario schools) that "it is unfair that her students were being assessed individually since they were used to working collaboratively." I almost choked on my Canadian bacon. In the United Kingdom, it is reported that "progressive ed banished competition and testing as harmful and elitist; the result is underachieving young males," referring to the tendency today to pit boys against girls and for an anti-competition culture to privilege the latter. On the other side of the globe, Japanese schools, which long have had tracking in high school and strict discipline and homework throughout all grades (resulting in Japanese students outperforming American students on most international tests), are now considering responding to criticisms that they put too much pressure on students to "study, study, study."

One of the best examples of the way in which the line between academic and nonacademic activities is becoming blurred in bizarre ways can be seen in the new way of teaching English literature that has been adopted at Pattonville High School, located in St. Louis County not too far from Clayton. Taking psychosocial behavior modification and situational learning, along with team teaching and interdisciplinary coursework, to a new level, a Pattonville ninth-grade teacher has teamed with an officer from the Maryland Heights Police Department to teach such classics as *Romeo and Juliet*, *A Tale of Two Cities*, and *To Kill A Mockingbird*. According to a news article, the teacher in question "called the police—for a little teaching help....The goal of her lesson plan was for her students to understand the importance of communication, respect and tolerance to promote harmony. Her use of articles from the *Post-Dispatch* about curfew violations, teen drinking, teen-age love and behavior earned her recognition as a 1998 Teacher of the Year.... [In *Romeo and Juliet*], the officer added relevance to the play by relating the characters and the plot to problems he deals with involving teens in everyday life. 'This turned out to be the highlight of our year' [said the teacher]." Note the assumption that kids cannot deal with abstraction but need somebody like a police officer to come in off the street to bring literature down to their level.

Another St. Louis County high school, Webster Groves, is also promoting harmony, in a manner reminiscent of the demise of the U. City jazz band. The high school recently adopted a new policy mandating that all students in the concert and jazz bands had to participate also in the marching band, since "marching taught students to work together as a group." A group mentality is found everywhere in St. Louis, from the most elite college-prep schools like Clayton to the St. Louis Career Academy, the voc-tech school in St. Louis city. A news article reported recently about the latter that "the St. Louis Career Academy isn't your traditional vocational school. Students will learn by doing [group] projects....The idea is to create a family-like environment and to get students used to working together, officials say." No, this is not your father's trade school. It sounds more like the multiage classroom in Clayton. Why would Clayton seek to mirror the St. Louis Career Academy, or vice versa? Because pack pedagogy cannot seem to distinguish between different school settings and different student needs. The explanation you constantly hear from K-12 reformers is that business people want schools to teach teamwork. The contradiction is that most of the business community thrives on competition.

In yet another St. Louis-area school district, Francis Howell, some staff members recently gave glowing reports on what they had learned from a Dr. Charles Schwann at an Outcomes-Based Education Conference in Custer, South Dakota. In an unambiguous reference to the shift away from academics, they proclaimed in a memo to colleagues: "Today the purpose of schools is to ensure that our graduates are ACADEMICALLY COMPETENT students. Tomorrow we must ensure LIFE-ROLE PERFORMANCE SUCCESS for our graduates. We must define what will be necessary to insure our students will be successful in their workplace and future life." Apparently, neither the speaker nor the staff had ever heard of the disaster that was the life adjustment movement of the 1940s and 1950s. I have noted how K-12 educators suffer from amnesia, but this seemed an especially acute case.

Clayton, Ferguson-Florissant, Pattonville, Webster Groves, and Francis Howell are all members of The Cooperating School Districts of St. Louis (CSD), which, in addition to spreading the gospel of multiple intelligences theory, also has been spreading the gospel of character education. Character*plus*, coordinated through CSD, reaches fifty Missouri districts with more than 425 schools and 250,000 students. Founded by the former head of McDonnell Douglas Aviation, it calls itself "the nation's largest community-wide response to the challenge of character education." The current director of the program wrote an op-ed piece defending the program: "Within days of assuming office [in 2001], Gov. Bob Holden announced that he wants the state to set aside $1 million to expand a program to teach character education in public schools....I was asked: Why would we want to spend a million dollars to pull children out of math and science classes to be taught character education? Values can be taught along with math and science and in all the curriculum. The goal is not for a separate program, but to integrate character education into the daily life of the school." If the character education envisioned here simply meant embedding basic virtues such as honesty and hard work into the everyday rhythm of a school, it would be one thing. The fact is, however, that it *is* a program unto itself, and a potentially distracting one at that, involving forty-eight different character traits that are supposed to be worked into lesson plans. When one adds this mandate to diversity training and all the other diversions of the contemporary classroom, it is hard to see how academics will not suffer. There would seem to be better ways to spend a million dollars.

Perhaps nowhere in America has there been a greater effort to bring together all the most progressive elements of the therapeutic classroom than at Celebration School in Celebration, Florida, a "highly planned brave new town" created by the Walt Disney Company. When it opened in 1997, Celebration School was the epitome of the child-centered commune, the educational version of the New Left workplace democracy model. It was designed to serve kindergarteners through twelfth-graders under one roof, complete with multiage classrooms, computers in lieu of textbooks, and unstructured classes that dispensed with tests and individual letter grades and in their place substituted a different sort of regimen built around group projects. As often happens with Alice-in-Wonderland ideas, "the happiest school on earth" failed to withstand reality-testing. Parents complained about the lack of homework, the antipathy toward standardized testing, and the absence of any grade point averages, practices which did not augur well for their kids getting into Harvard. When the school, in an effort to address the concerns of these parents, redesigned some elements of its program, it was accused by the more progressive parents of betraying the initial vision of the school. All the cooperative learning that the school had prided itself on could not prevent conflict and turmoil. Three years after its opening, parents "were queuing up to withdraw their children."

What's More Important, Feeling or Knowing?

As ubiquitous as character education programs are, they are eclipsed by those programs dearest to progressive educators, the ones, such as anger management and conflict resolution, that are most emotive in nature and that have become especially popular as hoped-for deterrents to the spate of recent shootings at Columbine and other schools. Even if there were evidence that these diversions from academic pursuits are producing more feeling human beings, there would still be the question of whether the school day is better taken up with lessons in feeling or lessons in knowing. The focus on building better people and communities has a proper and inescapable place in schools. It has, however, come to dominate our schools in a perverse way that I have only partially described in the above stories. Let's look more deeply into the inner workings of the therapeutic classroom and the extent to which affective learning has replaced cognition as the primary purpose of K-12 education.

The High Esteem K-12 Places on Self-Esteem

Diane Ravitch places what she calls "the self-esteem movement" in historical context: "In the late 1930s, the Progressive Education Association—an advocacy group for child-centered education…—launched a new campaign to persuade school officials that the academic curriculum conflicted with the 'needs of youth.' Several major PEA publications contended that the nation's high schools should concentrate on their students' personal, emotional, and social problems rather than academic studies.... By the 1980s, self-esteem was touted in professional literature as both a means and an end of education. Anything that might encourage higher academic standards—such as grades, standards, deadlines, homework, correction of grammar or spelling—was potentially a threat to students' self-esteem," which, if damaged, could then undermine their achievement. Ravitch notes it has become hard to separate self-esteem from multiculturalism and the other strands of the therapeutic classroom: "The big theory that many seized upon [in the 1980s and 1990s] to resolve the yawning achievement gap [between African-American and Hispanic-American pupils on the one hand and European-American and Asian-American pupils on the other] was that low-performing students would achieve more if they had higher self-esteem.... In short order, this theory evolved into a generalized belief that the schools should help all children develop higher self-esteem." Here again we see the pattern of educators allowing the bottom to drive the entire curriculum for the entire student body. What recently has been called "the middle school philosophy"—that is, nurturing students' emotional needs at a time when their hormones are commonly depicted as "raging"—has become the operant philosophy for pre-hormonal and post-hormonal development throughout K-12 education.

Few would question the proposition that self-esteem is important and that liking oneself may make it easier to like others. But there is little scientific evidence that self-esteem programs in themselves produce better "feelers." Indeed, a recent study by researchers from Case Western University and the University of Virginia found that high self-esteem, particularly artificially inflated self-esteem ungrounded in real accomplishments, seems to be correlated with violent tendencies. Based on an examination of dozens of empirical studies of behaviors ranging from bullying to murder, the authors concluded that "violent and criminal individuals have been repeatedly characterized as arrogant, confident, narcissistic, egotistical, assertive, proud, and the like." A related study found that many college students have unrealistically high opinions of themselves and are often unable to tolerate criticism, sometimes becoming violent when their exaggerated self-image, cultivated by years of ego-stroking in grade school, comes up against someone who dares to say "you are wrong."

If there is scant evidence that K-12's emphasis on self-esteem-building will necessarily produce better feelers, there is even less evidence that it will produce better thinkers and knowers. Research commissioned by a 1990 Task Force to Promote Self-Esteem created by the California legislature failed to find any link between self-esteem and improved academic achievement. Indeed, one of the researchers commented that "one of the most disappointing aspects of every chapter in this volume...is how low the associations between self-esteem and its consequences are," calling them "mixed, insignificant, or absent." Harold Stevenson of the University of Michigan has found that American fifth-graders and eleventh-graders surpass their Asian counterparts in labeling themselves as having high self-esteem, at the same time that Asian students surpass American students in terms of actual academic performance. While Asian students may be too hard on themselves, their American peers may be too easy. Stevenson says that "self-esteem theorists have it backward. Meaningful self-evaluation and positive self-esteem are usually results, not antecedents, of accomplishment.... Feeling good is fine. It is even better when we have something to feel good about." The same sentiments are echoed by Carl Lutz, the former president of Chrysler Corporation: "I believe that self-esteem comes only from hard work and legitimate achievement. I think failure is a wonderful teacher, and that shielding a student from failure is a form of child abuse."

The nicest and most satisfying communication I ever received from a former student was a copy of a letter that he had submitted for my tenure and promotion file, thanking me for flunking him:

> During my first two years at the University of Missouri, I had very little direction and almost as little ambition. Then one fall I enrolled in a course called "World Politics." The professor was Martin Rochester. I approached the course half-hearted. I missed a good deal of the lectures but assumed that I would slide through with my usual "C" grade. I was wrong. I failed the course. Despite my failing grade, I learned something from the class. I learned that there are professors who really care about their students. One might believe that failing a student is hardly a show of affection; but it sent the right message to me. If I had received another "C" I would have continued to drift through my education. Instead I was shocked into reality. I can honestly say that Professor Rochester

changed my life. For the next three years I consistently made the Dean's List and eventually graduated *cum laude.*

I quote at length because it conveys a message of simple common sense, that "tough love" is the best overall approach to take in motivating students to learn. I also include the letter here as an object lesson for today's progressive educators, who take their cues from the likes of Alfie Kohn, whose *Punished by Rewards* argues naively that the "intrinsic satisfaction" of learning is a more effective motivational tool than "extrinsic" rewards and punishments in the form of grades. Kohn is a devotee of the gradeless report card; if teachers must give grades, he urges they give only two kinds, As and incompletes—anything to avoid the dreaded F, even if it encourages students to procrastinate and accumulate delayed grades in course after course. While Kohn cites research he contends supports his position, he conveniently ignores, as progressives are wont to do, the larger body of research and the even larger body of professorial experience that refutes him.

Fortunately, there is of late some evidence that K-12 education may be in a period of adjustment where the pendulum is slowly swinging back from the excessive emphasis on self-esteem that characterized the 1980s and 1990s. One recent article notes that "in a sea change from the gestalt of recent decades, many educators and child psychologists are concluding that less praise is often better and frequent praise for unexceptional actions can actually have a negative impact on children. 'Praising every time lowers a child's motivation' [says one expert]." The question that continues to nag at me is why it takes such experts so long to figure out what the average man or woman on the street already knows, and why they cannot get it right the first time. Even the "middle school philosophy"—the apotheosis of therapeutic thinking in K-12 education—is undergoing rethinking. A recent *Education Week* article entitled "Muddle in the Middle" observes that "thirty years after districts began shifting away from junior versions of high school, the middle school model has come under attack for supplanting academic rigor with a focus on students' social, emotional, and physical needs." The article cites the backlash felt in one school district in particular, Howard County, Maryland, where a report commissioned by the Board of Education and compiled by a parents group concluded that the district's middle schools had "sacrificed academic excellence by putting too much emphasis on fostering students' self-esteem." The report quoted a teacher as confessing that "the lesson [students] learn from the middle school philosophy is that they do not have to do anything they don't feel like doing."

It is still unclear whether the K-12 profession as a whole is capable of learning any lessons from the many backlashes that progressive reforms provoke, of which the revulsion against the self-esteem movement is only one. In addition to the fading of the self-esteem fad, there is a backlash waiting to happen over cooperative learning and other progressive hobbyhorses associated with the therapeutic classroom that are beginning to come under greater scrutiny, again mostly from observers outside the K-12 establishment—outside the schools of education and curriculum offices, where stubborn pride and the fear of damaged reputations often prevent acknowledgment of mistakes that are readily apparent to parents, teachers, and others at ground-zero who see the fallout first-hand.

Conflicting Views on Cooperative Learning

Although there is good reason to encourage children early in life to appreciate the importance of "we" rather than "me," our schools have taken the "it takes a village" slogan to such excess that they risk producing a growing number of village idiots.

Cooperative learning has been described as "an instructional method in which small groups of students of varying abilities...are expected to work together as a team to complete a daily assignment or a long-term project. In theory, each individual in the group is accountable for contributing to the end product. In reality, the work usually ends up falling on the shoulders of one or two more capable students whose sense of personal responsibility and motivation keeps everyone else from failing." While it is axiomatic that children should be encouraged to help each other, this should not be the key pedagogical principle around which the classroom is organized, as in the case of multiage classrooms and many other school settings today. I have spoken to countless parents who rightly resent their high-achieving children being exploited by being asked to mentor slower learners, by being denied teacher instruction pitched to their level, and by having to accept a group grade that either penalizes them for the poor work produced by other group members or rewards the latter for work done by the former. Although supporters of cooperative learning often wrap themselves in the rhetoric of democracy to justify this pedagogy, it is hard to see how principles of justice and fairness are served by elevating the group to such an exalted plane. And, for high and low achievers alike, it is hard to imagine a pedagogical practice more likely to produce the kind of "dependent learners" progressives claim to abhor.

It is especially disingenuous of progressives to defend cooperative learning as something that has been practically forced upon schools in response to the new demands of the workplace, when, as I noted earlier, schools often are critical of the values of big business and, in social studies classes especially, tend to present American capitalism generally in an unfavorable light as uncaring and greedy. Cooperative learning has become chic in schools not because of the new demands of capitalism but because of the heightened commitment of schools to a collectivist ethos that is as old as John Dewey, who, after visiting the Soviet Union in the 1920s, applauded "the marvelous development of progressive educational ideas and practice under the fostering care of the Bolshevik government." Shortly before Dewey's pilgrimage to Moscow, a group of his fellow progressives had issued a landmark report on secondary education in which they stated: "Among the means for developing attitudes and habits important in a democracy are the assignment of projects and problems to groups of pupils for cooperative solution...[in order to] give training in collective thinking." Since socialism is now passé, today's progressive educators are forced to look to capitalism to legitimize their collectivist tendencies. There is more hype than reality, though, behind the claim that the modern firm is all about teamwork:

> "A great many more firms talk about teamwork than do it in any meaningful way" [admits a professor at the Harvard Graduate School of Education].... In a recent article in *The Harvard Business Review* titled "The Myth of the Top Management Team," [a consultant with McKinsey and Company] argued that groups of top managers that called themselves teams seldom actually worked together in pursuit of a particular goal.... [In an interview he said] too often teamwork becomes a feel-good mechanism that can get in the way of actually accomplishing something.... "The notion of the team-based organization is dangerous because you will try to do everything as a team. It's a crazy idea."...[A management professor at MIT adds that] it can be hard to square the fact that at the same time managers are ruthlessly pursuing bottom-line profits and their

bonuses, they are also urging workers to consider themselves part of the company team. And for all the talk of the need for team players, the star system remains alive and well in business.

As one researcher who analyzed fifty-six studies from twelve countries concluded about the grouping practices in multiage classrooms, the best case that can be made for them is that "these classes are simply no worse, and no better, than single-grade or single-age classes." That's not exactly a ringing endorsement and high return on investment for a pedagogy that has been sold as a cure for everything from school shootings to academic failure and has entailed high costs in terms of upsetting normal building routines. Let's have less hype and more serious research on this issue. (I do not much care if the research is done individually or collaboratively.) And let's have less professional development in such areas as "Advanced Cooperative Learning," the title of a one-credit course advertised by a St. Louis-area school of education.

The Multiculturalism Nursery

Mao Zedong, the father of Communist China, wrote the book on "manipulated empowerment." He called it the Red Book. One of his most famous sayings was "let a hundred flowers bloom," referring to the unleashing of creative energies associated with China's catastrophic Cultural Revolution of the 1960s. Today the multiculturalism crusade in K-12 education in America might well be best captured in the phrase "let 1,500 flowers bloom."

Why 1,500? Because that is the estimated number of distinct ethnic groups that are found around the planet, each of which, according to the prevailing logic of multiculturalists, needs to be studied, understood, respected, and honored, whether such groups have any representatives in the United States or not. There are not enough days, much less months, in the year to devote to all 1,500, so that we risk some groups being privileged more than others. Is it fair, after all, that we should now celebrate African-American Heritage Month (February), Asian-American Heritage Month (May), Hispanic-American Heritage Month (September), and American Indian Heritage Month (November), with all the other minorities having to scramble to stake a claim to the remaining months? Things are further complicated by the fact that some months are reserved for non-ethnic tribal units, such as National

Women's History Month (March) and, if the National Education Association has its way, Gay and Lesbian Month. Things get even stickier, when one realizes that "Hispanic" is an artificial, catch-all category. Perhaps we need special weeks slotted for Cuban-Americans, Chicano-Americans, Puerto Ricans, and just plain Spanish-Americans.

There may be as many as 7,000 distinct languages spoken in the world. The United States is a nation of immigrants that includes virtually every dialect spoken anywhere. Why should Hispanics be privileged with special bilingual programs in American schools when, it could be argued, newly arrived Bosnian immigrants and the other 6,999 foreign tongues are no less deserving of bilingual accommodation? Were multiculturalism to be carried to its logical extreme, one could see entire school budgets taken up with bilingual programs. Then there is also the matter of "student learning styles." As hard as it is for a teacher to teach to Gardner's seven different intelligences, imagine having to teach to thousands of different learning styles based on a child's "distinctive" oral or other tradition.

Ethnic cheerleading is now part of the fabric of our schools. Walk into any school building in America, especially any elementary school, and you will see walls plastered with drawings in tribute to every conceivable minority, most of which are assumed to be oppressed.

On the surface, there is nothing wrong with multiculturalism and much that is right, if we interpret the term to mean getting students to appreciate the richness and diversity of the human species. But rather than emphasizing either the singular, unique humanity of each of six billion human beings, or what all of them have in common, our schools are stressing what amounts to tribal groupings. In the United States in particular, as I suggested earlier, we are promoting balkanization, not unity. We are distancing ourselves from the melting pot history that has defined the American experience. If schools in the past were at times guilty of teaching a sanitized, exclusionist history that did not fully cover the flaws in the American experiment and the range of peoples who contributed in a positive way to that experiment, today we are guilty of other distortions. Arthur Schlesinger has put it best in his recent work, *The Disuniting of America*:

> The new ethnic gospel in its militant form rejects the unifying concept of a unique American identity, rejects the ideal of individuals

from all nations melted into a new race, rejects the ideals of assimilation and integration, rejects the common culture—its underlying philosophy is that America is not a nation of individuals at all but a nation of groups, that ethnicity is the defining experience for most Americans.

William Pfaff, a leading student of nationalism, adds that "American education is no longer didactic about citizenship or deliberately assimilative with respect to minorities, as it was in earlier periods of immigration. Then it insisted upon the acculturation of immigrants' children by teaching them English and American literature, American history, and...'civics'. [Today, such teaching] is denigrated as elitist, ethnocentric, imperialist, and patriarchal.... [We now] see American society in census terms: white, plus African-American, Hispanic, Asian-Pacific Islander, etc."

Higher education is just as much at fault for bean-counting as K-12, perhaps even more so, since a "roots" approach to history is rooted in the many multicultural studies programs that have blossomed across American campuses. (My own university has an entire bureaucracy housed in a Multi-Cultural Relations Office whose primary job is to implement the various monthly observances and to root out supposed institutional racism on a campus which during the course of the 1990s had a black chancellor and vice-chancellor in the top two leadership posts.) The K-12 social studies profession bears special blame. One critic explains, echoing Schlesinger and Pfaff:

> The critical question is what kind of multicultural education is most appropriate for our children? Although the treatment of ethnicity in social studies is complex, two visions of multicultural education seem to have emerged. There is a vision of multiculturalism that emphasizes cultural and ethnic differences and the nation's failure to live up to our ideals. There is a second vision...that, while recognizing our differences, accentuates what Americans have in common and our positive evolution in a diverse society....A disproportionately high number of leading multicultural theorists within the social studies profession are advocates of a critical separatist multiculturalism.... In fact, the theorists are less interested in multicultural content than in affective multicultural education. [They] place a high priority on multicultural education as a tool to improve ethnic group relations, raise specific groups' self-esteem...and stimulate citizen action to transform America.

Identity politics, of course, is not limited to ethnicity but extends to gender as well. Progressives have taken as an article of faith the proposition that females continue to be discriminated against in K-12 education, especially in math and science, partly because of the traditional emphasis placed in those fields on logical intelligence as opposed to the more creative intelligences and partly because boys are seen as more competitive and able to dominate the classroom. There is little empirical evidence to support this proposition. If anything, it seems girls are doing better than boys today in the nation's schools. As just one example, in 2001, for the first time, women were about to outnumber men in law school admissions. Christina Hoff Sommers writes: "This we think we know: American schools favor boys and grind down girls. The truth is the very opposite. By virtually every measure, girls are thriving in school; it is boys who are the second sex." Perhaps, it is because, as teachers increasingly have employed cooperative learning that is thought to favor girls' affinity for teamwork, girls are now more at home in school. If boys have become the "second sex," perhaps it is simply a function of the relentless feminist drumbeat that has led teachers to feel sorry for girls and, possibly, to practice reverse discrimination against boys. (At a middle school assembly, my son's science teacher, a woman, once ridiculed males with the line that "in the case of our boys, it's like a dog's life but in reverse," meaning that fourteen-year-old boys often act with the maturity of seven-year-olds; it would have been unthinkable to utter such an insult against girls, for fear of NOW being sicked on you.) Boys and girls obviously are different anatomically and probably even temperamentally, but we do both a disservice when we engage them in a battle of the sexes and base educational judgments on gender pigeonholing.

I once told the Clayton school board that as a teacher, when it came time for me to grade papers and exams, I still followed the quaint practice of not wanting to know whether the student was white, black, male, female, or belonged to any other categorical group. I do not teach to learning styles. I have one common standard to which all are held. I find this enables me to avoid stereotyping and other malicious effects that flow from obsessing over group identity. I work especially hard to resist racial profiling, which liberals object to when done by police departments in New Jersey and elsewhere but otherwise condone in the context of schooling. I take seriously Thurgood Marshall's admonition, stated before the U.S. Supreme Court when he was representing the NAACP in the 1954 *Brown vs. Board of Education* school desegregation case, that "distinctions by race are so evil, so arbitrary and insidious that a state bound to defend the equal protection of the laws must not allow them in any public sphere."

But such a view puts me squarely at odds with the latest thinking in K-12 education. Typical of the stereotyping and "soft bigotry" that now dominates American schools is the statement made at a recent seminar on race and education sponsored by the St. Louis Cooperating School Districts: "African-Americans come from an oral tradition....What is killing them is that standardized tests are not the right approach to measure intelligence." The K-12 scholarly literature often calls for sensitivity to group learning styles: "Research about the African-American culture shows that students often value oral experiences, physical activity, and loyalty in interpersonal relations....These traits call for classroom activities that include approaches like discussion, active projects, and collaborative work. Descriptions indicate that Native-American people generally...have reflective thinking patterns and generally value and develop acute visual discrimination....Thus, schooling should provide quiet time for thinking and emphasize visual stimuli."

Such a vision is perilously close to racism. It also risks defeating the major purpose of education, that is, forcing a young person to get outside of his or her "skin," to stretch experiences to include foreign ideas, indeed to imagine things that have no empirical references anywhere, such as "dinosaurs or lost civilizations." Rather than enriching children's lives, multiculturalism can have the opposite, parochializing effect. Multiculturalism can also have the effect of distorting reality, when we rewrite history in order to make everybody feel good about their ethnicity. We certainly should not overlook the contributions made by African-Americans and other people of color, but we also should not exaggerate them, as Afrocentrists do when they claim that the Ancient Greeks stole all their novel ideas from the Dark Continent—one of the views that is unfortunately present in many inner city public schools. The same can be said for histories of women, whose everyday lives no doubt are worth chronicling but who, precisely because of centuries-old oppression, were not positioned to shape history as powerfully as men. If we give equal coverage to Beethoven and Beethoven's mother, as one feminist recommends, we trivialize history. For better or worse, the fact is DWEMs (Dead White European Males) have dominated much of the history of the world, certainly the history of the United States. If one really believes in situational learning, then one should heed Edwin Yoder's advice to social studies teachers in America's classrooms:

> [Young people] need to learn first about our own traditions, and those from which they derive. You can't understand the ideas in the Declaration of Independence without knowing a bit about John Locke's treatise on government. Locke leads back into the English revolution of 1688. And that may lead back to Magna Carta....We should learn who we are before we venture to learn who we aren't.

When multiculturalists talk about cultural imperialism, they could be referring to the little empires they are building for themselves, as multiculturalism may be the leading growth industry in K-12 education. Not far behind, though, is the violence prevention industry.

Taking Violence Prevention Too Far

We need to be careful not to exaggerate the problem of school violence, since school shootings are still relatively rare. We also need to recognize that no amount of preventative measures can hope to eliminate completely the kind of random, lunatic mayhem committed by extremely disturbed kids. Still, there is reason to be concerned about the recent flurry of such episodes, and reason to try to respond with deterrent policies. The question is whether the approaches now in vogue are likely to work.

I have noted that the proliferation of school shootings has coincided with the growing emphasis schools have placed on self-esteem and other such bromides. One cannot blame the therapeutic classroom as the cause of school violence, but neither can one credit it with any visible success. One social psychologist goes so far as to suggest that the delivery of the entire K-12 academic curriculum be predicated upon violence prevention, through a "jigsaw classroom" structure that "requires students to cooperate and to share their knowledge with one another." Why a few pistol-packing students should now be the driving force dictating the restructuring of our schools and what evidence exists that "required cooperation" will make even a dent in the problem leave me puzzled.

Following the Santana High School shooting spree in a San Diego suburb in 2001, the *New York Times* quoted a state education department official as saying that Santana "was a school that did basically everything that we suggested they do," including training students in mediation techniques. The *St. Louis Post-Dispatch* added, "It did everything right [such as] programs to help youngsters get along, including one called 'Names can really hurt us,'" an anti-bullying program. Although the perpetrator was new to the school, having just arrived from Maryland, he was not new to a K-12 culture which for years was promoting the therapeutic classroom across the country. The *New York Times* reported that the number of school health clinics, including mental heath services, had jumped from 200 to 1,380 over the decade of the 1990s. The post-mortem done at Columbine High, the suburban high school in Littleton, Colorado where two teenagers murdered thirteen fellow students in 1999, revealed that the pair had just performed forty-five hours of community service and had received extensive counseling that included an anger management class. Indeed, a few years earlier the *Wall Street Journal* had run a story on Littleton, Colorado as a school district run by "educational faddists" who had made the district a leader in progressive education.

It would appear that progressive nostrums are no more likely to guarantee protection against future incidents of school violence than more metal detectors or more gun control laws. Matthew Rees notes that the track record of the Safe and Drug-Free Schools Act, the federal program that funds most violence prevention projects in the public schools, is quite dubious: "Hundreds of millions of dollars are being spent on activities with little or no record of success.... [Grant money has been] used to pay for questionable activities like motivational speakers...and magic shows. The Center for the Study of Prevention of Violence has surveyed more than 400 violence-prevention programs used in schools and communities and found that most had not been subjected to credible evaluations or had no record of effectiveness. This includes such fashionable approaches as conflict resolution, peer mediation, and individual counseling."

We should not be overreacting to news headlines about school shootings by instituting excessive suspensions and expulsions, although some are necessary as part of a "zero tolerance" policy. We should also not be overreacting by instituting excessive touchy-feely conflict measures. Some school systems, such as one in Austin, Texas, have gone to the extreme of banning dodgeball. A "curriculum specialist" in the Austin schools was quoted recently as stating that "this is something that should not be used in today's classroom," since "what we have seen is that it does not make students feel good about themselves." Most of us remember dodgeball as a light-hearted recreational outlet, as a relatively harmless way to expend energy during lunch break. Now the activity is a target of condemnation and the subject of weighty Ph.D. dissertations and journal articles calling for an end to all "elimination sports." It is tempting to surmise that, indeed, some of the people behind these reforms may well have been hit in the head by one dodgeball too many when they were youngsters, but that would be discourteous.

Let Schools Be Schools

In 1994, the Committee for Economic Development, which includes executives at 250 large U.S. corporations, issued a much publicized report entitled *Putting Learning First* that warned that K-12 staff were expected to be "parent, social worker, doctor, psychologist, police officer, and perhaps, if there is time, teacher." The committee chairman noted that school programs were "diluted, distracted, and diffused from the basic mission of education." As U.S. Secretary of Education Richard Riley said at the time in summing up the report at a news conference, "American public schools are being spread too thin." One newspaper editorial, entitled "Let Schools be Schools," added that "recent education reform efforts have fallen short because they...did not concentrate on academic excellence to the exclusion of other concerns." Sadly, "other concerns" continue to crowd out academics. The study of Shakespeare, the Peloponnesian War, the U.S. Constitution—to the extent they are taught at all—are now seen as mere vehicles whereby we cultivate character and teamwork, promote self-actualization, and improve society.

Toward the end of his life, Albert Shanker, the head of the American Federation of Teachers who saw up close the failed promise of American education, wrote a column applauding the Committee for Economic Development report, in which he commented that "CED's insistence that the academic mission should be at the center of our educational arrangements is refreshing and important....The idea might seem pretty obvious, but many people around the schools still frown at the mention of 'academic mission.'...And the majority believe that the chief purpose of the schools is the socialization of youngsters—teaching them how to get along together rather than how to do math and science." As much as K-12 gurus frown at the phrase "academic mission," they are even more contemptuous of the phrase "the 3 Rs" and the assumption associated with that phrase, namely that schools above all else are expected to provide young people with a solid grounding in "the basics." In the early 1900s, one of the most popular texts used in schools of education, amazingly, contained the following advice to future teachers:

> Traditionally the elementary school has been primarily devoted to teaching the fundamental subjects, the three R's and closely related disciplines.... Artificial exercises, like drills on phonetics, multiplication tables, and formal writing movements, are used to a wasteful degree. Subjects such as arithmetic, language, and history include content that is intrinsically of little value.

Succeeding generations of K-12 practitioners learned their lessons well over the course of the twentieth century, so much so that, as they entered the twenty-first century, educators had managed to turn "basics" into a dirty word inspiring ridicule, except among parents who were left wondering what K-12's charter was if not to pour a solid academic foundation for their children.

6

Basic Training in the Three R's

I have shown how a sizable fraction of the school day around the country is consumed by nonacademic fare. The same people who are behind this trend, mostly progressive educators, are also the ones who proclaim the most loudly that our schools do not have time to teach the basics as in the past, when kids were drilled in grammar, spelling, computation, and the like. I used to hear this constantly from the trendy assistant superintendent for curriculum in Clayton who, upon becoming the superintendent of a neighboring school district in 2000, counted among her administration's first decisions the floating of a bond issue for a new athletic track and the institution of "relaxation exercises" in classrooms.

Many of today's progressives who criticize traditionalists as "back to basics" dinosaurs are themselves merely going back in time and recycling earlier theories advanced by John Dewey and others. Perhaps Dewey and his followers can be excused for wanting students to go beyond merely "rote memorization" and to engage in more challenging intellectual activity, but some early progressives carried such logic to ridiculous lengths, as in the case of G. Stanley Hall, who, addressing the NEA annual convention in 1901, remarked that "we must overcome the fetichism of the alphabet, of the multiplication table, of grammars, of scales, and of bibliolatry."

Listening to modern progressives such as Alfie Kohn, they sound eerily like Hall. If they have their way, the solid basics education my generation received at places like Baltimore City College High School will become extinct. With even greater vigor than their predecessors, K-12 educators now take the position that it is *beneath* them to expend much energy teaching the academic basics to *any* kids, whether they are at the top or bottom of the achievement ladder, since our schools are now supposedly about teaching "critical thinking" and "higher-order skills." These end-lessly repeated phrases make for a great sound-bite. The idea is that, rather than boring children with sequenced, systematic instruction in diagramming sentences, avoiding split infinitives, or executing long division, the teacher is expected to intervene with such instruction only intermittently, on an "as needed basis," i.e., divining whether a student's latest essay reveals excessive gram-matical errors meriting a lesson in language usage, or whether his or her latest math exam reveals excessive computation errors mer-iting more extensive math drill. (Of course, in the age of the self-esteem-based classroom, where there is a rather high thresh-old for defining "excessive" error-proneness, intervention tends not to be triggered as often as it should be.)

The problem with this ambitious mandate is that kids either (1) have to hope they get the basics through some sort of osmosis process by the time they graduate from high school, or (2) other-wise need to have their parents hire a tutor as a surrogate teacher (which more and more parents are being forced to do, judging from growing enrollments in Kumon math and other such pro-grams), or (3) as often happens, *never* do get the basics, leaving it up to colleges and universities to remediate them.

Nationwide, 80 percent of all public colleges and 70 percent of all private colleges, including Ivy League institutions, offer such remedial courses, which are euphemistically called "academic development." Twenty-nine percent of all incoming college fresh-men enroll in at least one remedial course in reading, writing, or math. In New York's state university system, the figure is 36 per-cent; Georgia's is 39 percent; Kentucky's is 48 percent. In the twenty-two-campus California state university system, almost half the freshmen require remedial education in math or English com-position; according to the *Los Angeles Times*, in 2000, "the California State University system kicked out about 2,000 stu-dents—more than 6% of last year's freshman class—for failing to master basic English and math skills within their first year of classes."

Even "top 25" universities, which attract the very best stu-dents, are experiencing these problems. I am reminded of a campus visit I made to the University of Michigan in the late 1990s. I happened to stop in the UM bookstore to see, out of curiosity, what textbooks were being assigned in his world politics course by Professor J. David Singer, a fellow political scientist and a renowned scholar who was a former president of the International Studies Association. To my shock, alongside books on international relations theory, he had ordered a pocket manual containing the elemental rules of grammar, punctuation, and citation of sources. When I later asked him why he was requiring such reading in of all things an international relations course, he explained that he had no alternative since he found the writing deficiencies of his students "very serious" and getting worse with each passing year. Although I had suspected that writing problems were widespread, I had assumed naively that only at places like UM-St. Louis, "bottom 500" universities which attracted students of wide-ranging ability, did professors find basic literacy problems in their classroom. When I related this story to a progressive-minded *Washington Post* reporter who had just written an article featuring Alfie Kohn, he dismissed this as the rantings of an "old fart," neglecting the fact that he and Kohn could trace their own beliefs to an even "older fart" named John Dewey.

Our education systems are being turned upside down. While precollegiate educators are pretentiously referring to their charges, including pre-schoolers, as "a community of scholars," we in higher education often feel we are surrounded by graduates of South Park and are having to devote ever more time to remedial work.

Educators rarely have the guts to say publicly that they have abandoned the basics, instead defusing possible parental anger by touting "the new basics." I once told my school board, "I don't care whether you go back to basics, forward with basics, or sideways with basics, but I am going to insist that the basics are taught." The reader may see some contradiction in, on the one hand, my call for high-powered academics and, on the other hand, my call for emphasis on basics. Nonetheless, *all* kids need the basics, no matter what their brainpower. Moreover, acquiring a solid grounding in the basics is extremely *hard*, in terms of the disciplined effort required for mastery. Indeed, it is not a concern about higher-order thinking that is driving the current wave of anti-basics thinking, but instead a concern about some students failing.

The key intellectual rationalization not only for the anti-basics movement but for the entire progressive project is what is called in the halls of academe, particularly in university schools of education, "constructivist theory." As defined by progressives themselves, constructivism "is not a theory about teaching. Constructivism is a theory about knowledge and learning. Drawing on a synthesis of current work in cognitive psychology, philosophy, and anthropology, the theory defines knowledge as temporary, developmental, socially and culturally mediated. Learning from this perspective is understood as a self-regulated process of resolving inner cognitive conflicts that often become apparent through concrete experience, collaborative discourse, and reflection." Note, first, that this document was written primarily by the Dean of the School of Education at the University of Missouri-Columbia, describing in impenetrable educationese something called "Project Construct." Note, secondly, that education is no longer about *teaching* but learning, with no distinction to be made between adults and children as "learners."

Translated, what the dean was essentially saying, though he would hardly admit it, is that there are no building blocks to the knowledge process—no heavy lifting that young people must do to acquire a solid foundation of factual information and basic competencies before moving up the ladder to higher-order analysis and application—and, indeed, no store of knowledge to be transmitted between teacher and student. Constructivism is an offshoot of postmodern thought, which, as I've mentioned, rejects the existence of any objective body of knowledge. Reality is whatever one makes of the world, depending upon one's skin color or other personal/group circumstances and experiences. Tom Loveless, a former schoolteacher and now head of an educational policy center at the Brookings Institution, explains how constructivism is "the academic fad that gave us Ebonics," referring to the decision made by the Oakland, California school district in 1996 to allow African-American students to substitute their "home" language for standard English:

> The policy presents formal English as knowledge with no intrinsic rightness, as simply an artifact of the dominant culture and an accident of history.... This reasoning, though nonsense, exemplifies a prominent educational philosophy, one that transcends race and penetrates subjects other than language. The most influential doctrine in instruction over the last few years has been "constructivism," the idea that learners construct their own knowledge.... In mathematics, a student's "mathematical power" is awarded equal status with the ability to perform basic computations accurately. The influence of constructivism can also be found in current

approaches to teaching spelling, in the acceptance of invented spellings; written composition, in the emphasis on creative writing over the crafting of grammatically correct sentences; reading, in the use of "whole language" techniques instead of phonics; and history, in projects allowing students to express their interpretations of the past rather than learning the names, dates, and events that give history its shape. And this is where Ebonics is solidly in the mainstream of modern educational thought. It shares with constructivism the same relativism, the same reluctance to let students know when they are wrong. Ignorance is no longer a recognizable condition—distinguishable from competence and treatable through a teacher's guidance and a student's hard work.

There may be no "right" answers (certainly no simple answers) to what caused, say, the American Revolution or Civil War. But surely there is a right answer to what date did it start (or, at the very least, the century when it occurred), how you spell the names of the battlefields, where they were, and which historical figures were important actors in these events. True, we don't want to stifle creativity, and much of education has to do with getting students to cope with ambiguity rather than with feeding them right answers to regurgitate on multiple-choice tests. In a country in which barely half of the public knows that there are two U.S. Senators from each state, however, can we really be at risk of overdosing our students on facts? It is hard to do a lot of critical thinking about American democracy if one does not have the most elemental grasp of the basic roots and features of the Republic. Moreover, even if there are no clear "right" answers as to what caused the above conflicts, there are clearly superior or inferior answers—that is, more and less sophisticated analyses. There are still clearer answers to such questions as what is the product of 2 x 2, and when does one use "its" as opposed to "it's" in a sentence. It may be true that knowledge consists of few if any eternal truths, but it's silly to argue that there are no verities when it comes to the rules of grammar, the performance of mathematical operations, or the timing, locale and other particulars of historical events.

The dark secret today in many schools is that there are *no* rules, that is, no standards that are consistently enforced. The operative principle is, as the ad in the buffoonish 1995 Chris Farley *Tommy Boy* movie put it, "If at first you don't succeed, lower your standards." When asked by traditionalists why they are so cavalier about holding students, particularly in elementary and middle school, to strict grade-level benchmarks relating to spelling and other basics, progressives often invoke the ideas of Jean Piaget and other early constructivists, who stressed that teachers must be careful to offer education that is "developmentally appropriate"; that some kids develop certain competencies more rapidly than others, that insisting that kids master these skills before they are ready may destroy their fertile imagination and love of learning; and that, hence, we should avoid a "factory" model of simply operating an assembly line that turns out widget-like products. All this is well and good, but it effectively plays havoc with any effort to enforce common, minimal expectations regarding what kids should be learning at what level of schooling.

What we are left with, then, is the *nonjudgmental* classroom, one that is marked by atmospherics. David Gelernter, the Yale computer scientist who gained celebrity as a victim of the Unabomber during the 1990s, captures the problem:

> Our schools are in crisis. Statistics prove what I see every day as a parent and a college educator...students who can't write worth a damn, who lack basic math and language skills. Our schools are scared to tell students to sit down and shut up and learn; drill it, memorize it, because you must master it whether it's fun or not. Children pay the price for our educational cowardice.

Gelernter is no doubt guilty of hyperbole; I know of few, if any, educators who want students to simply "shut up and memorize." But he is expressing the frustration many traditionalists have with a K-12 reform movement that has gone to the opposite extreme of drill-and-kill in adopting a totally laissez-faire attitude toward learning regimens. In place of the old maxim "no pain, no gain," the new slogan is "if it ain't fun, it can't be done." In the words of Frank Smith, one of the founding fathers of the whole-language movement, "that learning requires effort is another myth."

Why the concept of drill and practice should be so alien to today's educationist remains a mystery. Michael Jordan, Itzhak Perlman, and any number of other highly successful people can speak to the importance of repetitive routines in the development of their skills. The Nobel laureate Herbert Simon and colleagues at Carnegie Mellon University note that science supports what would seem intuitively obvious: "The criticism of practice (called 'drill and kill'...) is prominent in constructivist writings. Nothing flies more in the face of the last twenty years of research than the assertion that practice is bad. All evidence, from the laboratory and from extensive case studies of professionals, indicates that real competence only comes with extensive practice." Washington University biologist George Johnson, citing numerous studies, similarly notes how recent neuroscience has confirmed "why repetition enhances learning." Reflecting on his own experiences, he says "I learned to multiply by memorizing the 'times tables' by rote when I was a child. Now today I don't have to use new math to figure out what 9 x 7 is. I know it's 63. Millions of GAP-43 molecules created by thousands of repetitions when I was 10 contributed to the formation of the nerve connections that tell me so. It may not be the trendy way to learn, but repetition works."

As evidence of how far K-12 education has strayed from this simple proposition, and from the teaching of basics, let us look at a few case studies of reading wars, math wars, and other sorts of conflicts occurring throughout the country. I will start with a reality check from my own experiences.

The Joys of Inventive Spelling and Fuzzy Math

The Clayton school district prides itself on teaching solid basics, as well as taking children beyond the basics. As our superintendent likes to say, he believes in "basics plus," which is a perfectly sound concept. The problem is that there is so much constructivist thinking permeating the staff that the formula at times seems to be "higher order plus," with the basics almost an afterthought. For example, a district science teacher recently told me that, in his judgment, "parents should be responsible for teaching their kids multiplication tables rather than relying on the schools to do it." This sentiment was echoed by another local teacher in a different school district, who said, "It is not a good use of the time of a $50,000 professional to drill students on multiplication." Both of these teachers were bright individuals who should have known better. In the case of the Clayton science teacher, he was a great supporter of an "expeditionary" learning program that took kids on numerous distant field trips away from the classroom, apparently on the assumption that it *is* a good use of the professional's time to spend hours riding on a schoolbus and organizing kids into small groups for camping adventures.

Many Clayton parents, in fact, do send their children to private Kumon math classes, styled after Japanese instruction aimed at developing automaticity in number usage, since they feel they cannot count on their public school to provide this training. I noted earlier that, out of frustration, one Clayton parent tried to mount a Parents and Teachers for Academic Basics campaign, only to be subjected to insults by district staff. The district conducted a survey in 1999 to assess how satisfied parents and residents were with the Clayton schools, including the teaching of basics. In summarizing the survey results, the Attitude Research Company (ARC) hired by the district stated: "We read a list of possible programs or projects the District could implement over the next few years, and asked survey participants to rate these on a seven-point scale, on which a 7 indicated the highest priority, and a rating of 1 indicated the project was not very important at all. By far, the highest priority was given to improving programs to make sure students are proficient in basic skills. A majority (51.3%) assigned the highest priority (7) to this, and almost four in five (74.9%) of the survey participants gave it a rating of 5 or more. Only 12.8% thought this priority rated below a 3."

There was one survey question, in particular, that was phrased in a highly loaded manner designed to elicit an anti-basics response from those polled. Respondents were essentially asked to choose between supporting "innovative programs" and "concentrating on the basics," an absurd choice to force people to make, as if "the basics" and "innovative programs" were mutually exclusive. Almost anyone with half a brain would, of course, opt for both. ARC produced the result desired by its customer, reporting that "in many school districts across the country, there are widespread complaints that schools are not doing a good job teaching the basics. This is *not* the case in the Clayton School District. Nearly two-thirds (65.8%) of respondents *disagree* that 'schools should eliminate new and innovative programs and concentrate on the basics.'" Such are the shameful games school districts play across the country to cover up the fact that parents resent their abandonment of the basics. I afterwards suggested to the administration that, if it was serious about getting feedback from parents, instead of artful obfuscation it should put the question more directly (e.g. "Are you satisfied with your child's ability to use correct standard English conventions, including proper spelling, grammar, and punctuation? Are you satisfied with your child's ability to do mathematical operations without a calculator, including multiplication and division?"). Needless to say, I don't expect to be hired anytime soon to design survey research for the district.

Two recent episodes, one having to do with mathematics and the other with language arts, are a graphic commentary on the constructivist mindset that has taken hold in the Clayton school district and the lengths educationists will go to in order to shut out dissident views. I mentioned in my discussion of excellence vs. equity that the district some time ago had adopted two popular new "fuzzy math" programs in K-8—Everyday Math in elementary school and Connected Math in middle school—which were to be the standard curriculum taught to virtually all students even though the authors of these programs themselves explicitly said they were designed specifically for the weakest and most mathphobic of students. In an article entitled "It's Time to Abandon Computational Algorithms," one of the chief publicists for these programs, Steven Leinwand, stated that "it's time to recognize that, for many students [i.e., low achievers], real mathematical power, on the one hand, and facility with multidigit, pencil-and-paper computational algorithms, on the other hand, are mutually exclusive." It should be noted that these curricula had the endorsement of the National Council of Teachers of Mathematics (NCTM), a major standards-setting body which included both K-12 and college-level math educators and which had become constructivist in its orientation. When the NCTM issued its new national standards in 1989, it found itself at odds with the Mathematics Association of America, a rival professional group which supported the "real-world problem-solving" focus of the standards but was worried about the lessened emphasis on drill, rigor, and precision.

While "fuzzy math" was being implemented in K-8, Clayton High School still offered a rather traditional, rigorous math curriculum, with most students enrolled in either advanced honors/AP courses or regular college-prep courses in geometry, algebra/trigonometry, and calculus. In the spring of 2000, however, the district Math Committee, while agreeing not to eliminate the honors/AP courses for top students (which would have produced a near-riot among many parents), proposed to adopt Core-Plus, the high-school equivalent of Everyday and Connected Math, for the majority of students. In a journal article that the Math Committee circulated, the Core-Plus authors openly confessed the populist impulses behind their curriculum, asserting that "using calculators removes the 'skill filter' that paper-and-pencil symbol manipulation has become for some students" and that their curriculum was aimed at "expanding access to...mathematics for all students." There could not have been a clearer indication that the bottom was suddenly driving the high school math curriculum for the bulk of the student body. Nonetheless, the Math Committee contended in its presentation to the school board that Core-Plus was meant to be a challenging new program that would provide a richer curriculum for students. The Committee cited the NCTM imprimatur, arguing, as such committees are wont to do, that "all the research" supported their proposal.

What the Math Committee failed to point out, and what it took parents like myself to reveal, was that some two hundred of the leading research mathematicians and scientists in the United States were so strongly opposed to NCTM's and the U.S. Department of Education's endorsement of Core-Plus and its sister curricula that they took the extraordinary step of publishing an open, signed letter in the November 18, 1999 *Washington Post* calling upon U.S. Secretary of Education Riley to withdraw his approval due to "serious mathematical shortcomings" in these programs. The signers included four Nobel laureates, a former head of the NCTM, the chairs of the math departments at Harvard, Yale, Stanford, Cal-Tech, the University of Chicago, and the University of Rochester, and dozens of distinguished professors from other major universities. One of the signers, Betty Tsang of Michigan State, summarized the sentiments of her colleagues in noting that Core-Plus and the other programs "teach to the lowest common denominator," referring to the stress on calculator dependency rather than basic skill acquisition, on positive attitudes toward math rather than academic rigor, and socialization through group learning rather than individual mastery.

When I brought all of this to the attention of the board, a parent member of the Clayton Math Committee maintained that this was part of the "vast right-wing conspiracy." I had become used to progressive parents dismissing other parents' concerns as ideologically driven while characterizing their own motives as purer. (In my experience, few traditionalist voices are chosen to represent parent opinion on curriculum committees.) The position taken by this parent, however, seemed especially untenable. Aside from the fact that it was hard to make the case that the chairs of the leading math departments in the country were all right-wingers, or that math as a field of study even lent itself to ideological biases, the parent was also unaware that three of the founders of Mathematically Correct, the California-based group that had been leading the fight against constructivist math, were self-described liberal Democrats, while one of the organizers of the *Washington Post* letter project was a socialist!

I alerted the *St. Louis Post-Dispatch* to the brewing controversy in Clayton, whereupon a reporter wrote an article commenting on the upcoming school board meeting at which the Core-Plus proposal was to be discussed. One of the persons who came to the board meeting to speak against the proposal was Christopher Byrnes, a math Ph.D. and the Dean of the School of Engineering at Washington University in St. Louis. Byrnes addressed the board with a public comment, telling them it would be "foolhardy" to proceed with the proposal, and afterwards remarked to me that "[Sir Isaac] Newton said there was no royal road to geometry, but these folks seemed to have found it." Split between a progressive faction that favored Core-Plus and a traditionalist faction that opposed it, the board put off a vote on the issue, so that they could study the matter further. Meanwhile, one board member who was wary of the proposal asked Steve Krantz, the chairperson of the Washington University Mathematics Department and one of the two hundred signers of the *Washington Post* letter, to examine the proposed Core-Plus textbook to be used at Clayton High School. Krantz sent the board a devastating, detailed five-page critique, echoing the concerns expressed by Betty Tsang and others and concluding, "You would be doing your students, and your school district, a great disservice to adopt this book." For his efforts, the board member who had solicited the review was bitterly criticized by fellow board members, as were parents who supported the effort to get more information.

In March 2000, a divided Clayton school board voted in favor of adopting the Core-Plus curriculum. In so doing, they ignored the advice of two hundred of the leading math minds in the world and some of the most respected mathematicians in the local metropolitan area, not to mention many parents upset with the proposal. Rumor had it that, amazingly, some board members blew off the opposition of Byrnes, Krantz, and others with the line "what do they know about teaching math?" (Krantz had written the book on teaching college math, 30,000 copies used nationwide, while Byrnes was about to be recognized by the Academy of Science of St. Louis for excelling in "teaching and communicating science to future researchers and the public.") If the argument was that college teachers should not be looked to for advice about high school math curricula, then, using the same logic, high school teachers presumably have nothing to tell K-8 math teachers; yet the Clayton Math Committee prided itself on an integrated K-12 program. If the argument was that professors from Yale, Washington University, and other elite schools should not be consulted about curricula aimed at non-honors students, then one would hope at least that professors from more pedestrian places like the University of Missouri-St. Louis would be consulted. Yet math colleagues at my own institution were as vehemently against Core-Plus as the two hundred signers were. (After I wrote an op-ed piece in the *Post-Dispatch* criticizing Clayton's decision, the chair of the UM-St. Louis Mathematics Department e-mailed me that "I felt compelled to let you know how well your article is being received over here. I have passed out copies to the entire department.")

There are several morals to this story. First, one cannot trust K-12 curriculum committees to present *both* sides of the issue and *all* the relevant research relating to a proposed reform, including research that undermines their position. Although it is true that there was a sizable body of research supporting Core-Plus as well as some heavyweight names in NCTM endorsing it, the same could be said for the opposition; yet it took parents to unearth the *Washington Post* letter, which at least should have been included in the committee report presented to the board and in the district conversation on this matter, whether one ultimately agreed with it or not. Parents and taxpayers have a right to expect truth in advertising, that is, full, balanced, professional disclosure of all research as a basis for making curriculum decisions, especially when curriculum committees almost always claim their proposals are "research-based." Second, even very able curriculum leaders, such as those on the Clayton Math Committee, who were highly skilled math teachers, often fall victim to pack pedagogy and, in almost robotic fashion, accept the latest nostrums emanating from the educational establishment, in this case the NCTM. My guess is that, if NCTM had told these folks to jump off a cliff, they would have done it, but not before telling us what a wonderful idea it was. Add to this the cultural pressures of educational populism, and you have a recipe for knee-jerk decision-making. Finally, even when a parent thinks he or she has an enormous weight of evidence and argument on his or her side, one cannot count on being taken seriously and being listened to by a district's leadership. The central administration, and especially the school board, rarely will exercise independent judgment and go against staff desires, tending instead to rubber-stamp curriculum proposals; critical parents end up being demonized as "right-wingers" or troublemakers of some sort, and are accused of being disrespectful by those who themselves show little respect for contrary views.

I saw this same pattern at work in another episode worth describing, one involving the recent evolution of the Clayton language arts curriculum. As with its math curriculum, Clayton long had had a strong language arts curriculum, including a "conferenced writing" program entailing intensive one-on-one mentoring in English composition. As with the math curriculum, however, the school district undertook in the 1990s a major overhaul of the entire curriculum aimed at incorporating the latest constructivist fads that were being trumpeted by the National Council of Teachers of English (NCTE), a clone of the NCTM. These fads included "inventive spelling" in writing assignments, "whole-language" in reading instruction, and broadening the concept of literacy to include "oralcy," "media-viewing," and all conceivable forms of communication (leading to the aforementioned Play-Doh and cut-and-paste scrapbook projects my son did in "English" class).

The much publicized whole-language vs. phonics controversy bears more discussion. For now, it is enough to note that the whole-language approach, which could trace its roots to the early twentieth century but which gained momentum especially toward the century's end, "proposed that children read literature connected to their interests rather than textbooks and that they read for meaning and pleasure rather than study the mechanics of language. Whole-language was a rebellion against drill, workbooks, textbooks, and the other paraphernalia associated with phonics that, overdone, could deaden students' interest in reading." Learning to read through immersion in rich literature certainly seemed a reasonable pedagogical strategy, as long as it was supplemented with the usual training in consonants, vowels, and other parts of language. It was the latter half of the equation that whole-language devotees had forgotten. Whole-language and the non-judgmental, therapeutic classroom were made for each other.

Inventive spelling and other more relaxed uses of language followed easily from whole-language assumptions.

Inventive spelling was the last innovation that Russ Hogan would have allowed in his classroom. Hogan was a legendary "old school" English teacher at Clayton High School who, according to a *Wall Street Journal* article written by a former student of his (who went on to author the definitive biography of the boxer Hurricane Carter), "was a successful one-man army fighting the good fight against ambiguous antecedents, superfluous commas and creeping colloquialisms. 'He was on a mission [added a classmate]. He broke down the language and made you feel as if you were studying it for the first time.'" By the 1990s, after thirty-five years of teaching, Hogan saw the handwriting on the wall; his taskmaster style, his brand of systematic instruction, his exacting standards, and his passion for the language were out of vogue. He had become "the grammarian who lost a war of words." He retired in 1993. Although many able colleagues remained, they gradually were being replaced by a new generation of teachers who dismissed spelling and grammar as "superficial concerns."

A year after Hogan left, Clayton approved the new constructivist literacy curriculum despite protests on the part of many parents and misgivings on the part of some board members. Among the comments I made before the school board were the following: "You are paying less and less attention to the *careful* use of language. This is partly due to the constructivist philosophy that there are no right and wrong answers, and partly due to the self-esteem movement. Heaven forbid you correct any mistakes—you might scar Johnny for life if you point out a dangling participle! You say you have taken the lid off the curriculum. Sure, Johnny in second grade is told to write a novel. He cannot even write his name, but he is being asked to write a novel. My only question is, why wait until second grade? Why not start the kids on novel-writing at the Family Center at age 3? Whatever the child writes, you can be assured that the teacher will tell him he is the next Hemingway."

A more telling set of criticisms was offered by another parent in attendance at the latter meeting, in a letter she subsequently sent to me. It is long, but deserves to be quoted for the insights it conveys about what's wrong with the new literacy:

> I am enclosing a copy of something called the "Death List." I used this list when I taught English to eighth graders at University School

of Nashville. This private school had once been Peabody Demonstration School, connected to Peabody Teachers College [at Vanderbilt], and the caliber of both teachers and students was extremely high. The "Death List" was a tool that was already in use by other Middle School English teachers, and I incorporated it happily into my teaching strategy. At the beginning of each year the students were given a copy of this list. They were told that these were to be considered inexcusable errors to be made by seventh or eighth grade students, and that any finished paper turned in that included one of these errors would receive an automatic "F" grade.... In two years of teaching at this school and using the "Death List," I think I only had two students who received an "F" because of one of these errors. I think the "modern" thinkers would be appalled at this methodology; I only know that the standard was clear, and that the tool worked.... I just do not understand why there cannot be some middle ground.

The reference to the "Death List" sounded similar to the "Fatal Flaw" policy I had heard about at John Burroughs School, the premier private school in the St. Louis area, where papers were returned ungraded if they had more than three spelling or grammatical mistakes on the same page. Clayton had no such policy.

One did not have to be a graduate of Burroughs or on the faculty at Vanderbilt University to appreciate such a common sense call for a "middle ground." Still, the district's Language Literacy Committee, increasingly dominated by progressives, persisted in its view that there was no need to blend old and new pedagogy. Clayton made an effort to be responsive to the concerns raised by parents, developing special "parent fact sheets" to communicate how the district was using new ways to teach grammar and other elements of writing. These efforts to reassure parents that the basics were being taught as seriously as before would have been more persuasive had the district not plainly devalued such things in its new assessment instruments. The district was testing more and more for atmospherics and less and less for whether students were dotting their i's and crossing their t's and producing polished prose. As concrete evidence, I went back and compared my son's fourth-grade Educational Records Bureau (ERB) writing assessment which my wife and I received shortly after we first arrived in Clayton in 1989 with the ERB assessment used by the district a decade later; whereas the 1989 assessment explicitly provided detailed feedback for parents on how proficient their child was at "spelling," "capitalization," "punctuation," "verb and pronoun problems," and other such specific skills, the more recent assessment collapsed all this information into a vague, generic category labeled "mechanics," which became further diluted by its juxtaposition next to even vaguer categories such as "overall development" (having to do with "voice"), "organization," and "support." Similarly, whereas my son's elementary report card had devoted considerable space to special, highlighted sections labeled spelling and grammar (e.g., "uses correct spelling"), these categories now were competing for attention with "writes with confidence" and other such airy rubrics while the word "correct" had mysteriously disappeared from all forms. (Such masking of deficiencies in basic skills has been aptly called "the holistic hustle.")

The lip service the district paid to the idea of a balanced "basics plus" curriculum would have also been more persuasive had it not been contradicted by a particularly revealing incident in the spring of 2001. The Language Literacy Committee was having to present a five-year curriculum review to the Clayton school board in May, preceded by a presentation to the Citizens Curriculum Council in February. At the February meeting, the committee report stated, "We started [in 1992] from a shared set of beliefs that emerged from the research on best practices in literacy instruction at the time." Indeed, these were truly "shared beliefs," insofar as it was hard to find a single voice on the committee that dissented from the prevailing whole-language orthodoxy, which was based more on theology than science. The committee not only "started" with these beliefs; a decade later they were still wedded to the same exact tenets, despite the fact that in the intervening years many studies had appeared which questioned the excesses of whole-language. In particular, in April of 2000, an important report was released by the National Reading Panel—a body appointed by the U.S. Congress, under the auspices of the prestigious National Institutes of Health, consisting of experts from Yale, Columbia, Chicago and other major universities—which called for blending phonics and literature-based activities as the best strategy for teaching reading. As described by NIH, "in the largest, most comprehensive evidenced-based review ever conducted of research on how children learn reading, a Congressional mandated independent panel has concluded that the most effective way to teach children to read is through instruction that includes a combination of methods." *Education Week* added: "The report suggests that teaching all children phonics—how the sounds that make up speech are linked to letters of the alphabet—beginning in kindergarten can help them read more proficiently later on. The report also concludes that helping children develop fluency in reading words and building their comprehension skills is critical for them to become successful readers.... The panel...based its findings on some of the 100,000 published studies in five areas of reading."

Not all agreed with the NIH/National Reading Panel's conclusions. Within the panel itself, a few members issued a minority report. Whether one agreed or disagreed with the study, however, it was almost impossible to ignore such a highly regarded, highly publicized report as food for thought in the literacy debate. That is precisely what the Clayton Language Literacy Committee did—amazingly, the committee pretended the NIH study did not exist, as it was nowhere to be seen among the dozens of materials displayed at the February meeting. But the committee took care to alert parents to the "Standards for the English Language Arts," a national standards document produced in 1996 by the National Council of Teachers of English (NCTE) in conjunction with the International Reading Association (IRA), which was so devoid of attention to basic skills that the U.S. Department of Education withdrew its funding and major newspapers and major scholars ridiculed it as a national disgrace. For example, the *New York Times* called it "pedagogical molasses" that failed to provide "a clear, candid case for greater competence in standard English," while Diane Ravitch called it "an unmitigated disaster." Never mind; the Clayton Language Literacy Committee proudly displayed it. The committee added insult to injury by attaching to its February report an incendiary article labeling all critics of whole-language "right-wingers."

Such is what passes for "balance" today in Clayton and many other school districts. As Louisa Moats, the project director of the National Institute of Child Health and Human Development Early Interventions Project, has noted, there is the "illusion of balanced instruction" designed to appease recalcitrant parents. In May 2001, in its report to the Clayton school board, the Language Literacy Committee, at the behest of the central administration (which to its credit had recognized the earlier sin of omission), did acknowledge the existence of the NIH/National Reading Panel study, but dismissed its findings as "flawed." No such characterization was used to describe the NCTE national standards; the report stated that "Clayton's Language Literacy Document is aligned with the philosophy of language learning underlying the IRA/NCTE standards. All twelve IRA/NCTE standards are encompassed in our literacy curriculum." Notwithstanding the heavy criticism of the NCTE standards by respected national sources, the Clayton school board quietly accepted the committee report with hardly a whimper, except for mild questioning from a traditionalist faction which had become the loyal opposition, three members who nobly but vainly tried to stop the constructivist steamroller.

At the May meeting, the chair of the committee said that the committee members saw themselves as "continuous learners," constantly updating their knowledge about their field. However, their behavior betrayed a certain narrow, almost closed-mindedness, an unwillingness to rethink established views or at least cast a wider net in considering alternative perspectives as a basis for their deliberations. The only two parent members on the committee were two peas out of the same pod—two pre-school educators who shared not only an identical, constructivist view of the world but even worked at the very same business address, one being the school director and the other her employee—hardly a recipe for "diversity." And in response to questions from board members about the relative merits of whole-language vs. phonics, the committee suggested that the board read the writings of Kenneth Goodman and Carolyn Weaver, two of the people most closely associated with the whole-language movement—akin to being told to read consumer reports prepared by the advertising department of Coca-Cola in order to ascertain whether Coke or Pepsi was the superior brand.

The threefold moral of the story I told about the math committee applies equally to the literacy committee. One could discern a similar *modus operandi*—the tendency by staff to withhold relevant information in reporting research to parents and school boards (in this case the NIH study), the tendency for intelligent educators to be victimized by pack pedagogy (in this case that prescribed by NCTE), and the tendency for curriculum proposals to be rubber-stamped and for critics to be stamped with epithets such as "right-winger" (or, as in my case, "worshipper of conservative thinkers"). Even if you have on your side "the world's leading medical research organization," that won't help you.

At the May board meeting I told the board: "I am reminded of the fanatic Japanese soldiers who wandered the South Pacific islands for years after World War II, refusing to surrender. I don't know how to break the news to this committee, but the war's over. You won...and you lost! The NIH study is the peace treaty, the final word to all but the most fanatic whole-language zealots. It's called a *compromise*, a word that does not seem to be in your vocabulary." It is a word that is all too often missing in many school districts today, as can be seen in stories being told all across the United States.

A Spreading Conflict

Fuzzy math, fuzzy English, as well as fuzzy history and fuzzy science, are now commonplace features of the K-12 landscape in America. Many districts are mirror images of Clayton in terms of the battles being fought over basics education. The stories I just related are being repeated everywhere, although every superintendent I have ever encountered has told me that, of course, *his/her* own district does not deserve to be tarred with the same brush, that it has not followed the pack, that this is not happening *there*.

Just across the border from Clayton, the Rockwood School District has been sending mixed signals regarding such skills as spelling. On the one hand, their curriculum materials state that "developing student writers cannot be expected to spell all words correctly every time they write. If they were, few would write. Many of a beginning writer's words should be accepted with approximate [invented] spellings." Furthermore, "spelling expectations for student writers in everyday writing should not be as high as for writing that is part of an ongoing process that produces a writing piece over time through many revisions." On the other hand, the same document, in a bow to critics of inventive spelling, acknowledges that at some point in a child's education "invented spellings need to be phased out and replaced with conventional spelling. This spelling transition must begin early for the highest-use words, usually by the second half of grade one.... If the highest-use words (the, of, and, a, to, in, is, you) are written incorrectly repeatedly, the misspellings are reinforced and become increasingly difficult to change." It is reassuring that Rockwood believes it is not excessively self-esteem damaging to insist a student be able to write the word "a" correctly! The document is less clear regarding when the "transition" should occur for tougher words.

To the district's credit, it issued a mea culpa rarely found in K-12 circles:

> It once was thought that invented spellings would not lead to the formation of bad spelling habits. However, the evidence began mounting that led educators to modify this belief. The totality of the invented spelling philosophy reduced the importance of spelling in the minds of both teachers and students. The outcome emerged as major student spelling deficiencies in writing.

Why this "outcome" could not have been readily foreseen by K-12 educators is mystifying, but no more so than their failure to grasp many other truths that are obvious to non-educators. Equally mystifying is the document's admission that "teachers need a plan for the development of spelling skills in writing. *They need confirmation that spelling literacy is indeed an instructional goal* [italics mine]." It is an amazing commentary on our times that an upper-middle-class school district feels its staff needs to be reminded that it must have a conscious strategy for teaching spelling. I imagine such "confirmation" will come from "professional development" workshops where facilitators will be paid large sums to disseminate cutting-edge techniques for using red ink on student essays.

As a footnote to the latter story, I should add that I was invited by a group of Rockwood parents of gifted children, concerned about district instruction in the basics, to join Rockwood administrators in a special public forum on language arts the parents organization had scheduled. The Rockwood officials backed out the last minute, and I was left to carry the ball for the entire two-hour meeting. I later discovered that my comments, some of which were rather off-the-cuff, were secretly taped by opposition forces and distributed to various parties, including my "home" superintendent in Clayton. This is yet another dimension of the Great American Education War—the frequent use of dirty tricks to delegitimize, discredit, and silence critics.

Fortunately, K-12 critics are supported by Public Agenda and other national public opinion polling organizations that keep reporting data showing a disconnect between the public and the education establishment. As *Education Week* notes, "Polls and surveys have shown concern about safety, discipline, and the academic basics for 20 years. Part of the disconnect stems from the word 'basics.' To the public, it is associated with a solid foundation. But to many educators, the word has almost a pejorative meaning, conjuring images of rote, low-level learning. 'Reformers keep saying that basics aren't enough,' said Jean Johnson, Public Agenda's director of programs. But the public, she added, has dozens of real-life examples that suggest students are not getting even that much education."

One such "real-life example," involving highly educated parents of high-achieving children who had become frustrated with the anti-basics philosophy of their local school district, was captured recently in a front-page *New York Times* story entitled "Parents Hungry for ABCs Lead New School Movement." Parents in Princeton, New Jersey, who had become "horrified by…progressive education run amok," founded their own charter school:

> Signs of quiet revolt are everywhere: children tracing neat cursive letters in penmanship class, memorizing multiplication tables, taking spelling quizzes and learning the value of a strong topic sentence. Today's model classroom tends to avoid these things, deeming them uninspired and uninspiring…. Here, the new Princeton Charter School is embracing them unabashedly…. In a desire to…satisfy multiple intelligences and foster self-esteem, these parents say, most schools have moved so far away from the fundamentals that their children come home knowing about the Holocaust but not World War II, Babylonian math but not fractions. Children cannot think critically, they retort, if they do not have the basic content to think about.

The frontline for math wars, reading wars, and other education wars has been not New Jersey or New York but California, where the latest progressive fads first appear, and also where the first backlash occurs. Its trends often become the nation's trends, since, with over five million schoolchildren, it exercises a dominant market influence on what standards are incorporated by textbook publishers in their newest editions of K-12 curricula. A 1996 *Education Week* report traced the rise of Mathematically Correct as a grassroots parents movement—a textbook lesson in how to mobilize a counterattack against ill-conceived constructivist curricula:

> In the past year, well-educated parents in at least nine communities

around the state have formed grassroots organizations to fight [the new constructivist math]. They charge that with its emphasis on higher-level thinking, California has abandoned the basics.... Many of the parents making such noise about math are middle-class and affluent professionals, including engineers and scientists. They use electronic mail and the Internet as tools in their highly organized campaign....

For Mr. Clopton [Paul Clopton], a statistician with the U.S. Department of Veterans Affairs in San Diego, it all began one evening last fall as he watched his 7th-grade daughter struggle with her homework.... Although his daughter was getting an A in the class, she often made simple errors, Mr. Clopton said. Mr. Clopton, Mike McKeown, an engineer at the Salk Institute, and several other parents founded a group called Mathematically Correct and began lobbying the San Diego schools to abandon the program.

The efforts of Mathematically Correct and other such groups paid off in 1997, when the California Board of Education voted to restore an emphasis on basic skills in their endorsement of a more traditional set of state math standards, a decision that figures to have an eventual ripple effect across the country.

The website operated by Mathematically Correct has become a rallying point for dissident parents nationwide. As the *Education Week* article notes, "though the voices are loudest in California, the debate over math standards isn't limited to the West Coast. 'It may have started there a little earlier, and the volume may be a little higher, but it is popping up everywhere' [says a senior scientist at the Education Development Corporation]."

The volume is getting especially louder of late in New York City, where recent newspaper headlines have announced "The New, Flexible Math Meets Parental Rebellion," a reporter noting that "the new curriculum has enraged many parents who find that their children cannot multiply easily or understand basic algebra.... Parents said they were stunned as they talked to their friends and realized how many had hired tutors.... [One parent] said she was appalled when her daughter, a sixth-grader at East Side Middle School, came home with assignments to write her math autobiography and to write about her favorite number." Teachers are also joining the rebellion, at the risk of alienating their administration. I received via a listserve the following poignant e-mail from a NYC high school math instructor in March 2001:

I can tell you that I teach in a school which has won its state math competition every year since its inception, which won the first ever regional last year, which just qualified 24 students for the American Invitational Mathematics Exam, and which routinely produces students who go to Harvard, Stanford, and MIT. Why, you ask, could a math teacher in such a school be frustrated? We [this teacher and many of her colleagues] are supremely frustrated with the [constructivist] textbook we use and are wanting to adopt a new text—a so-called "traditional" series as opposed to a "standards-based" series. There is a strong push to adopt Connected Math at our junior high, and many of the junior high teachers want to use it with heterogeneous groups. It seems to me a gigantic leap backward to throw all of these kids into one program such as CM in junior high. I have a tremendous fear that our highly talented math students will lose their love for the subject. Without fail, those of us who teach the higher level students at my school are all opposed to these [new] programs because we do not feel they will meet the needs of those students who will go on to study math in college. I am passionate about mathematics and I cannot stand still and watch "fuzzy math" get adopted at my school.

As evidence of how deep the passions are running and how heated the math wars are becoming in New York City, the *New York Post* reported that in reaction to a 2001 forum held at New York University sponsored by critics of fuzzy math, a constructivist math teacher at a private Quaker institution, Friends Seminary, created a website on the eve of the meeting which hinted at violence. As the *Post* article noted, "the words on the website were written in red, and the message was chilling: Will there be a bloodbath at NYU?" Elizabeth Carson, a parent activist and a leader of the protest movement, was quoted as saying about the teacher: "He's one of these very evangelical supporters of this math reform." A New York University math professor concurred, "Some of the attitudes I see among [constructivist math supporters] haven't been seen since the '60s, with Mao's Red Guards....We're talking serious ideology here. They believe they have the truth, and nobody else has the truth." The teacher in question later apologized for his militant, threatening statements.

Although math wars in California and New York tend to attract the most publicity, one can find similar news headlines in other locales. In the Washington, D.C. area, in addition to the Montgomery County, Maryland math war I alluded to earlier, the *Washington Post* recently has reported on "How Math Is Taught

Has Fairfax Squabbling," referring to the northern Virginia sub-urban school system described as "the 14th largest school district in the country, and one of the best." In addition to the St. Louis area, there have been other Midwestern "firestorms" occurring in Waukesha County, Wisconsin (the *Milwaukee Journal Sentinel* reporting on "Math Problems: New Curriculum Divides Tradi-tionalists, Constructivists"), Bloomfield Hills, Michigan (the *Detroit News* reporting on "Math Debate Heats Up"), and other places.

The Bloomfield Hills story has special relevance for many Clayton parents, since one of the Bloomfield high schools, with an m.o. like Clayton High, had adopted Core-Plus in 1993, with poor results:

> A plaque in Andover High School's main office announces that this Bloomfield Hills, Mich. school is no ordinary place—it is ranked one of America's "100 best" high schools. Mathematics is a serious matter here. Andover students are drawn from a community of auto-industry engineers and business elites who expect their chil-dren to use high-level math skills in a variety of high-tech careers.... Andover's math test scores soar above those of most other schools in the state. Despite that, the prestigious school stopped offering its traditional math curriculum to new students in 1994 and began an experimental program known as Core-Plus...based on NCTM standards.... "We really believed in what we were doing and had a strong belief in making the study of math applicable to daily life" [remarked Andover's principal]. But Melissa Lynn felt differently. A freshman at Andover in 1993, she became worried her Core-Plus class wasn't very hard. She asked to switch into a traditional class. But she would have had to travel by bus to another school. So she threw herself into the Core-Plus program and received straight A's. She graduated in 1997 at the top of her class, with a 3.97 grade-point average. Then she took the math placement test at the University of Michigan at Ann Arbor and bombed it. She found herself in "remedial math."

Melissa was not alone. According to one survey done by a Wayne State University mathematician, 96 percent of Andover graduates who took Core-Plus and responded to his questionnaire (nearly half of all graduates) had to take remedial math in college. There was sufficient dissatisfaction with the curriculum that the Bloomfield Hills school board, in 2000, voted to give students a choice between Core-Plus and traditional math.

A parent involved in the New York City math wars, testifying before the Education and Workforce Committee in the U.S. House of Representatives, said bluntly: "If medical doctors experimented with our kids in the same fashion school districts do, they would be put in jail." In medicine, if one takes perfectly healthy patients and tries to find something wrong with them so as to justify operating, it is called malpractice. In K-12 education, it is called school reform.

As with the math wars, the reading wars started in California and experienced their most virulent reaction there. Nicholas Lemann, writing in 1997, describes the role of Bill Honig, the former superintendent of public instruction in California, in leading the state into the whole-language era in the 1980s, and then leading a retreat from that pedagogy in the 1990s:

> Honig...wanted not merely to make teachers and students submit to tests of competence but to change what was taught. A privileged idealist from San Francisco, tall, skinny, and enthusiastic to the point of obsession, Honig worked tirelessly to convert the California curriculum into an immersion in [rich literature].... [After being forced to resign due to a personal scandal], Honig threw himself into the study of elementary-grade instruction. He concluded that under his direction many of the policies of the state education department had been terribly mistaken; he publicly disowned them, and started an organization to undo what he had done only a few years earlier. One Sacramento lobbyist...called him "the Robert McNamara of reading."

> The policy that caused Honig's recantation was whole-language reading instruction.... In each of the past three years California legislators have passed bills designed to force the state's public schools to move the needle in reading instruction away from whole language and toward its archenemy—the phonics method.... In California everybody now claims allegiance to a "balanced approach" incorporating whole language and phonics, but the truth is that the two sides have one of the purest and angriest disagreements.... "We're in the midst of a huge war," one California state legislator told me. "This is worse than abortion," another of the combatants gleefully reported.

California's reading scores on the NAEP test plummeted following the implementation of whole-language, with the state finishing next to last, ahead of only Guam. Then came the admission by Honig's successor as state superintendent, Delaine Eastin, that whole-language had been adopted mistakenly, that "good people do believe in alchemy at various points in our history." By 1997, Lemann notes, "whole language [had] been isolated. Support for it [was] limited to an enclosed community of devotees, including teachers, education-school professors, textbook publishers, bilingual educators, and teacher trainers. Virtually no one in the wider public [seemed] to be actively promoting whole language." The final chapter of this saga has not been written, however, as there is ongoing concern that the new phonics-based language arts professional development training authorized and funded by the state legislature in the late 1990s has been hijacked by the very "enclosed community" that has an egoistic and financial stake in continuing whole-language instruction.

Such battles continue around the country, even though "most research backs the need for lots of phonics, the sooner the better." I mentioned the 2000 NIH/National Reading Panel study earlier. Emblematic, also, of the heavy firepower which the traditionalist side is able to muster but which is often ignored by progressives was a 1995 letter written "from forty Massachusetts specialists in linguistics and psycholinguistics to the Commissioner of Education, Commonwealth of Massachusetts" on the subject of "standards for reading instruction in Massachusetts." The forty individuals were, in fact, among the leading language researchers in the state, and indeed the world, many representing Harvard, MIT, Massachusetts General Hospital, and other major institutions and including in their ranks four former presidents of the Linguistic Society of America and several members of the National Academy of Sciences—all stating that the whole-language curriculum proposal being circulated by the state department of education "replaces the common-sense view of reading as the decoding of notated speech with a surprising view of reading as directly 'constructing meaning.'" The letter went on to say:

> We want to alert the educational authorities of Massachusetts to the fact that the view of language research presented in this document is inaccurate....The facts are as follows. Language research continues to focus on the components of language, because this focus reflects the "modular" nature of language itself. Written language is a notation for the structures and units of one of these components. Sound methodology in reading instruction must begin with these realities. Anything else will shortchange those students

whom these standards are supposed to help. As linguists, we are concerned that the Commonwealth...should presume to legislate an erroneous view of how human language works, a view that runs counter to most of the major scientific results of more than 100 years of linguistics and psycholinguistics.

What more could be said in support of the traditionalist position? Yet in Massachusetts and elsewhere, such expertise tends to be received with indifference by the K-12 establishment. (When I brought the above letter to the attention of members of the Clayton administration and Language Literacy Committee, they gave it the respect they might have accorded a journal entry in a first-grader's diary.) Although the Massachusetts state education department is currently led by thinkers sympathetic to the views expressed by the forty scholars, there is a continuing struggle to overcome the resistance mounted by the same sort of "enclosed community of devotees" found in California.

The education wars extend beyond reading and math to every subject. The *Washington Post* reports that a "traditional, fact-based guide" for social studies teachers adopted by the Virginia Board of Education under a conservative state administration "has proved both popular and controversial across the country. It has influenced the work of several other state school boards...and incited an education brawl in Massachusetts, where the state board is trying to incorporate the Virginia approach despite complaints that it reduces history to a game of 'Trivial Pursuit.' Virginia's guide appeals to educators and parents who fear that children are no longer learning the names of presidents or the dates of wars as they once did and who worry that students can't think clearly about history without first knowing the facts.... Besides the Massachusetts board, educators in Texas, California, North Carolina, Kentucky, Maine, Vermont, Wisconsin, Pennsylvania, Arizona and Louisiana have sought information about the Virginia approach.... But in many of those same states, some teachers and parents have said the Virginia guide demands too much memorization and leaves too little class time to learn how to analyze history and apply its lessons."

Creativity Is Wonderful, but What Happened to Rigor?

At issue here are first principles: what constitutes an "educated" person, and how does one become "educated"? Leo Botstein, the president of Bard College, says "a good education teaches you how to ask a question. It's knowing what you don't know, the skills of critical thought." One might add that a good education also provides you with the ability to produce good answers, grounded in a solid knowledge base. A timeless quote offered by Jeremiah Day and James Kingsley in *Reports on the Course of Instruction in Yale College*, in 1830, speaks to the essence of a good education: "The two great points to be gained in intellectual culture are the *discipline* and *furniture* of the mind—expanding its powers, and storing it with knowledge."

Benjamin Bloom once offered a helpful taxonomy of lower-level to higher-level "educational objectives" that included the development of memorization, comprehension, application, analysis, synthesis, and evaluation capabilities. The clear implication was that the higher-level skills (such as analysis and evaluation) were built on the lower-level ones (memorization and comprehension). That is, it is almost impossible to play intelligently and effectively with English (do "creative" or "persuasive" writing) unless one has achieved a degree of mastery over and command of the language, as a result of having gained familiarity with grammar, vocabulary, and other elements of expository expression. Likewise, one cannot become adept at doing sophisticated statistical analyses until one has developed some facility and automaticity with numbers, with the manipulation of what mathematicians call algorithms (and others call arithmetic). One cannot meaningfully reflect on civil liberties questions, constitutional law, and the intent of the Founding Fathers if one has no historical bank of information, including who were the Founding Fathers and what are the relevant amendments in the Bill of Rights they gave us. And one should not be trying to save the homeless, much less the planet as a whole, until one has a clear idea of roughly how many homeless people there are, what causes homelessness and poverty, and other such "minutiae."

When progressives disparage the "furniture" of the mind as "mere facts," as they incessantly do, they undermine the possibilities for true education. There is something to the notion that if you can't remember it, that means you don't know it. Even if knowledge does not require total recall, memory is still vital. One of the best statements I have ever seen about the indispensable function memorization serves for a learner came from an Eastman Kodak scientist, whose e-mail read (with some paraphrasing) as follows: Even at a fairly sophisticated level, memorization is useful and probably essential. Consider some bright high school students learning physics. Their teacher tells them Newton's first law—a body in motion will continue in a straight line at a constant speed unless acted upon by an outside force—and they memorize it. At first, they do not understand the factual basis of the law. Indeed, the law's claim appears to them to be obviously false; everything eventually slows down, and virtually nothing travels in a straight line. Here, the students are memorizing a proposition. But, just as memorizing words helps children learn concepts, so memorizing this proposition helps them to learn mechanics. Their crude understanding of the memorized proposition guides them in accumulating empirical support for the law; they may never have wondered what forces might act on a knuckleball, a planet, or a compass needle, but the claim of the law urges them to do so. As they acquire data, the memorized proposition provides a mental locus at which they can integrate them.

True, memorization can be oversold as a skill. I confess I cannot remember all that I was taught in my own elementary and secondary education. What I do remember, however, are not only many important bits of information but also the fact that my teachers did not merely inundate me and my classmates with dates and other particulars but also engaged us in conceptual understanding, analysis, and other larger intellectual processes. Progressives are guilty of unfairly caricaturing traditional education, and setting up straw people, when they depict the education my generation received as amounting to little more than ingesting and spitting out a bunch of facts forgotten three days after the exam.

To appreciate the hubris and lack of historical memory that mark the modern-day constructivist, one need only examine some exams given to grade-school students in the nineteenth century. Note a few of the following items found on an eighth-grade final exam given in 1895 in Salina, Kansas. In addition to tapping the careful, rigorous use of language that is now viewed with disdain (e.g., "name the parts of speech and define those that have no modifications"; "give rules for principal marks of punctuation"), the exam presaged the "performance assessments" that are now all the rage among cutting-edge types (e.g., "write a composition of about 150 words and show therein that you understand the practical use of the rules of grammar"). As for problem-solving, the exam went beyond "name and define the fundamental rules of arithmetic" and asked students to answer this puzzle: "District No. 33 has a valuation of $35,000. What is the necessary levy to carry on a school seven months at $50 per month, and have $104 for incidentals?" How about historical acumen? The exam, in addition to daring to ask "who were the following—Morse, Whitney, Fulton, Bell, Lincoln, Penn, and Howe?" and "name events connected with the following dates—1607, 1620, 1800, 1849, 1865," required students to "give an account of the discovery of America by Columbus" and "relate the causes and results of the Revolutionary War." Geography? "Name all the republics of Europe and give capitals of each" and then "describe the process by which the water of the ocean returns to the sources of rivers."

Obviously, many educators in the past had high expectations for students to demonstrate strong skills of *both* the "low-level" *and* "high-level" variety. They truly believed in and practiced a philosophy of "basics-plus"! In contrast, today, in the age of atmospherics, we have "higher, but hollow, academic standards," which is the way Diane Ravitch characterizes the expectations associated with the new New York State Regents examinations. In the area of language arts, for example, she notes the standards formulated by the state education department "consisted of [several] vacuous statements [such as] 'students will read, write, listen, and speak for social interaction.'" Once the gold standard of American education, the Regents exams now have a tin quality.

One critic of constructivism wisely calls for a "moratorium" on the banalities uttered by progressives:

> Wouldn't it be nice if we could declare a moratorium on the use of certain grand sounding but effectively pernicious phrases and ideas? Near the top of our list would come "critical thinking."... [In K-12 education] the phrase is supposed to denote an important intellectual advance beyond the old-fashioned concern with "content." Remember content? It is an important part of what, in the bad old days, one would go to school to obtain: a mastery of particular names, dates.... Critical thinkers are beyond all that.... For devotees of critical thinking, there is something indescribably naif about mastering any particular body of knowledge or affirming any traditional conclusions. That is what drudges do. Critical thinking is held to be so much more creative....The ideology of "critical thinking" continues to be enormously popular. It is the hardiest of hardy perennials. Nor is this surprising. Talk about a labor-saving device! How many hours of difficult study have been circumvented by a timely dose of "critical thinking."

Perhaps a moratorium should also be imposed on the word "creativity." It is not the antithesis of rigor, but progressives have made it so. In praising rigor, I mean a commitment to painstaking diligence in aiming for perfection in one's work, even if perfection is virtually unattainable. A common saying is that the best is the enemy of the good, in that we often reject good, sound proposals because they are not perfect. K-12 education has turned this saw on its head—the good is the enemy of the perfect, in that the unattainability of perfection has meant that students should not strive for such a goal. The result has been academic rigor mortis. Aristotle once wrote that "the diner, not the cook, is the best judge of a meal." Not so in a constructivist eatery, where the chef, not the customer, is always right.

Basics and the Rich-Poor Gap

Rigor begins with basics. While all kids need schools to train them in the basics, kids from poor, disadvantaged backgrounds need them even more than kids who grow up in well-to-do households, since—if schools fail to teach the basics—the former kids, unlike the latter, normally cannot fall back on hovering middle-class parents, book-abundant home life, or outside tutors to fill in the gaps. There is less margin for error from misguided reforms in schools which serve poor neighborhoods than wealthy ones. Most of the examples of anti-basics pedagogy I cited in my survey of the "spreading conflict" were drawn from affluent Clayton-type districts, such as Fairfax and Bloomfield Hills, but it is the poorest children from the poorest school systems who suffer the most from trendy methodologies, and whose voices are the least heard.

Although constructivism is a relatively new term, Diane Ravitch has documented how it is merely a reincarnation of earlier doctrines espoused by G. Stanley Hall and other progressives who, by the 1930s, already had penned the now omnipresent cliché "we teach children, not subject matter" and had decided to spare masses of those same children any serious academic work. E.D. Hirsch shows the great irony of liberal, progressive educators posing as champions of the poor. It is conservative, traditionalist educators who in fact offer a more promising way out of poverty. He compares the views of Antonio Gramsci, a 1930s Italian communist who understood this irony well, with those of Paulo Freire, a Brazilian contemporary of Gramsci who spoke of traditional education as "the pedagogy of the oppressed" and whose progressive ideas only increased the oppression of the poor:

> Gramsci saw that it was a serious error to discredit learning methods like phonics and memorization of the multiplication tables as "outdated" or "conservative." That was the nub of the standoff between himself and another prominent educational theorist of the political Left, Paulo Freire. Like Gramsci, Freire...was interested in methods of educating the poor. Unlike Gramsci, Freire has been quite influential in the United States.
>
> Like other educational progressives, Freire rejected traditional subject matter and derided the "banking theory of schooling," whereby the teacher provides the child with a lot of "rote-learned" information. This conservative approach, according to Freire, numbs the critical faculties of students and preserves the oppressor class.... In short, Freire, like other modern educational writers, linked political and educational progressivism.
>
> Gramsci took the opposite view. He held that political progressivism demanded educational traditionalism. The oppressed class should be taught to master the tools of power and authority—the ability to read, write, and communicate—and should gain enough traditional knowledge to understand the worlds of nature and culture surrounding them. Children, particularly the children of the poor,...should learn the value of hard work, gain the knowledge that leads to understanding, and master the traditional culture in order to command its rhetoric.... History has proven Gramsci a better prophet than Freire.

The famous African-American intellectual W.E.B. Du Bois, writing in 1935, pointed out that, in order to help the less fortunate, "the school has again but one way, and that is, first and last, to teach them to read, write and count. And if the school fails to do that, and tries beyond that to do something for which a school is not adapted, it not only fails in its own function, but it fails in all other attempted functions." Hirsch made these same arguments in his 1988 work *Cultural Literacy*, where he suggested that all children, especially disadvantaged ones, be exposed to a common vocabulary of major historical figures and events, which included especially the Western canon. Although he was widely accused by progressives of promoting establishment, right-wing views, he started his own foundation, the Core Knowledge Foundation, that targeted its efforts especially at educating underprivileged inner-city children.

Some progressives, like Howard Gardner, lately have grudgingly come to accord Hirsch some respect, at least in regard to the education of minority and disadvantaged children. Gardner has written that "progressive education works best with children who come from richly endowed homes.... It is optimistic to...expect success with children who come from impoverished backgrounds, who lack the knowledge...to explore an environment and learn from their own activities.... A large and possibly growing number of students need the kind of help, support, [and] modeling...that has often been seen as antithetical to the unstructured atmosphere of progressive education.... [Regarding Hirsch's "core knowledge" curriculum], for those disadvantaged children who do not acquire literacy in the dominant culture at home, such a prescribed curriculum helps to provide a level playing field and to ensure that future citizens enjoy a common knowledge base." The flaw in Gardner's analysis is, first, that today's full-inclusion, heterogeneously grouped classroom is incapable of differentiating instruction as he suggests—the equity crusaders tend to be unwilling to separate out the "advantaged" from the "disadvantaged" kids—and, second, he puts the onus on affluent parents to teach their kids the basics when they are paying taxes for schools to do so. Despite the compelling arguments against the progressive position on the basics, the leftist Freire, indeed, has prevailed in the United States—he was named in 1997, in a special *New York Times* survey, as one of "13 innovators who changed education."

Just as rich districts are fighting back against the progressives' anti-basics onslaught, so, too, are poorer districts. The M.C. Terrell Elementary School in inner-city Washington, D.C., home to some three hundred students, nearly all African-American, sent several staff to the 10th Core Knowledge National Conference in Boston in 2000 to learn more about Hirsch's principles. Eight-five percent of Terrell's teachers voted to adopt Core Knowledge, which they felt would "lead to more creativity, not less." Meanwhile, Barclay School, in the Baltimore inner city, with a low-income student body over 90 percent African-American, has borrowed from a local private school "a distinctly old-fashioned program," according to an editorial in the *Baltimore Sun*. "It emphasizes penmanship and it keeps repeating exercises until the student gets the spelling and syntax right. The reading program is a mixture of children's classics and phonics. As for history, it uses a text that has been revised but was first published more than seven decades ago. [This approach] has produced students who consistently score at or above the national average in reading and comprehension. Math scores glow, too. Tried and true methods may be what public schools need."

Among the most impressive back-to-basics success stories reported on lately are the ones catalogued in Casey Carter's *No Excuses: Lessons From 21 High-Performing, High-Poverty Schools*. Fifteen of the schools he studied were public schools. In all cases, over three-fourths of the students came from families whose incomes qualified them for the federal lunch program. Despite their humble origins, students in all the schools scored well above the national average on national achievement tests, with students in eleven of the schools scoring above the 80th percentile. Among the keys to academic success in the twenty-one schools was a common focus on fundamentals.

I referred earlier to the NCTE and NCTM national standards that now set the agenda for K-12 curriculum development in English and mathematics in most schools. In the 1990s, these and other national standards projects were developed by task forces authorized and funded by the U.S. Congress, spurred by the bipartisan education summit held in Charlottesville, Virginia in September 1989, which called for tougher, "world-class" standards in America's schools. They became a central feature of both the Bush administration's America 2000 school improvement plan as well as the Clinton administration's Goals 2000 program. The aim was to define what today's students should be expected to know and do in the various academic disciplines. The controversies that continue to swirl around these standards-setting projects indicate much confusion and disagreement over the age-old question of what constitutes an "educated" person.

The Controversy Over the National History Standards

I noted the "brawls" occurring in Massachusetts, Virginia, and other states over social studies education. These state-level conflicts owe their genesis to the larger fracas that followed the unveiling of the national history standards in 1994, a three-volume set of curriculum guides for grades K-4 as well as grades 5-12. The idea behind the history standards project was to try to identify key knowledge and skills students should learn in U.S. and world history. This daunting task was undertaken by the National

Center for History in the Schools at UCLA, directed by historian Gary Nash, who involved a panel of some two hundred historians and social studies educators. The standards document released in 1994 sparked a firestorm of protests because of the perception that the authors had gone overboard in PC thinking, in failing to give adequate attention to important features of the American experience and Western civilization and, to the extent these topics were covered, loading them with negative connotations.

Witness just some of the reactions. Lynne Cheney, who as head of the National Endowment for the Humanities had initially supported funding for the project, wrote in the *Wall Street Journal* that "the authors tend to save their unqualified admiration for people, places, and events that are politically correct....To understand West Africa, students are encouraged to 'analyze the achievements and grandeur of Mansa Musa's court, and the social customs and wealth of the kingdom of Mali.' Such celebratory prose is rare when the document gets to American history itself [where, for example, John D. Rockefeller, is put on 'trial' for his wealth accumulation].... One of the most often mentioned subjects, with 19 references, is McCarthy and McCarthyism. The Ku Klux Klan gets its fair share, too, with 17. As for individuals, Harriet Tubman, an African-American who helped rescue slaves by way of the underground railroad, is mentioned six times. Two white males who were contemporaries of Tubman, Ulysses S. Grant and Robert E. Lee, get one and zero mentions, respectively. Alexander Graham Bell, Thomas Edison, Albert Einstein, Jonas Salk, and the Wright brothers make no appearance at all."

The historian John Patrick Diggins, the author of a Yale University Press volume on Abraham Lincoln and the Civil War, remarked that the history standards document "lies somewhere between comedy and farce. [It] minimized the importance of the Western Enlightenment and replaced political knowledge about human nature with cultural mystiques about races and racial heritages." The historian Walter McDougall of the University of Pennsylvania derided the assumptions upon which the standards appeared to be based: "If Europeans braved the unknown to discover a new world, it was to kill and oppress. If colonists carved a new nation out of the woods, it was to displace Native Americans and impose private property. If the 'Founding Fathers' (the term has been banished) invoked human rights, it was to deny them to others. If businessmen built the most prosperous nation in history, it was to rape the environment and keep workers in misery." U.S. Secretary of Education Richard Riley added that the standards "portray American history in a bad light....Those aren't our standards. We had nothing to do with them." In January 1995, the U.S. Senate, by a vote of 99-1, also disowned the standards.

Albert Shanker's response was somewhat more muted but nonetheless critical. Shanker was a strong advocate of national standards, but not these:

> Admittedly, the history standards have some serious flaws. They also offer much that is worthwhile....The first piece of good news...is that they are substantive and demanding.... Are the standards marred by political correctness? They give more attention to groups—like African-Americans and Native people—that were largely ignored by traditional history, but that in itself is not a problem. This reflects...an attempt to correct previous distortions.... On the other hand, there is no question that the picture of U.S. history the new standards present is grim.... [Our] history looks like a history of oppression. This is unfair, [as] these people [the authors] do not apply current standards when they are judging the histories of other countries or groups.

Efforts have been made since 1995 to refine the standards in response to criticisms, but differences persist over striking the right balance between America Firsters and America Worsters.

What lies beneath the history standards controversy is not only the matter of political correctness or incorrectness but also some profound differences over educational objectives. In some respects the standards document both overreached and underreached in the demands they placed on students. As Shanker said, they were quite "substantive and demanding." Indeed, one could argue they were absurdly so, to the point of pretentiousness. Among the stated goals was that students should be able to "demonstrate understanding of China's sustained political and cultural expansion during the Tang period" and to "demonstrate understanding of the synthesis of Hindu civilization in India in the era of the Gunta Empire." Difficult as these standards are, they pale next to "analyze the relationship between Muslims and Hindus in the [Mughal] empire and [compare] Akhbar's governing methods and religious ideas with those of other Mughal emperors, such as Aurangzeb." Most Ph.D.s I know in history and political science, except for South Asian specialists, would be clueless about this historical subject, masters degree and baccalaureate graduates even more so.

The authors of the national standards scoffed at the notion of history as factual literacy, at Hirsch's notion of core knowledge. Gary Nash, the project director, stated that his group's objective "was to bring about nothing short of a new American revolution in history education...we want to bury rote learning and the emphasis on dates, facts, places, events, and one damn thing after another." He wanted to "let children out of the prison of facts and dates and make them active learners," staging mock trials, debates, and other performances.

It was here where the standards underreached. As the Princeton historian Sean Wilentz warned, educators "like to pose as courageous progressives dedicated to liberating schoolchildren from the tyranny of rote instruction.... But if they have their way, the widely lamented historical illiteracy of today's students will only worsen in the generations to come." The fact that Al Shanker felt a need in 1996 to write a column entitled "Knowledge Still Counts" was a telling commentary on the obsession of the modern educationist with process over content and the latter's failure to understand the connection between the two. In the column, Shanker reported on a study that found, not surprisingly, a direct correlation between "cultural literacy" and a successful career (defined as high-income and high-status occupations). There are the examples of such "factgrubbers" as former U.S. Secretary of State Madeleine Albright and Microsoft tycoon Bill Gates. Albright recently acknowledged the importance of her early training, noting that "when I was a sophomore in high school, I won the United Nations contest in Colorado because I could name all the countries of the United Nations." About Bill Gates, Hirsch writes:

> Bill Gates is independent-minded, has higher-order accessing skills, is a critical thinker...and exhibits the various creative competencies that American experts say are much more important than just knowing a bunch of facts. But it happens that Bill Gates knows a lot of facts.... Cognitive psychologists tell us that if competent people like Gates didn't know a lot of facts, they couldn't be critical, creative, independent thinkers. The research literature is very clear on this point: that highly skilled intellectual competence comes after, not before, you know a lot of "mere facts." First facts, then facility.

Teenagers seem to be able to remember the names of rock stars and the lyrics of their songs, however fleeting their presence on the cultural scene. (Who in my generation can forget Sam Cooke's recording of "Wonderful World," which included the words "Don't know much about history"?) Although schools have never done a great job of getting kids to remember more important, durable cultural names—as Wilentz says, there has always been "widely lamented historical illiteracy" in the United States—at one time there were expectations in many schools that such knowledge was worth the effort to teach and test. Now we have thrown in the towel. Ignorance has never been more blissful, and never more in evidence. Note the following evidences:

- On a recent National Assessment of Educational Progress (NAEP) test, "fourth-graders were asked which of these states were among the original 13 colonies: Illinois, California, New York, and Texas. Only 32 percent—fewer than one out of three—knew the answer was New York. Asked which war the United States fought to try to contain communism—Mexican-American, World War I, World War II or Vietnam—only 31 percent could identify Vietnam.... Results from eighth-graders or high school seniors weren't much better. Overall, 36 percent of fourth-graders scored below basic; only 2 percent were advanced. By eighth grade, 39 percent were below basic and only 1 percent advanced. For seniors, a depressingly large 57 percent were below basic, with 1 percent advanced."

- Summarizing the same NAEP exam, journalist Lewis Lapham notes that the test results "can be read as a coroner's report.... [They] returned a finding of mortal ignorance. More than 50 percent of all high school seniors were unaware of the cold war. Nearly 6 in 10 were bereft of even a primitive understanding of where America came from."

- Other recent NAEP data: "Two out of three seventeen-year-olds, most ready to go on to college, did not know the meaning of Abraham Lincoln's Emancipation Proclamation. Less than half the 16,000 high school seniors tested recognized Patrick Henry's defiant challenge, "Give me liberty or give me death." Even fewer teenagers...knew of the existence of the War of 1812, the Marshall Plan that saved Europe, or Lyndon Johnson's Great Society."

- Columnist Bob Herbert, commenting on "a nation of nitwits," reports that the ignorance-is-bliss condition exists as well in the wider public, including older adults who perhaps were victims of the "great meltdown" of American schools in the 1950s that Ravitch described. He notes: "According to a new poll, 60 percent of Americans are unable to name the President who ordered the nuclear attack on Japan, and 35 percent do not know that the first atomic bomb was dropped on Hiroshima. One out of every four people surveyed...did not even know that Japan was the target of the first atomic bomb."

- David Broder has noted that "young people are in danger of losing America's civic memory." Writing on July 4, 2000, he commented: "Who was the American general at Yorktown? William Tecumseh Sherman, Ulysses S. Grant, Douglas MacArthur, or George Washington? When that question was asked late last year of 556 randomly chosen seniors at 55 top-rated colleges and universities, one out of three got it right. Stunningly, more of those about to graduate from great liberal arts colleges like Amherst and Williams and Grinnell and world-class universities like Harvard and Duke and the University of Michigan named Grant...rather than Washington....That was not the worst. Barely one out of five (22 percent) could identify the Gettysburg Address as the source of the phrase 'Government of the people, by the people, for the people.'"

It is now asking too much of students to know the identity of Patrick Henry, even if, apparently, they are expected to know who Aurangzeb was.

The Controversy Over the National English Standards

Historical illiteracy may well be exceeded by verbal illiteracy, which creates even greater shackles. Echoing Benjamin Bloom, E. D. Hirsch notes "there are no real-world examples of adults with information-age competencies who are functioning with a 4th grade vocabulary."

I spoke earlier of the national standards document produced by the National Council of Teachers of English (NCTE) in 1996, which reflected progressivist ideas about inventive spelling, whole language, and media-viewing as a surrogate for reading. Since the late 1960s, NCTE had campaigned for a "writing process" model that placed emphasis on students doing multiple drafts in which they were encouraged not to worry about standard English conventions; far less stress was placed on a final draft as a polished, perfected piece of work. The 1996 standards simply confirmed what had become the dominant paradigm. At the time, rumor had it that the NCTE was considering removing the word "English" from its organizational name. One of the chief architects of the standards document boasted that "it doesn't even tell you to teach grammar." Around the same time, the president of the Assembly for the Teaching of English Grammar, a renegade group of traditionalists, noted that at a recent NCTE annual meeting "out of some 340 sessions on the NCTE program and...well over 1,000 individual papers, not a single one was devoted to language structure or linguistics. In fact the word grammar appeared only once in the [entire] program—and that was in a negative way." She added that "our profession has not been well served by the anti-grammar policies based on dubious research and on distorted conclusions."

One of education's harshest critics has been Sandra Stotsky, a former editor of the NCTE journal, in the days when rigor still mattered. In *Losing our Language*, Stotsky blows the whistle on how America's schools of education have systematically ratcheted down K-12 literacy training over the past several decades out of a misplaced obsession with multiculturalism. She offers a scathing critique of how educators—based on condescending assumptions about the inability of minority children to meet high academic expectations—have altered the curriculum to accommodate what they see as the needs of the latter children, in the process doing a disservice to all students.

Most revealingly, Stotsky notes that a NCTE-sponsored journal awarded a best article prize in 1993 to an essay in which the authors (from Indiana University of Pennsylvania) stated that "writers should be encouraged to make intentional errors in standard form and usage. Attacking the demand for standard English is the only way to end its oppression of linguistic minorities." The editor of the journal described "the matter of standard edited English as an emotional political issue" and praised the authors because they "exposed the tyranny of standards." My own colleagues in the UM-St. Louis English department, which like many college English departments is dominated by postmodernists, once told me they "have to respect diverse dialects" when grading English composition papers. English comp instructors today make a big deal of getting students to write for different "audiences" and in different "genres," such as "persuasive essays." One of my students once asked about a term paper I had assigned, "Do you want it to be written as a persuasive piece?" to which I replied, "Yes, persuade me you know how to use the English language!"

Again, the problem starts in K-12. Inventive spelling is supposed to end by around third grade, but it is permitted in perpetuity. Spelling bees are widely disparaged for committing the twin sin of fostering competition and fostering right answers. The literacy gurus contend that kids' egos are so fragile that the mere correction of errors by a teacher will produce instant "shutdown." Yet, out of the other side of their mouths, they talk about empowering kids to develop higher-order skills. Regarding the latter, what is harder to master—communicating in jumbled gibberish, or communicating by using careful syntax and concise, tight expression of ideas? As I stated in an article that was published in *Education Week* as a counterpoint to a companion piece written by the NCTE executive director, "With the new English standards, we are at risk of producing increasingly illiterate kids who are good at talking off the tops of their heads or from the seats of their pants, or writing stream-of-consciousness prose baring their innermost feelings, but who cannot spell or punctuate their way out of a paper bag."

The official newsletter of the Duke University Talent Identification Program had this to say: "From kindergarten through secondary education, fear runs roughshod among educators that to teach grammatical rules and punctuation will inhibit the writer's expression. Arriving at such a conclusion defies all logical thought." No reasonable person would wish to unleash the grammar police on a child, but neither should one be unleashing the anti-grammar police on America's teachers, as assistant superintendents for curriculum have been known to do. David Mulroy, in "The War Against Grammar," writes, "I learned about grammar in a parochial school from no-nonsense...nuns who had me diagramming complicated sentences in the fourth grade. This gave me an understanding of the structure of language that is by far my most valuable intellectual possession.... How could any sane person object to the proposition that high school graduates should know the parts of speech and understand the structure of sentences?" Yet this is now contested terrain in K-12 education. Diagramming sentences is virtually banned in Clayton. It was especially revealing when, at a Curriculum Council meeting in April 2002, I asked a Wydown Middle School English teacher

point blank whether she would repudiate the "tyranny of standards" statement in the 1993 NCTE journal article, which I
quoted aloud, and she refused.

It is hard to be a good writer if you are not a good reader.
Compelling arguments were made by Rudolf Flesch in the 1950s
(*Why Johnny Can't Read*) and Jeanne Chall in the 1960s (*Learning to Read: The Great Debate*) for teaching reading through
phonics (decoding text by learning the smallest sound units that
combine to produce words), as opposed to relying on "whole
word" or "look-say" reading methods. Nonetheless, the latter
methods, re-labeled "whole language," won out in the reading
wars in the 1980s and were privileged in the NCTE 1996 standards. One of the leaders of the whole-language movement,
Kenneth Goodman, sounding like a walking billboard for Ebonics, summarized the movement's philosophy, in urging teachers to
"reject negative, elitist, racist views of linguistic purity that would
limit children to arbitrary 'proper' language." The 1996 NCTE
document itself defined standard English as "English as it is spoken and written by those groups with social, economic, and
political power in the United States."

If the key standard-bearers of the English language take this
view of the mother tongue, should we be at all surprised that our
kids are lacking strong literacy skills? Reading comprehension
scores on the NAEP and other national tests have been stagnant
for the past several decades, with the whole-language movement
unable to show any gains. As with the teaching of history, there
are overwhelming data showing the failure of American education
in the field of language arts:

- I noted earlier the California reading disaster of the 1980s and
  1990s. Stotsky points out that "despite the efforts of the defenders of whole language to claim that the teachers in California
  had not been given sufficient training in whole language and
  that the rise in the number of immigrant children was the real
  cause of the decline in reading scores, the fact is that the scores
  of native 'white' children declined as much as did the scores of
  other children."

- Sandra Stotsky also notes that we "need to take a close look at
  what children were expected to read in the primary grades one
  hundred years ago and compare that with what...children are
  expected to read today. If [we] did, [we] would discover that the

language base needed for understanding mature academic and literary texts began to erode before midcentury. The decline in the difficulty level of the selections used to teach children how to read has not been a steady one over the course of this century. But there is no mistaking the direction of the movement.... We can find clear testimony to a decline in the total number of hard words offered in the various editions that leading reading series have put out in the past two decades by looking at their glossaries." Based on an extensive content analysis, she concludes: "Not only are children being given fewer hard words in their readers than just one or two decades ago, worse yet, their vocabulary knowledge is not being accelerated over the course of upper elementary grades."

- Donald Hayes and Loreen Wolfer of Cornell University also found "long-term use of simplified texts," based on a computerized system to grade the relative difficulty of reading material. A 1993 *New York Times* article reported their contention that "the nationwide decline in verbal [SAT] scores since 1963 is a result of simplified schoolbooks introduced after World War II. Scores started falling in 1963, when the baby-boom generation began taking the test. The scores continued to drop for 16 years and have remained low ever since. The...average score on the verbal [SAT] was 420 out of a possible 800 last year, compared with 478 in 1963. The drop of 56 points does not take into account the declining difficulty of the test.... [Scores were "recentered" after 1993.] Dr Hayes sampled 788 school books used between 1860 and 1992. 'Honors high school texts are no more difficult [today] than an eighth-grade reader was before World War II.'"

- About "the latest dismal NAEP scores," reported in 2001, E.D. Hirsch says that "this latest reading report from the National Assessment of Educational Progress documents a steady state. It shows no significant overall shift in American students' reading proficiency.... In 2000, there were minor gains at the top, and slight declines at the bottom, but no global change in overall achievement or in the gap between middle-class and low-income students, a gap that has been a disturbing feature of American schooling for at least 50 years." In other words, the very population that equity-oriented progressives purport to serve through whole language and other such pedagogies has been ill-served.

Also commenting on the 2001 NAEP results, the *New York Times* pointed out that "two-thirds of students tested fell below the level the federal government considers proficient, and 37 percent fell below even basic knowledge of reading."

Criticism of the NCTE has been bipartisan. Michael Cohen, senior advisor to Secretary of Education Riley in the Clinton administration, remarked about the national standards that they "are so remarkably vague, most of the time I don't even know what they are saying." As fuzzy as the NCTE English standards are, the math standards produced by the NCTM are a close second. They have been called "ebonics with an equals sign."

The Controversy Over the National Mathematics Standards

The 1960s saw the wide-scale adoption of the so-called "new math," built around abstract logic that turned out to be incomprehensible to most children as well as adults. Supported by the National Science Foundation, the idea was that teachers should stress the conceptual rather than computational aspects of mathematics. When test scores then dropped, critiques such as Morris Kline's *Why Johnny Can't Add: The Failure of the New Math* (1973) called for a return to basics. The math profession went back to the drawing board to determine the right mix of traditional and non-traditional numeracy training that schools should provide. The result was the "new-new math," unveiled in the national standards document released by the National Council of Teachers of Mathematics in 1989, which, like its predecessor, had the endorsement of the National Science Foundation.

Supporters called the new standards "integrated math," rejecting the "fuzzy math" label used by detractors. The mix of methods NCTM promoted in the 1990s was weighted heavily toward constructivist pedagogy, with an emphasis again on conceptualization. As Diane Ravitch described the NCTM standards, they seemed to draw no lessons from the debacle of the 1960s: "Like the new math of the 1960s, the NCTM standards were an immediate success; every mass-produced mathematics textbook claimed to have adopted them.... Intended to encourage critical thinking and problem-solving, the NCTM standards put a premium on student-led activities, mathematical games, working with manipulatives (e.g., blocks and sticks), using calculators, and group learning, and discounted the importance of correct answers.

Rote learning was out, and computation was also downgraded because students in every grade were expected to use calculators at all times."

Tony Snow, the newspaper and television commentator, put it more plainly: "Heap praise on kids if they get close. Theorists say precision matters less to young minds than developing comfort with their ordinals and cardinals. The new-new crew thus recommends letting students 'discover' their own personal methods for performing simple calculations. Don't make them memorize tables. Stimulate their imaginations." Once again, the emphasis was placed on "creativity" over rigor. It reminded one of satirist Tom Lehrer's song in the 1960s: "So you've got thirteen, And you take away seven, And that leaves five...Well, six actually. But the idea is the important thing." What we used to laugh at as goofiness is now the conventional wisdom in K-12 progressive circles.

What has driven the new-new math is the usual blend of good intentions aimed at enriching the curriculum while reaching the most impoverished minds, with the latter being the overriding concern, resulting in the usual charade of dumbing down disguised as smarting up. Few can quarrel with the desire to improve student problem-solving capabilities, which no doubt is one of the features that attracted the interest of NSF. As noted earlier, however, the populist impulses have been even more evident, in wanting to make math more fun and more accessible to mathphobes, particularly girls and minorities thought to be disadvantaged by traditional math instruction. This goal is especially dear to many math educators affiliated with K-12 think tanks and schools of education, such as Steven Leinwand, who was on the federal panel that approved Core-Plus and other new-new math curricula. Leinwand has said it is "downright dangerous" and exacts a "psychic toll" to teach students things like "six times seven is 42, put down two and carry four." Such instruction is a "sorting mechanism" for "anointing the few [who master these procedures] and casting out the many." He argues as a matter of democratic theory that the calculator now provides an opportunity to remove "the discriminatory shackles of computational algorithms."

Aside from the fact that calculator dependency threatens to harm inner-city children the most, such thinking also ignores all the evidence indicating that, in Singapore and other Asian countries that outperform the United States in international K-12 math competitions, calculators are used only sparingly, especially in the early grades. David Klein of California State University-Northridge has noted:

> According to the Third International Mathematics and Science Study (TIMSS), the use of calculators in U.S. fourth-grade mathematics classes is about twice the international average.... In six of the seven top-scoring nations...teachers of 85 percent or more of the students report that students never use calculators in class. Even at the eighth-grade level, the majority of students from three of the top five scoring nations in the TIMSS study (Belgium, Korea, and Japan) never or rarely use calculators in math classes. In Singapore, which is also among the top five..., students do not use calculators until the seventh grade.

Harold Stevenson of the University of Michigan, a leading authority on TIMSS, adds: "Japanese and Chinese teachers do not permit the everyday use of calculators or computers in mathematics classes because they want the students to understand the concepts and operations necessary for the solution of problems.... Only at the high school level, after students have developed a clear understanding of mathematical concepts are East Asian students given the opportunity to use a calculator as a tool in solving mathematical problems." Progressive educators in America probably cannot appreciate the humor in a cartoon that depicted a school-age child commenting to his friend that "I think I'm going to do better in math this semester. I got new batteries for Christmas."

The *Wall Street Journal* has suggested that more self-serving motives than the promotion of democracy lie behind the new-new math: "The reason for the New Math...is that teachers, school administrators and their unions are tired of being blamed for...poor student performances. So...such educators work to destroy or reject the standards that brought them trouble in the first place. Children are different nowadays, goes the line, and cannot be measured by old benchmarks." Also at stake have been the professional egos of mathematicians as well as millions of dollars in project funding and royalty payments going to curriculum developers able to demonstrate a superior product. The *Christian Science Monitor* has voiced the concerns of traditionalist critics that "the [U.S.] Department of Education's expert panel, assembled to find the best math programs in the United States,...relied heavily on studies of student achievement that were authored or co-authored by the directors of the programs themselves." "Several panel members were affiliated with programs being judged. Most notable was the co-chairman of the panel, Steven Leinwand, who also sat on advisory boards of three programs being judged, two of which were later selected as 'exemplary' programs."

Whatever the factors contributing to the rise of the new-new math, the anti-basics posture adopted by supporters like Leinwand provoked an understandable backlash in the form of the "second great math rebellion" described in the previous section. Even Secretary of Education Riley, whose department blessed Core-Plus and other constructivist math curricula, chimed in that "in my view, a test of eighth-grade students should measure...whether students have learned how to do arithmetic accurately without a calculator." Many parents around the country emphatically embraced this common-sense position. One of the parents mobilized by Mathematically Correct was Marianne Jennings, an Arizona State University professor, who gained national attention when she "wrote a vivid critique of her teenage daughter's algebra textbook, an 812-page full-color tome replete with Dogon art from Africa, poetry, maps of South America, and warnings about pollution and endangered species," dubbing this "rain-forest algebra." U.S. Senator Robert Byrd of West Virginia, upon examining the latter text, called it "wacko math," remarking on the Senate floor that "I still don't quite grasp the necessity for political correctness in an algebra textbook. Nor do I understand the inclusion of the United Nations Universal Declaration of Human Rights in three languages."

The main check against such abuses is the use of achievement tests that can be employed to determine whether American kids are truly learning about math, as opposed to group dynamics or ecological threats to the monarch butterfly. Here is where the TIMSS international comparisons have been telling. In 2000, the head of IBM and the governor of Wisconsin, co-chairs of Achieve, Inc., a business-government partnership aimed at promoting higher academic standards in U.S. schools, commented on the latest TIMSS results in math and science:

> The new results, from the Third International Mathematics and Science Study, in which 38 countries participated, show American eighth-graders about where they were four years ago—average, putting them on par with students from Bulgaria, Latvia and New Zealand.... It's especially troubling that four years ago, when

today's American eighth graders were in fourth grade, as a group they ranked better—well above the international math average on an earlier version of the same test, scoring behind their peers in only seven countries. The message here is extraordinary and irrefutable: Every day our public schools are open, the gulf between our children and the world's top performers grows wider.

The *New York Times* reported at the time that "the most comprehensive and rigorous international comparison of schooling ever undertaken reveals American high school seniors, even many in advanced classes, to be among the industrial world's least prepared in mathematics and science.... Particularly devastating was the bleak performance of the best American students in advanced subjects. In physics and advanced mathematics, not one of the countries involved—even less well-off nations like Greece, Cyprus, and Latvia—scored lower than the United States." Although the K-12 establishment often tries to dismiss the TIMSS results as unfairly measuring Asia's very best students against a broader sample of American students, such rationalizations for ignoring the evidence are becoming harder to justify. NAEP and other standardized tests taken only by American students likewise show little progress. We should not be surprised, then, that almost half of all the 13,000 Ph.D.s awarded annually by American universities in math, physics, and the hard sciences are earned by non-Americans.

The latest skirmishing in the math wars has seen the NCTM come close to issuing a mea culpa. As reported in the *New York Times* in 2000, "While not abandoning its original agenda, the council added strong language to its groundbreaking 1989 standards, emphasizing accuracy, efficiency, and basic skills." Many traditionalists greeted the news with great fanfare: "Now school districts throughout the country will have to re-evaluate the 'content-lite' mathematics programs they purchased over the past ten years." Others, while encouraged, were more skeptical, concerned that school districts would find it hard to undo their investment in teacher training that had been tied to the 1989 standards.

From the Nonjudgmental to the Nonhierarchical Classroom

Most teachers are caring professionals who want to do a good job. However, they find themselves in a system, starting with their preparation in schools of education, followed by in-service professional development workshops, where they are practically brainwashed to accept constructivist ideas. It literally is drilled into them, even as they are taught the evils of drilling. Typical was the statement made by the 2000-2001 "teacher of the year" in the largest school district in the St. Louis area, who explained that her distinctive teaching philosophy was that "my students are always pushed to be their best, to be critical thinkers and to be creative problem-solvers."

Such is the pabulum that all too often comes out of schools of education and professional development workshops, which are the twin engines of pack pedagogy. We turn now to an examination of teachers and teacher-training, and how today's nonjudgmental classroom is also the nonhierarchical classroom, where the teacher plays the role not of manager but merely "coach" cum cheerleader.

7

The Teacher as Coach

The subject I teach, world politics, is characterized by what is called anarchy—the absence of any hierarchical authority, of any "ruler" who governs the members of the international community. In a sense, our classrooms have also become anarchical, since they are now places where everybody is supposedly a coequal member of a "learning community," where no one individual is superior to (possessing more authoritative knowledge) than anyone else. Progressives make no distinction between teaching and learning. They proclaim "we are all learners." While it is true all of us (toddlers and professors) are, or should be, continuous lifelong learners, progressives lose sight of important distinctions in terms of who it is worth learning *from*. There is reason to believe that adults, although not omniscient, know more than children. Although all people in any given college classroom are adults, one adult in particular usually has read approximately several hundred more books and scholarly articles than the others, and has spent approximately several thousand more hours in deeper study reflecting on the subject matter. Traditionalists understand these distinctions. Progressives are not so sure.

It is easy to see how the current popularity of the teacher-as-coach paradigm can be traced intellectually to the rise of constructivist theory in the 1980s, and ideologically to the radical egalitarianism and radical libertarianism that came out of the 1960s. As I noted previously, however, the idea of "discovery learning" has a long pedigree that goes back several centuries. Jacques Barzun, for example, describes the seventeenth-century thinker John Amos Comenius: "He was another in the long line of school reformers who, with interesting variations, always say the same thing; it is their fated role.... Anyone who has had much to do with education or has dipped into its history can guess what

175

Comenius said: Change school from a prison to a *scholae ludus* (play site), where curiosity is aroused and satisfied. Stop beatings. Reduce rote learning and engage the child's interest through music and games and through handling objects, through posing problems (the project method), stirring the imagination by dramatic accounts of the big world.... He added the substance of the twentieth century thought-cliché: education goes on as long as life."

Jean-Jacques Rousseau, writing in the eighteenth century, influenced the growth of "child-centered" education as much as any historical figure. Known more as a political philosopher than educationist, Rousseau nonetheless was instrumental in promoting the Romantic vision of schooling, the notion that "children can and should learn all things naturally," exploring the world around them through their innate curiosity, relying on their senses more than books or other artificial devices. In *Emile*, Rousseau made the case for a pedagogy based on experiential learning guided by the interests of the child, where the tutor was to "do nothing." (Rousseau, indeed, did nothing in his own parenting, abandoning all five of his children while they were infants.)

Rousseau was neither the first nor the last educational theorist to advance ideas based on virtually no hard empirical evidence. Barzun, a former Dean of Faculties and Provost at Columbia University and a critic of progressive education, notes how child-centered educational philosophies had become an article of faith in many circles by the twentieth century: "Ellen Key, the Swedish feminist, declared on the eve of the new century that it would be 'the century of the child,' and in her book of that title the first chapter heading is 'The Right of the Child to Choose His Parents.' Many parents and other persons sharing their concern set about reforming the school. As always, it was 'ossified,' 'stultifying,' and therefore cruel. The child must be freed from dull teachers and rote learning; his naturally inquisitive mind redirected from words to things. John Dewey and his friends at the University of Chicago started a school [in 1896] that would effect the emancipation from all these errors.... The pupil could choose his line of studies, would not recite memorized facts but discuss them, and would progress at his own pace. The teacher would be a mere guide."

To this day, John Dewey remains the pivotal figure in the development of child-centered education—the direct descendant of Comenius and Rousseau, the star pupil of G. Stanley Hall at

Johns Hopkins University (who had criticized the teaching of basics), the founder of the Laboratory School at the University of Chicago which inspired the establishment of the activities-oriented Lincoln School at Columbia University's Teachers College in 1917, the later colleague of William Heard Kilpatrick at Teachers College (who trained thousands of students in Dewey's ideas and out-Deweyed Dewey as the father of "the project method"), and the precursor to Freire (who condemned direct instruction as "the pedagogy of the oppressed"), and to Gardner, Kohn, and all the other contemporary progressives who now dominate K-12 education in America.

For a while, in the 1950s, it seemed Dewey's progressivism had run its course and had collapsed under the weight of its accumulated failures, including the much-ridiculed life adjustment movement that momentarily took over the nation's schools following World War II (with the school day consumed with peer learning about etiquette and other such subjects). The Sputnik episode of 1957, which ushered in a swing back to traditionalist pedagogy, coincided that year with the magazine *Progressive Education* ceasing publication. But progressivism would not die. It was resuscitated by the arrival of the 1960s and the Woodstock nation. Diane Ravitch describes *Summerhill*, a best-selling 1960 book written by A.S. Neill, the director of an ultraprogressive British school by that name which became almost as influential in some American education circles as the Beatles did in the larger culture:

> [It was] the perfect book for the age of individualism and student freedom. Neill believed above all in freedom for youth. No student in his school was ever compelled to learn anything against his will.... [Neill wrote] *"I believe that to impose anything by authority is wrong. The child should not do anything until he comes to the opinion—his own opinion—that it should be done.* The curse of humanity is the external compulsion, whether it comes from the Pope or the state or the teacher or the parent. It is fascism in toto." (italics in original)

In Neill's world, teachers, and even parents, who dared to exercise the slightest bit of discipline and impose the slightest measure of structure were equated with Hitler and Mussolini. Ravitch notes that by 1970, *Summerhill* was *required* reading in some 600 university courses in schools of education, as "Neill's paean to student freedom" was being force-fed to future teachers. The single-minded zeal with which progressives promoted child-centered education reached a crescendo with the constructivist movement in the 1980s and 1990s; in the words of one educator, constructivism had become "something akin to a secular religion," complete with a "mantra-like slogan that 'students construct their own knowledge.'"

To be fair, constructivists were right to argue that too many teachers relied solely on lecturing and on the mechanical transfer of information from lectern to rows of students, and that more active learning could dramatically enhance the schooling experience. Most progressives, however, did not stop at calling for direct instruction to be supplemented with indirect "facilitating" of learning. They went further, calling for it to be *replaced*, disparaging almost any traditional teaching as worthless, and ridiculing anyone who continued to employ such pedagogy as "a sage on the stage" engaged merely in "chalk and talk"or "yell and tell" routines. When teachers were not being compared to pretentious pedants, they were portrayed as dull, droning drill instructors. Rather than celebrating the good instructor alongside the good facilitator, only one mode of education received the seal of approval from progressives. And it is this model—the teacher-as-coach or, as it is sometimes called, the guide-on-the side model—that is now predominantly taught to future teachers in America's schools of education and subsequently reinforced in professional development workshops. As one critic put it, "a generation of absentee parents now wants a generation of absentee teachers."

Typical is the view of an instructional technology specialist on my campus (a fellow named Bob Clapp), who recently told me "we are moving from the old model of teacher 90 percent-student 10 percent to teacher 10 percent-student 90 percent." This claptrap is called "authentic learning." Robert Hutchins, the president of the University of Chicago who was Dewey's contemporary, argued that advocates of child-centered classrooms were reducing teachers to the role of mere "chaperons." Even though such advocates today use the term "coach" to describe the proper role of the teacher, teachers are not even performing the duties of coaches, who in football and other sports typically build learning sequentially and formally around lots of drawing of x's and o's on a blackboard along with drill and practice. Pointing out the silliness of constructivism, Ravitch comments "It's like going to a golf pro who says: 'However you feel like swinging is okay. You figure it out.' You wouldn't pay him."

Constructivism has made it to Clayton, Missouri and virtually every school district in America. Progressives feel threatened by the standards and testing regime that the federal and state governments have been attempting to implement, because calling for clear documentation of results ("scorekeeping") is the one thing that could derail the constructivist express. That is why many elements of the K-12 establishment, from teachers unions to schools of education, are mounting a full-scale attack against efforts aimed at increasing accountability. When confronted, they will deny this. But it is all too apparent in my own experience and, judging from reports from around the country, the experiences of other observers.

Expeditionary Learning and Other Adventures in Education

Each spring semester I team-teach a Global Ecology course with a biologist that is specifically targeted at elementary education majors. Funded by a National Science Foundation grant, the course was conceived as a highly innovative course that was interdisciplinary, examined environmental issues from both a global and local perspective, combined a traditional lecture format with many field trips, labs, and other learning-by-doing activities, and proceeded from the assumption that future teachers should have not only pedagogical expertise but also content expertise in the subject matter they are expected to teach. After a decade of teaching this course, my colleague and I have found it nearly impossible to get the students to embrace it, since their training in the school of education (with some exceptions) has generally led them to devalue *any* lecturing, *any* necessity to learn content, and *any* work ethic. They are not used to listening to subject matter experts present information to them and to having extensive reading and writing assignments, even though we try to soften these aspects of the course with plenty of "fun" stuff. Taught to be facilitators who will one day preside over the therapeutic classroom, they have trouble functioning in a teacher-led class. Typical of their cohort group was one student who admitted to me that she "did not like listening to lectures, since they go in one ear and out the other."

Here was a future teacher confessing she was an airhead, and was proud of it! We are now building entire curricula around such students. She may soon be teaching *your* child. It won't be me; even if I wanted to teach in grade school, I would not be permitted to do so. The K-12 establishment does not rate my credentials as high as this young woman's. I could not walk into an elementary school, middle school, or high school and teach without first getting "certified," that is, taking courses in some education school. It might help me get a teaching job at a school if I could also coach the men's water polo team or girl's volleyball team, since these days such skills are very much in demand, but I am afraid I again come up short. (The Clayton school district recently has adopted a policy that is a variation of the teacher-as-coach model. This coach-as-teacher policy encourages the hiring of staff to teach history or science or other subjects who can also service the athletic department; given a choice between an excellent history teacher who cannot coach sports, and a good one who can, the latter is likely to get the nod. So much for the supposed primacy of academics.)

As evidence of the devaluation of subject matter expertise on the part of K-12 teachers, even in an academically serious school district such as Clayton, let me recount the story of an experiment in "expeditionary learning" that was tried during the 1990s at Wydown Middle School. Two superb science teachers decided to turn their relatively traditional classrooms into student-centered learning environments revolving around a series of field trips to local and faraway places. The teachers were to take responsibility between the two of them for not only science education but English, social studies, and math, and they were to stay with the same group of students from sixth grade through eighth grade so as to develop a special rapport with them (a practice called "looping"). An "Expeditionary Learning Informational Packet" sounded the usual progressive themes—"keep learning groups heterogeneous," "promote the primacy of self-discovery," and so forth. Even as progressive tracts go, however, this one was over the top. In a particularly insulting reference to faculty members, the document stated that students had little to gain from "listening to a large person talk about" anything. We used to call the "large person" a teacher, but no more.

Some questions about this new instructional model never did get answered. First, why all the hype that attended expeditionary learning, when previous generations of school-age kids, including my own, had always been treated to field trips such as visits to the

local zoo? What seemed new and different was that the Wydown
field trips were not supplementary features of the classroom but
substitutes for the classroom, and they were consuming not just a
few hours of bus-riding time through Greater St. Louis but taking
children hundreds of miles to Maryland's Eastern Shore and to
other exotic locales around the country. Among the questions
never answered were whether this was a good use of student and
teacher time. And how realistic was it to expect science teachers at
the secondary level to teach about Ancient Greece, the American
Civil War, and Shakespeare's sonnets and to instruct students in
sentence structure and algebraic equations (while on the go)?
Would they have been equally willing to have history or English
colleagues teach about molecular structure? Also, rather than cod-
dling students by providing a friendly face throughout middle
school through the looping arrangement, would teenagers not be
better served by being exposed to a variety of instructors and a
variety of viewpoints, especially when they must learn to cope
with such complexity in high school and later in college?

I was never able to get anyone to address these concerns. The
experiment eventually was terminated, not because of any of the
obvious problems but because it proved to be prohibitively expensive and was judged unfair to those students on the other teams
who were denied the thrill of experiencing summer vacation during the school year. Commenting on the financial and other costs
of the program, one school board member asked the right question but also failed to get a clear answer from Lewis and Clark
(the pseudonyms adopted by these science teachers turned camp
counselors): "What's wrong with expeditions of the mind?"
Another school board member could not help observing that expeditionary learning seemed to be education for kids who did not
like school.

Another experiment still underway in Clayton is the adoption of the "Reggio" theory of teaching in preschool. Reggio is
essentially Montessori pedagogy, that is, constructivism for tykes.
(Maria Montessori opened her House of Tots in 1912, inspired by
Rousseau's notion that the infant is capable of "self-teaching.")
The reason it is not called the Montessori method is that it would
not then be considered cutting-edge and would not therefore qualify for funding grants and for all the hoopla that accompanies
every new K-12 innovation. The Clayton school district spent
thousands of dollars to send several staff members to Reggio

Emilia, Italy to come back with the remarkable finding that we should not be force-feeding learning to preschoolers and should not be browbeating toddlers (as if traditional preschooling fails to promote a warm, nurturing environment and instead encourages teachers to administer fifty lashes to any three-year-old who makes a mistake with his letters or numbers). Reggio enthusiasts, like most progressives, tend to caricature traditional education. Where Reggio does differ from traditional preschool education is that it tends to downplay structure, especially academic structure, allowing students total freedom to pursue whatever grabs them based on their "interest." If they prefer mudwrestling or puttering in the sandbox rather than looking at alphabet charts and mathematical tables, no problem. Hence, Reggio is the perfect preparation for expeditonary learning and the constructivist classroom in K-12.

In cultivating critical thinkers from the cradle to the twelfth grade, teachers are now supposed to "get out of the way," especially when it comes to the highest achievers, who are expected increasingly to teach themselves and each other—that is, when they are not busy mentoring lower achievers. A Clayton High School history teacher recently used exactly those words, thinking I would be impressed with the respect he was showing his students. Instead, I had to wonder why my taxes were going to pay for, in this case, someone who defined his job as that of a $60,000 a year day-care provider/cheerleader, someone who naively assumed that youngsters—even the brightest in the class—did not need constant supervision of their education, including regular direct instruction. Homeschooling would seem cheaper, with a superior per pupil ratio. The average salary of the Clayton teaching staff is approximately $50,000 a year; nationally, it is roughly $40,000, which includes excellent benefits and the luxury of a work year of only 180 obligated days. I happen to think the best teachers deserve higher salaries, but for teaching, not for coaching or cheerleading or getting out of the way. Progressives risk making K-12 teachers expendable, and denigrating their own profession if they continue to chatter about teacher-as-coach.

Lest one think I am exaggerating the extent to which direct instruction is now considered passé in places like Clayton, see the following passage authored recently in the *Clayton Curriculum Quarterly* by the district social studies coordinator, who, to his credit, was offering "a defense of the lecture":

Listening to a story or a speech can be a very important, effective, entertaining, and powerful way to learn. And what is the counterpart of the story or speech in the classroom? It is the lecture. Currently, lecturing is not in favor as a form of pedagogy. Most books and essays on "best practice" [in K-12 education] consider this form of teaching as antiquated and less effective than "hands-on" experiences. When I interview candidates for social studies positions, they invariably, and proudly, claim that they don't lecture, assuming that I will consider that to be a positive attribute. When I hear my colleagues talk about their teaching, if they mention that they lectured, it usually comes attached to an apology. I have no problem with the lecture. It is a great teaching tool. Indeed, there are times when there's nothing better than the lecture to get essential information across or drive a point home.... It takes a great deal of knowledge and skill to construct and deliver a great lecture.... Should we only lecture? Of course not. That would be absurd, but let's stop apologizing or feeling guilty when we do lecture.

Just as it is a sad commentary on K-12 education for Albert Shanker to have felt a need to author an article entitled "Knowledge Still Counts," it is equally sad that curriculum leaders feel a need to defend direct instruction as a mode of teaching. Not every lecturer is a great one, any more than every active learning specialist is tops at what they do. Boredom and inanity can characterize any classroom, teacher-centered or student-centered. Education, however, rarely reaches its apotheosis in the absence of a *"teachable moment"* and a *teacher* able to take advantage of that opportunity by providing the benefit of his or her insight and wisdom. If you have nothing worth saying, then you probably should not be lecturing; in fact, you probably should not be paid to be at the front of the classroom or anywhere else in the room.

I was reminded about the lasting virtues of a good lecture when I attended my older son Stephen's graduation from Yale University in 1997. In his commencement address, David McCullough (Class of '55), the respected biographer of Harry Truman and John Adams, paid tribute to his Eli teachers, whose lectures he and his peers treasured. Of one such professor, he said "the last lecture he gave on *Othello* I would remember for the rest of my life." Not once did he refer to his "coaches" or "facilitators." There were no demeaning references to "large persons," except to acknowledge the intellectual giants upon whose shoulders generations of students had stood.

A Spreading Conflict

In the St. Louis area, from the Wellston school district, which serves the most economically disadvantaged, least educationally prepared children, to the Gifted Resource Council, which was established to serve the highest achievers, the message sent by K-12 educators is one and the same. The one-size-fits-all pedagogy is teacher-as-coach, child-centered, experiential, cooperative education, echoed in headline after headline.

For example, the Fall 2000 Gifted Resource Council (GRC) newsletter, drawing on multiple intelligences theory which treats each child as gifted, advertised "Open enrollment, no testing required.... Bright children are screened into the courses by their interest, not by having to excel on standardized tests.... GRC classes are inclusive.... More important than the enriched content of these courses is the hands-on way these students learn.... GRC believes strongly that bright children learn almost as much from each other as they do from their teachers.... Learning without grades bolsters self-esteem.... Cooperation, teamwork foster social skills." I once served on the board of directors of the Gifted Resource Council, but resigned when I realized that it had succumbed to educational populism and had surrendered its mission to foster extraordinary academic accomplishment. I was not surprised at the GRC newsletter, since at that same moment Clayton's recently retired director of enrichment was quoted in the school newspaper as specifically rejecting "the sage on the stage" paradigm. It is bad enough to presume that struggling kids need constant stroking as opposed to academic challenge; such patronizing of children is especially disgraceful when it occurs in so-called gifted programs.

Around the same time that the Gifted Resource Council proclaimed its conversion to the constructivist faith, the impoverished Wellston school district did likewise. The *St. Louis Post-Dispatch* quoted a Wellston middle school science teacher as putting down traditional instruction and intoning "the idea is to learn by doing." As with the GRC educators and the Clayton enrichment specialist, he no doubt learned this in a lecture given by some professional development expert housed in a school of education somewhere. It would seem that Maplewood-Richmond Heights, a working-class suburban district not too far from Wellston, has been sending its staff lately to the same professional development workshops. The *St. Louis Post-Dispatch*, apparently unaware that Clayton and most other school districts had long ago bought into trendy hands-on learning, ran a story in June 2001 noting that "the school board has approved a new learning approach called Expeditionary Learning for middle-school students." One teacher commented "when we told kids we were going to take them to the Science Center and make roller coasters, they thought they'd died and went to heaven." This teacher's innovative interpretation of the past tense of the verb "to go" says much about what kind of expedition this one would be.

A month earlier, in May 2001, the *Post-Dispatch* again evidenced unfamiliarity with the pack pedagogy phenomenon and the copycat mindset in K-12, when it reported that the College School of Webster Groves "uses novel teaching methods, a hands-on approach to learning." The College School is a St. Louis private school, in the vanguard of the progressive movement, known for never having seen a progressive reform it did not fully embrace. Being a private school, it put even Clayton to shame in terms of the reach of its commitment to expeditonary learning. One student's experience was described as follows: "Before Matt leaves...he will have likely gone camping for entire weeks, explored half a dozen caves, released monarch butterflies to their Mexico-bound migration, and taken road trips to the Smoky Mountains, Chicago, and points beyond." "We don't just read it in a book," Matt said. "We do it."

The Johnny-one-note quality of the St. Louis K-12 scene can be seen also in a newsletter distributed by the principal of Northeast Middle School in the Parkway school district, in which he urged his staff to "reduce the sage on the stage and increase the guide by the side" and lamented that "the greatest roadblock to learning is content coverage." It was not lack of subject matter expertise of the staff, or inadequate time spent reading by students, or any other such problem; no, the problem was excessive attention to content! Likewise, in University City, a recent teacher of the year honoree, referring to herself as a "facilitator," publicly ridiculed her own traditional education as characterized by "rows of quiet, well-disciplined children patiently soaking up knowledge." She confesses, "I was drawn to the reforms [of the 1970s and since] that converted classrooms into reflections of the 'real world,' where students became active participants of their own education." This was a first-grade teacher complaining about the discipline and the transfer of knowledge that had apparently helped mold her into an award-winning professional.

Railing against what they call "seat-time," modern educationists are big on feet-time. You can take your own expeditionary learning excursion around the country and see this everywhere. As Albert Shanker described one Summerhill-type private school far from St. Louis: "Alpine Valley [in Edgewater, Colorado] has dispensed with curriculum, schedules, classes—the works. On a given day, if students 'want to climb trees, read, bake a cake or learn physics, it's all OK and completely up to them.' And this goes for long-term learning, too. If a kid doesn't feel like finding out how to read until he is 12, that's no problem.... 'The school is based on freedom for the students,' is how one of the founders puts it. It is also based on the idea that adults have no knowledge or experience that makes their ideas about what to learn and when to learn it any more valuable than their students."

In an article entitled "Lost in Action: Are Time-Consuming, Trivializing Activities Displacing the Cultivation of Active *Minds*?," the director of the American Textbook Council notes that project learning, long a staple of American education, has gone way beyond its initial intent and is now out of control across the country. The article states, "No one contests some legitimate place for projects and activities in classrooms. But lost in the whirlwind, this doing and doing, is a sense of where the real action should be—in the minds of students. Activities enthusiasts are right not to want passive students. But they have made a dangerous error. They have substituted ersatz activity and shallow content for hard and serious work of the mind.... In many schools, activities more than supplement the text and lesson. Activities are the lesson." The article goes on to say:

> Activities expand exponentially because teachers think that's what they are supposed to be doing. Administrators, curriculum specialists, education gurus, workshop presenters...have told teachers that activities are the only way to engage students.... "Drill and kill" [and other such epithets] are the derisive names given to traditional approaches. Teachers, understandably, shudder at the thought of being associated with such dreary pedagogy. Should they resist [the new conventional] wisdom, they may face scorn and intimidation.... Pressed to be events coordinators and social directors, teachers have been robbed of traditional pedagogy's vision of quality: the carefully prepared lesson, rich with analogy, illustration,

and anecdote; focused and guided; demanding and lively; peppered with good humor; with frequent interchange between the student and teacher, student and student; interspersed with small-group work when appropriate; and with a clear sense of direction at the beginning and summary at the end.... At the core, always, is serious content approached seriously.... This is real action learning. This is the mind at work.

The author leaves no doubt as to what is driving this obsession with activities:

This content needs no dressing up or excuses. It stands on its own. In the upper grades, social promotion and detracked classrooms contribute to hands-on practices. Teachers are rightly eager that all students succeed.... Faced with the daunting task of teaching to a wide range of achievement, teachers feel they have no choice but to offer an array of activities accessible to even the most unprepared students.... Activity-based learning is vain. It presupposes that it alone is responsive to the "inner gifts" of children, especially children who are challenged or overmatched by traditional academic learning. A salting of high theory stands behind it, theory that is reinforced in faculty lounges and workshops and that has special appeal to those who face a rising number of children who seem alienated from words and numbers.

John Hoven, co-president of the Gifted and Talented Association of the Montgomery, Maryland school district—a parent who has perceptively observed how even supposed advocates of gifted education like GRC have been retreating from academic excellence—writes: "It is an enigma that so many professional educators are drawn toward an ideology that urges teachers not to teach.... They are attracted to it as a way to avoid making intellectual demands on the least able students."

The anti-intellectualism of the hands-on movement comes through in the comments of a St. Louis-area middle school principal from Pacific, Missouri who is on record as saying that "a student who is doing and experiencing rather than reading...is going to learn more science. It's much easier to remember what you've done than what you've read." The operative word here is "easier." Because many kids are now assumed to be incapable of reading for comprehension, as well as taking notes from a teacher, it is now considered a neanderthal notion to ask them to absorb and retain information, derived either from a book or a bookish mind. It is alright for today's student to sit on his posterior for an hour or more and watch a movie—cutting-edge types call this "reading" a work of "visual art"—but somehow it becomes "seat-time" when such stationary learning occurs through traditional pedagogy.

One motive for the anti-lecture campaign in K-12 education has sexist and racist overtones; this is the assumption, expressed at a recent workshop sponsored by the St. Louis Cooperating School Districts, that "when you ask a black male to sit down and listen to a lecture, you are setting him up for failure." We are setting many kids up for failure today—black, white, male, female, and others—not when we inflict lectures on them but when we engage in racial and sexual profiling that attributes attention deficit disorder syndrome to an entire categorical group.

One of the main inspirations for the nationalization of dumbing-down is an educator with Boston Brahmin roots who should know better. Ted Sizer is a former Dean of Harvard University's Graduate School of Education and former headmaster of Phillips Academy in Andover, Mass., who in 1984 founded the Coalition of Essential Schools. The Coalition has grown to include more than 800 public and private schools, all committed to the self-directed, Dewey-like learning principles Sizer articulated in his *Horace's Compromise—the Dilemma of the American High School*, which are now widely mimicked well beyond the Coalition—less is more (i.e., study a few topics in-depth rather than maximizing content), work in teams while avoiding grades and competition, substitute portfolios for standardized tests as assessment vehicles, stress critical thinking more than accumulation of knowledge, and, of course, don't teach but coach.

Although Sizer supporters can claim some successes—for example Deborah Meier, whose Central Park East Schools raised academic achievement levels in the East Harlem section of New York City—overall performance has not matched the rhetoric. As a *Wall Street Journal* article noted, there is substantial "research challenging the effectiveness of coalition schools. Five recent...studies, including a five-year research project sponsored by the coalition itself, suggest that Dr. Sizer's ideas may be a lot more workable in theory than in practice." Even the Coalition's former research director, Grant Wiggins, has expressed skepticism regarding the superiority of the coalition's pedagogical approach, commenting that "it has always been my sense that it's not better, it's not worse, it's just different." He adds about Sizer's principles, "they're just jumping off points, and to argue that they've been proven to be of value,...that's crap." Crap or not, it is testimony to the seductiveness of Sizer's vision that so many donors have been willing to fund it, including AT&T, Exxon, Citicorp, and the Walter Annenberg Foundation (the latter established by the former publisher of *TV Guide*, who made a $500 million grant in the 1990s to promote K-12 educational reform, with almost nothing to show for it).

The "Socratic Method Minus Socrates" Model

In constantly disparaging traditional instruction as the "sage on the stage" model, Ted Sizer and fellow progressives invite derision themselves, for supporting what could be called the "Socratic method minus Socrates" model. The Socratic method has been used for centuries as an educational technique in higher education. It consists of the teacher engaging students in the acquisition of knowledge and insight through a process of inquiry. The emphasis is on the teacher, who carefully frames questions and then elicits responses from students, all of this aimed at getting students to arrive at shared understandings. Although the Socratic method assumes no universal or eternal truths to be disseminated, it assumes that there is such a thing as wisdom and that it is more likely to emanate from the teacher than the student.

Socrates' pupil was Plato, Plato's pupil was Aristotle, and Aristotle's pupil was Alexander the Great. There is no historical evidence of these great teachers doing "facilitating" and their star pupils doing "projects." There was a lot of listening and a lot of learning going on, with the students usually studying at the feet of these scholars. (Alexander seemed to benefit from his education, creating before his death, at age thirty-three, an empire that stretched across the known world, at least that which was known to him. Not bad for a dependent, passive learner.) It is true it was not just seat-time. Aristotle, for example, had a reputation for lecturing at his school (the Lyceum) while standing in its covered portico or walking place (*peripatos*), which explains why the school came to be named Peripatetic. In the 1960s, progressive educators who promoted the "open education movement" took the concept of *peripatos* to an extreme, knocking down classroom partitions, encouraging students to float freely from one activity center to another, and cultivating "a certain noise level...as a sign of active learning." Clayton and other school districts are still living with the legacy of the open classroom era, their older buildings in many cases still lacking classroom sound barriers and an environment that encourages listening. These architectural wonders remain a monument to the foolishness of educators, although they do have a certain functionality, as they are well-suited for today's use of the Socratic method minus Socrates.

Also supportive of the Socratic method minus Socrates paradigm are two recent innovations that have taken the K-12 world by storm—block scheduling and computer-aided instruction. These both are aimed at forcing teachers to abandon their "tired classroom routines," in other words their role as teachers. When people outside the K-12 fraternity, such as myself, criticize teachers, we are blasted for appearing disrespectful toward such dedicated professionals. But when assistant superintendents for curriculum do it, telling teachers that they are blockheads, are sadly behind the times and must change for their own good and the good of their students, this is called "professional development."

Block Scheduling

Inspired by Ted Sizer's *Horace's Compromise*, an ever increasing number of schools have been adopting block scheduling as an alternative to the typical fifty-five-minute period, six-periods-a-day regimen found in most U.S. high schools and middle schools. Two types of block schedules are most popular. One, called an eight-block, consists of classes meeting for some ninety minutes every other day instead of the traditional fifty-to-sixty minute period five days a week. A second, called four-by-four, compresses a year-long course into a single semester, with students taking only four classes each semester. There are other variations, in some cases so complex (with week-to-week rotations between "A" days, "B" days, and other mutations) that I have found teachers hard pressed to explain the schedule to me when I have tried to reserve a time I could meet their classes during the semester in my role as the UM-St. Louis liaison for advanced-credit high school courses.

What purpose is served by block scheduling? Reformers tout a number of advantages. They argue that the fifty-five-minute class routine continues to exist only due to habit and inertia, that it is very inhibiting in encouraging teachers to lecture rather than to experiment with newer active learning pedagogies. Since the bell marking the end of a class does not ring as often, the extended class time permits greater class discussion as well as greater opportunity for students to work on independent and cooperative learning projects. Indeed, since no teacher realistically can expect to talk for ninety minutes, teachers are forced to abandon direct instruction as the dominant mode of education and to become more creative in time-management. The fewer bells also means less time is wasted with students traversing the hallways going from one class to another, and fewer attendance problems. In addition, science courses particularly benefit from the extra time that can be devoted to labs. All courses stand to benefit from learning occurring in more sustained, intense blocks rather than it being crammed into short, disruptive time frames.

What is rarely admitted is that block scheduling also is aimed at those students who have trouble with the lecture format, as well as those students who—because they are lazy, because they come from homes where there is little parental support, or for whatever reason—need time during the school day to do their homework. In many schools, block schedules have become simply "study hall" surrogates, where students spend many hours during the school day doing what they should be doing after school. Giving homework the fancy name of "project" is somehow supposed to legitimize using school time for its completion, but it seems hard to justify paying teachers to be *in loco parentis* homework overseers. Many teachers, finding they have to fill up ninety minutes, have taken to showing more and more videos. (At one high school I visited, which was just moving to a block schedule, the teacher's first question to me was whether I knew any good films she could use.) Even where block time is used constructively, there is a downside few reformers are willing to acknowledge. As one critic notes:

> It reduces the overall amount of time spent in individual academic classes (sometimes by as much as 10 to 15 percent; e.g., two fifty-five minute classes become one ninety-minute class).... Block scheduling is particularly disadvantageous for subjects that require frequent drill and repetition, such as math, music, or foreign language. It also shortchanges the very students for whom it is supposedly being implemented: the at-risk and unmotivated students who typically have shorter attention spans and are rarely well-organized.

One could add that it also disadvantages Advanced Placement (AP) courses and other courses where a premium is placed on learning a great deal of content, since there is less time and a less conducive environment for presenting information.

In response to an op-ed commentary I had written in 1994 in the *St. Louis Post-Dispatch*, a mother of twins at McCluer High School in the St. Louis area once wrote me about her own experiences with block scheduling: "Recently I helped form a committee of parents demanding input into the proposed restructuring of the high school along the lines of the Coalition of Essential Schools. The administration attempted, without significant parent input, to begin a 'block schedule' program. The result would have been the end of honors programs, as well as the end of continuity in areas like foreign language and mathematics. It would also have shaved 30 instructional hours from every core subject. The goal? To increase opportunities for 'hands-on' learning and the incorporation of more 'creative teaching strategies' to reach the underachiever. The good news is that when I got on my soapbox, I found countless other folks willing to fight for the kids who try. We won the first part of our fight, but won't stop until the concept of excellence is again part of the curriculum. No group of students, including those with the most deficient preparation, is ever served well by lowering standards and demanding less." Brave words but this woman ultimately lost the fight, as parents usually do, McCluer having since implemented block scheduling over their objections.

Thus far Clayton High School has managed to resist this fad, but neighboring Ladue High School has not. One Ladue English teacher, noting that Ladue had long dabbled with flexible scheduling, openly confessed "it brings equity. A lot of these kids don't have parents who might be able to help them with their homework. Now they always have the opportunity to have an adult who can help." (Of course, often it is children, the more able members of the class, who are exploited during block time to help their less able peers, begging the question why they are not entitled to a share of the teacher's paycheck.) The *Wall Street Journal* reports: "Some teachers are ending their lectures halfway through the class period to force students to complete at their desks assignments they used to do at home. A high school English teacher in a suburban Ohio school district days that if she doesn't leave time for students to read classic works of literature during class, they won't do it at all."

A Clayton school board member said that he is in favor of bigger teacher salaries because "teachers spend eight hours a day with our children." Were Clayton to adopt block scheduling, these monies would be going toward enhanced day-care services. My guess is that Clayton High School will eventually adopt this reform, given the pressures of pack pedagogy; Wydown Middle School has already implemented a modified block schedule. In addition to the Ladue school system going this route, the Parkway school district, another peer district, has also followed suit, the last remaining holdout among its four high schools finally forced to conform about a year ago. One of the Parkway high school principals rationalized that "having longer classes on alternating days decreases daily stress by giving the student more time." Most teachers, after initial resistance, come to like this innovation because it reduces their stress as well, particularly the stress of having to prepare for class. Not surprisingly, *Education Week* reported in 1996 that, nationwide, "interest in alternative forms of scheduling has been growing steadily. For example, less than a decade ago, only three schools in Virginia used some form of block scheduling. Now nearly 45 percent of the state's high schools use it." One can assume that well over half of Virginia's high schools now are on block schedules, and that similar trends are found throughout the country.

All this is happening without any clear evidence that block scheduling improves student achievement. *Education Week* asks: "But does block scheduling help students learn more? And do longer classes really propel teachers to shift from lecturing to a more active teaching style...? So far, there is a small body of research that can help answer these questions. [Although there is some data to support the claims of block scheduling advocates], some schools have found that failure rates increased, perhaps because when students miss a class, they miss more material and find it more difficult to catch up. And several studies of block scheduling in Canada, where the approach has been popular for a decade, found that it had a negative effect on achievement.... In North Carolina,...the state education department found that student scores on statewide tests had neither increased nor decreased on average in the schools using a block schedule." In my own backyard, non-blocked Clayton High School has done no worse than, and often has outperformed, blocked Parkway and Ladue schools on state tests. The jury is still out on block scheduling, but that has not stopped the K-12 establishment from issuing a verdict in support of it.

I am sometimes asked how I can be so skeptical of block scheduling when universities, at least in upper level courses, often have ninety-minute classes, two-hour seminars, and many independent study opportunities, while being careful not to crowd the student's day with wall-to-wall classes but instead allowing ample time for library research and "down time." The answer is that college students are at a different level of intellectual growth than K-12 students, or so we hope.

Computer-Aided Instruction

I am not a Luddite. I have been very open to technological and other innovations over several decades of teaching, including enhancing my courses lately with e-mail listserves whereby faculty-student exchanges can occur any time of day. Indeed, I headed an NSF project in the 1970s that pioneered "learning by doing" in the international studies field. Still, I worry about the misuses of technology.

Just as the television has become a babysitter at home, the computer has become a babysitter at school. Block time is being filled up not only with viewing videos but also with increased use of the latest "interactive" electronic toys that in some cases are only a slight improvement on Mortal Kombat. I mentioned earlier "the two double-edged swords of technology and culture" as having potentially negative impacts on K-12 education. On the one hand, a wondrous instrument, the computer has been welcomed by many educators as a liberating and equalizing technology. It is reasonable to be concerned about "the digital divide" between the haves and have-nots and to want to rectify this problem. On the other hand, like nuclear energy, the computer is double-edged in that it offers a Faustian bargain—the promise of unlimited intellectual power in every school building in America from the richest suburb to the poorest urban ghetto, but only if it can be harnessed in a way that does not cause damaging fallout and further "meltdown."

E.D. Hirsch frames the problem well. Referring mainly to the Internet, he states: "Undoubtedly, computers will be able to enhance pedagogical principles that are already known to work. One fears, however, that the enthusiasm for computers is based upon a confidence in technical solutions that has not been well explained in theory or well documented in experience. Most of all, one fears that enthusiasm for computers will simply reinforce and prolong the now discredited tool conception of education, which claims falsely that education consists ideally in learning the tools that will enable one to learn things in the future." In other words, computers only reinforce the progressive focus on teacher-as-coach, process as opposed to content, teach the child rather than the subject, and so on, even though "there is no evidence that a well-stocked and well-equipped mind can be displaced by 'accessing skills.'"

There is the old parable that one is better off giving a starving person a fishing rod and teaching him how to fish than simply giving him a fish, since the former gift will last one a lifetime while the latter gift will suffice for only one day. K-12 reformers have twisted the lesson to mean that we should teach students how to learn rather than what to learn, that is, we should not feed them daily information but should give them the skill for carrying on lifelong learning themselves. Students starved of facts and knowledge, however, will hardly have the capacity to make intelligent use of the Internet or other computer aids. It is all too apparent from my own experience and the experience of my colleagues that students use Yahoo and other search engines to go on fishing expeditions that are often a waste of time and result in only the shallowest learning.

Letting pedestrian minds loose on the information superhighway can be dangerous. As David Gelernter, the Yale computer scientist, puts it, "learn first, surf later." He rightly complains that "our children already prefer pictures to words, glitz to substance, fancy packaging to serious content. But the Web propagandizes relentlessly for glitz and pictures.... And while it's full of first-rate information, it's also full of lies [and] garbage.... There is no quality control on the Internet." As another professor comments, "search engines are closer to slot machines than to library catalogues. You throw your query to the wind, and who knows what will come back to you? You may get 234,468 supposed references to whatever you want to know. Perhaps one in a thousand might actually help you." It requires a teacher with subject matter expertise and scholarly familiarity with the most authoritative sources to help students navigate.

The same professor relates his frustration with the Internet-based "research" papers his students are now producing; comparing papers he received in the late nineties with those in previous semesters, he notes:

> I noticed a disturbing decline in both the quality of the writing and the originality of the thoughts expressed.... My class had fallen victim to the latest easy way of writing a paper: doing their research on the World-Wide Web. It's easy to spot a research paper that is based primarily on information collected from the Web. First, the bibliography cites no books, just articles or pointers to places in that virtual land somewhere off any map.... Then a strange preponderance of material...is curiously out of date. A lot of stuff on the Web that is advertised as timely is actually at least a few years old.... Another clue is the beautiful pictures and graphs that are inserted neatly into the body of the student's text. They look impressive as though they are the result of careful work and analysis, but actually they often bear little relation to the precise subject of the paper. Cut and pasted from the vast realm of what's out there for the taking, they masquerade as original work.... We all know that word processing makes many first drafts look far more polished than they are. If the paper doesn't reach the assigned five pages, readjust the margins, change the font size, and *voilà*! Of course these machinations take up time that the student could have spent revising the paper. With programs to check out one's spelling and grammar, one wonders why students make any mistakes at all. But errors are as prevalent as ever.... Instead of becoming perfectionists, too many students have become slackers, preferring to let the machine do their work for them.... Surf. Download. Cut and paste.

Cheating and cutting corners did not begin with the creation of the Internet, but the Internet has made academic delinquency far simpler and more efficient. Witness the creation of websites such as schoolsucks.com and studentu.com, which brazenly offer free term papers as well as free lecture notes taken by hired student note-takers to be made available to class-cutters at sixty-two universities. The *Cliff Notes* culture has been taken to a new, high-tech level, captured in a *New York Times* editorial entitled "Slacker.com." (For the less tech-savvy, one can purchase complete research papers through outfits like A-1 Termpapers, which, for example, offers a report on McCarthyism at $53.70 plus handling.) Term papers, when not completely plagiarized, are becoming elaborate exercises in hunting-and-pecking and xeroxing, requiring students to demonstrate mainly a deft touch at keyboarding. I suppose this is bodily kinesthetic intelligence at work. In a recent issue of *NEA Magazine,* the official publication of the National Education Association, a teacher is quoted as saying that "students become independent learners with resources like the spellchecker at their fingertips. They don't need to run to teachers as much." Sure, and they also don't need to know how to spell.

As Gelernter noted, students are becoming slick packagers of information, even as they become less and less informed. A *New York Times* headline reads: "Pupils Who Can't Even Spell 'Power-Point' Can Use It As Slickly As Any CEO." PowerPoint is a great skill to have in making oral presentations, especially in the corporate world. The question is whether producing computerized slide shows, involving tough decisions about what colors to use with what size bullets, is becoming a substitute in the K-12 world for substance, or is at least competing with the latter for time and attention in an ever-crowded school day. Another question is whether the huge financial outlays for computers and electronic media equipment now incurred by schools are competing with and crowding out other expenditures, such as the purchase of library books. Clayton can perhaps afford it all, but other districts must make hard choices.

In making these choices, it would be helpful if there was solid empirical evidence to draw on regarding the benefits of computer-aided instruction. As with block scheduling, however, the jury remains out. Stanford University's Larry Cuban, one of the more sober voices found in schools of education, has questioned the value of the Internet in K-12. He says, "It's what I call the romance with the machine, and it's happened before. It's driven by this dream of a magical solution that does not exist." Ethan Bronner, a *New York Times* education reporter, notes that "most of it is akin to glorified video games offered in the vague but firm belief that access to endless information, regardless of quality, must be good. Skeptics ask if schools are overwired and children undertaught." In an article entitled "The Computer Delusion," Todd Oppenheimer argues that "there is no good evidence that most users of computers significantly improve teaching and learning."

Nonetheless, the country moves to fulfill Bill Clinton's dream that every school and, indeed, every classroom be wired over the next decade. Even the chair of President Clinton's own Committee of Advisors on Science and Technology, David Shaw, admitted "the reality is we haven't the faintest idea what really works in a classroom." What studies have been done are of little value. Clinton's presidential task force that produced a report entitled "Connecting K-12 Schools to the Information Superhighway" cited a few studies which linked computers to enhanced student achievement. But, as one observer noted, "unfortunately, many of these studies are more anecdotal than conclusive. Some, including a giant, oft-cited meta-analysis of 254 studies, lack the necessary scientific controls to make solid conclusions possible. The circumstances are artificial and not easily repeated, results are not statistically reliable, or, most frequently, the studies did not control for other influences. Some studies were industry-funded, and thus tended to publicize mostly positive findings." Edward Miller, a former editor of the *Harvard Education Letter*, lambasts the lack of replicable, statistically significant findings, the lack of controlled experiments, and the incestuous relations between investigators and funding agencies: "The research is set up in a way to find benefits that aren't really there. Most knowledgeable people agree that most of the research isn't valid. It's so flawed it shouldn't even be called research. Essentially, it's worthless."

Of course, the same criticism can be made of almost all educational research. Meta-analyses, which are a widely practiced form of scholarship among educationists, simply survey and synthesize a body of literature on some topic, without examining in any detail whether any of the studies surveyed actually pass scientific muster and are worthy of attention. A newly popular mode of scholarship in K-12 education is called "action research," which produces purely anecdotal results, based on impressions teachers and other classroom observers glean from their experiences with computers or any other new pedagogy; the tendency to see what you want to see and to draw conclusions to support your predispositions is not checked by any external, objective validation procedures.

As one commentator states, "The complaint of the fair-minded critics is not that there is nothing good in progressivism but that the progressive educators decline to look at the results of their methods. Instead they elevate those methods into an object of near-religious veneration." I have suggested that The Great American Education War almost borders on jihad. Nowhere are truer believers to be found than in schools of education, which are now training cadres of teachers all over America to go out and construct constructivist classrooms.

Schools of Education and the Professional Development Industry

Ed Schools: Schools for Scandal

William Bagley, a traditionalist who taught at Columbia's Teachers College in the 1930s, once uttered the following remarks that ring just as true today as then: "If I were seriously ill and in desperate need of a physician, and if by some miracle I could secure either Hippocrates, the Father of Medicine, or a young doctor fresh from the Johns Hopkins School of Medicine, with his equipment comprising the latest developments in the technologies and techniques of medicine, I should, of course, take the young doctor. On the other hand, if I were commissioned to find a teacher for a group of adolescent boys and if, by some miracle, I could secure either Socrates or the latest Ph.D. from Teachers College, with his equipment of the latest technologies and techniques of teaching,...I am fairly certain that I would jump at the chance to get Socrates."

Actually, I have many good friends, colleagues whom I respect, in the UM-St. Louis School of Education and in schools of education at other St. Louis-area universities. There are education professors elsewhere, such as the aforementioned Larry Cuban and Sam Wineburg at Stanford, who also command respect. Still, there is built-in institutional vapidity in ed schools generally, having to do with the fact that by their very nature—due to their focus on process rather than content—they leave one wondering "where's the beef?" Only when they have sought to build strong links with the substantive disciplines in arts and sciences have ed schools managed to avoid the problem of the empty delivery truck that runs beautifully with the most advanced engine but lacks any cargo. Ed schools see their mission as refining the delivery of knowledge, particularly to school-age children, but under the influence of constructivist theory they have distanced themselves increasingly from the knowledge itself.

Ed school deans and faculty talk of "deep principles" of learning, but talk less of deep grounding in the stuff to be learned. Albert Shanker stated the obvious when he said that the greatest teachers "share an important quality—a passionate devotion to the subject they teach." He lamented "it is too bad, then, that there is a prejudice against content among many members of our educational establishment." Confirming the obvious, a number of studies have found that "the scores of students on standardized tests improve in direct relation to the amount of training teachers have in the subjects they teach." In examining the TIMSS data, for example, it is clear that "U.S. eighth-grade students are less likely than their international peers [in Japan and other countries] to be taught math by teachers who majored in the subject (41 percent versus 71 percent)" and more likely to be taught by teachers who majored in education. The same can be said for teaching science and other fields as well.

If one were to examine the coursework taken by America's future teachers (the classes taken by education majors in our colleges) and current teachers (in-service workshops and graduate-credit classes), one should not be shocked to find that, more and more, teachers are getting trained in pedagogy rather than in the subject matter they are expected to teach. Instead of upgrading their knowledge of history, by taking undergraduate or graduate work in, say, nineteenth-century European affairs, they are likely to receive training in how to teach history, usually offered not by a historian but by a social studies educator. In order to receive certification to teach in a public school in most states, undergraduates have to take a large number of education courses that often allow relatively little room for concentrating in any discipline, even in the case of students majoring in secondary education. Then, once they have a job, in order to make their way up the career ladder, teachers are encouraged to attend professional development workshops or accumulate graduate credits, more often than not emphasizing generic instructional techniques (e.g., how to teach to multiple intelligences) which may be only tangentially applicable to their field.

Although many teachers crave the additional intellectual stimulation that might be provided by taking courses in their subject area, there are perverse incentives to avoid such training. If those who define the K-12 education field and are the gatekeepers to career advancement constantly tell teachers they need to retool to learn about hands-on, active, cooperative, experiential, media-based learning, and you are a busy teacher having to decide how to spend your scarce professional development time, what workshop or short-course would you attend—one on understanding terrorism, taught by a Middle East expert, or one on understanding how to teach about terrorism, taught by a Middle School expert? Ideally, such a training session might combine both the subject matter specialist and the pedagogical specialist, but this rarely ever happens.

The American Council of Education issued a scathing report on teacher preparation in 1999, observing "that many students in America...are taught by unqualified teachers is a reprehensible form of malpractice." Diane Ravitch, citing the large number of teachers in K-12 who are now teaching out-of-field (with neither a college major nor minor in their main teaching field), rightly asks, "why is teacher certification based on completion of education courses, rather than on mastery of what is to be taught?" According to the U.S. Department of Education, approximately 40 percent of K-12 science teachers are out-of-field instructors, while in math the figure is 34 percent, in English 25 percent, and in history 55 percent. All told, one-third of the nation's public school teachers of academic subjects at the middle school or high school level are out-of-field.

K-12 apologists might argue that "seat-time" in university science or history courses does not necessarily translate into knowledgeable teachers of history or any other subject (although, curiously, seat-time in piling up education credits is valued highly in potential hires). Alright, then, let's assume on-the-job-training; let's go beyond inputs and focus on outputs in terms of what teachers know, not how they got their knowledge. The problem here is that the K-12 establishment in many parts of the country is unwilling to permit serious testing of teachers to assess their subject matter competency, partly because of the stake it has in the existing credentialing system and partly for fear of what they would find. Lee Shulman, head of the Carnegie Endowment for the Advancement of Teaching, has criticized his profession for abandoning the "deep-knowledge, content-based" examinations that teachers were expected to take over a century ago. He has stated that "the assumptions underlying those tests [in 1875] are clear: the person who presumes to teach subject matter to children must demonstrate knowledge of the subject matter as a prerequisite to teaching. Although knowledge of the theories and methods of teaching [was] important, it [played] a decidedly secondary role in the qualifications of a teacher." About today's competency exams, he asks "where did the subject matter go? What happened to the content?" The U.S. Department of Education asked the same question in its 2002 "Annual Report on Teacher Quality" presented to Congress, calling for ed schools to "alter curriculums to emphasize content over pedagogical theory."

Even in the best school districts, not only elementary school but also secondary school teachers are hired through a process that rarely tests the candidate's subject knowledge but instead relies heavily on a battery of psychological tests which tap the extent to which the individual is a team player. Clayton, for example, uses a commonly employed screening test called the perceiver. One could graduate with a math degree from MIT and have considerable K-12 teaching experience, but if you can't perform well on the perceiver test you are unlikely to be hired. There is nothing wrong with wanting to insure that future teachers can relate to kids, but why isn't at least equal weight given to subject matter competency? While most teachers in Clayton do have strong substantive expertise, my hunch is that we have lost many fine candidates over the years who fell victim to the perceiver test and that we have added many faculty whose main asset was their capacity to project warmth.

As Martin Gross notes, in 1998, the Massachusetts state department of education, concerned about teacher training and qualifications, instituted "a new examination for the licensing of would-be teachers, almost all of whom had received a bachelor of education degree shortly before. The test was not designed to challenge the teacher candidates at particularly high levels. But it did expect that they could at least write a lucid sentence.... Of the 1,800 test-takers, 59 percent—3 out of every 5—flunked." John Silber, the chancellor of Boston University and chairman of the Massachusetts Board of Education, who helped design the test, expressed outrage that "thirty percent failed a basic test in reading and writing, and the failure rate on subject-matter tests varied from 63 percent in mathematics to 18 percent in physical education." Does anybody believe that, were the test-takers from Missouri, Mississippi, or most other states, they would have done any better than those in Massachusetts? He put the blame squarely on schools of education: "Nowhere are standards lower than in schools of education.... Most have standards so low that they repel the highly qualified students who are desperately needed in our schools."

That ed schools attract lesser quality students is beyond doubt. Michael Kirst, an education professor at Stanford, acknowledges that "regrettably, when compared to applicants for professional training in business, medicine, and law, education students have low grades and dismal SAT and GRE scores." In one study reported by Kirst, teachers-in-training ranked fourteenth out of sixteen occupational groupings on SAT verbal scores and fifteenth out of sixteen on quantitative scores.

As Silber says, one reason ed schools tend to attract lower achieving students is the "mindless" coursework education majors must typically be prepared to endure. My wife, whose field is special education, has reported to me on what goes on in many of the graduate-level education courses she has had to take to maintain her certification and obtain salary increases. Her reports echo a letter to the editor in the *New York Times*, written by a teacher who had taken graduate work at Columbia University Teachers College, who observed that "in one of my courses we spent the first 10 minutes of three of our classes throwing a ball around the room in order to learn each other's names." I once received a letter from a stranger who could not attend the talk I gave to the parents of gifted children in the Rockwood school district but who wanted to share some thoughts. The letter read as follows: "I recently began a Masters program in education and I am very dismayed by the lack of standards urged on teachers. One of my professors does not grade us because she says that she cannot judge our experience." (The nonjudgmental ed school classroom did not prevent a Central Michigan University professor from sending me a few years ago the blistering reactions his students had to my "Decline of Literacy" *Education Week* commentary; reflecting the level of sophisticated criticism that the course apparently encouraged, one of his students wrote that "if I ever see you on the street, I'm going to kick your a—.")

If these were isolated stories, they could be forgiven. But they recur regularly. Although some ed schools have more rigorous programs than others, many are notorious for being diploma mills. If the sort of nonsense noted above occurs in graduate-level education courses, one only can imagine what transpires in undergraduate courses. Actually, one does not have to imagine. Read *Ed School Follies* by Rita Kramer, whom I quoted earlier. She documents her first-hand experiences observing several ed school classes and how students are trained to lead the therapeutic classroom. One can see how school of education graduates have an advantage over other candidates when it comes to taking the perceiver test in Clayton and elsewhere.

School of education graduates also have an advantage over other students when it comes to competing for Latin honors at commencement ceremonies. Although grade inflation may be rampant throughout the university today, nowhere is it greater than in ed schools. At my own university it has reached the point that the former dean of our Business School has made a crusade out of collecting data and exposing the laxity of standards. He found that the average grade point assigned to Business students by Business faculty during the 1990s was 2.68, while Business students received an average grade point from Education faculty of 3.70; on the other hand, the average assigned to Education students by Business faculty was 2.3, while the average assigned to Education students by Education faculty was 3.6. Not surprisingly, education majors annually are the most "honored" UM-St. Louis students at commencement time. For example, at the May 1999 UM-St. Louis graduation, out of 210 B.S. in Education degrees awarded, 128—61 percent—had at least the *cum laude* designation, in contrast to 23 percent for all arts and sciences degrees granted. Similarly, Maryville University, whose ed school is often cited as an exemplar of St. Louis-area schools, gave Latin honors to almost half of its education graduates at the May 1999 commencement, compared to roughly 25 percent of the arts and sciences graduates.

I have commented on the mediocrity of the research produced by most ed schools. As Alan Kreuger, Bendheim Professor of Economics at Princeton, has written, "reform after reform [in K-12] is being introduced with little supporting research." Although reformers always refer to "research-based" practices, these "suffer from a lack of scientifically sound studies." In *The Graves of Academe*, Richard Mitchell pokes fun at most academic departments. Pointing to the "soft," often lightweight research produced by humanities professors, he says that when the latter arrive at a college of arts and sciences meeting and enter the same room as the faculty in chemistry and the hard sciences, it is the equivalent of a touch football team visiting the locker room of the Pittsburgh Steelers. He reserves even greater skewering for faculty in schools of education. For these and other reasons, a number of elite universities have refused to create schools of education, while others, including Yale and the University of Chicago, have closed theirs.

The Professional Development Center Movement

What has opened increasingly are "professional development centers" (in the jargon of the trade, PDCs), usually housed in a middle or high school or in a district administration building and usually "partnered" with a school of education, supported by state education departments and various grantmaking agencies. PDCs are a chic way of establishing a district's credentials as being forward-thinking. If your district does not have a PDC, it is considered woefully behind the times, even though all it is is a fancy name given to what we used to call the unit within the office of the assistant superintendent for curriculum that was responsible for planning all those in-service training days and other activities that distracted teachers from teaching kids. (One of my UM-St. Louis colleagues whose kids attend a Ladue elementary school has told me he can't keep up with all the in-service days that now take teachers out of the classroom and require him to scramble to find alternative childcare.) It is your school district's PDC or comparable body that arranges for its teachers to take courses such as "Advanced Cooperative Learning" and other courses purporting to discuss "deep principles" of learning, and to attend workshops where all the participants wear orange vests in order to put them into a "constructivist" mood. I have a friend who is in the professional development business, so I hear about such things all the time. About the orange vests that were displayed at a recent conference, my friend told me "Marty, it looks like you have lost the battle." My retort was that at least I had not lost my marbles.

For those PD consultants who aim to provide content and not just pedagogical training, it is a tough sell. As one put it, "we try to offer these people [teachers] something substantial, not based on a lot of hypothetical mumbo-jumbo about brain-based, multiple intelligence, cooperative structure of the month stuff, and they don't know what to do with real content. I'm convinced that few of our clientele are truly interested in reform—they prefer to bask in the illusion of pseudo-reform." Why should teachers grapple with content when they can move up the career ladder and polish their credentials through programs such as Illinois' year-old teacher recertification program, where "teachers can claim professional development credits for gambling at the racetrack, enrolling in Tai Chi classes and learning to give massages"? As described by a reporter, "on a sweltering Saturday last month, 45 teachers from across the Chicago region gathered at Arlington Park to eat lunch, place bets and cheer for their favorite horses. The afternoon of gambling was part of a two-day, 15 credit hour class called 'Probabilities in Gaming,' where teachers discussed statistics, played bingo and talked about winning the lottery. Mostly, though, they talked about horse racing."

The "Day at the Races" expeditionary learning venture was questionable for reasons too obvious to need elaboration. Still, compared to other professional development activities one sees, it was arguably at least potentially useful. PDC newsletters around St. Louis can be found containing such inanities as "being and doing are regarded as important as knowing" and "educators in professional learning communities embrace the notion that the fundamental purpose of school is learning, not teaching—an enormous distinction." Apparently, judging from the topics that Missouri school administrators put on their list of "staff development needs," high-powered academics is not among the things to be learned. In a recent statewide needs survey, they listed the use of technology, strategies for students at-risk, inclusion, conflict resolution, block scheduling, active and cooperative learning, and assorted other fads. Nowhere on the radar screen was gifted education.

This is what E.D. Hirsch has called the "Thoughtworld," the "deep-seated intellectual uniformity that is aided and abetted by education schools" and their affiliated agencies, what I have referred to as pack pedagogy. Most teachers end up learning the exact same buzzwords and uttering them in uniform cadence. They emerge from their training behaving almost like the Laurence Harvey character in the movie *The Manchurian Candidate* or like the creatures depicted in the movie *Night of the Living Dead*." (The 1968 sci-fi film may be a superior metaphor for K-12 than *The Blob*, the fifties thriller that inspired the nickname former Secretary of Education William Bennett gave to the national educational establishment.)

This situation will only worsen as public schools pursue the misnomered "university partnerships" that are now spreading throughout almost every metropolitan area as well as rural region in the country. University partnerships are not really university partnerships, since they involve ordinarily only one unit on campus, the least respected one. They are school of education partnerships, that is, intensified links between a given school district and an ed school, which is expected to lend its research expertise in return for enhanced internship, practicum, and job opportunities for its majors.

Clayton, like most districts, has been considering possible university partnerships, but has put its plans on hold in the face of opposition from some parents and school board members. I have been among those waving red flags. In a memo to the board I wrote in 1999, I raised the following specific concerns:

"(1) University partnerships invite an excessive amount of time and energy to be spent by Clayton faculty on mentoring student teachers and helping schools of education carry out their mission, which promises to distract our faculty from their mission to teach our children. (2) This program will only increase the role of student teachers in our kids' education, something that most parents, especially those who are paying hundreds of thousands of dollars for a house, should find unacceptable. (3) This program will tend to increase reliance of the Clayton school district on local schools of education to provide future teaching staff, since they will be viewed as a natural pipeline, when districts, particularly world-class ones like Clayton, should have higher aspirations, i.e., recruiting from a national pool (from Harvard, Yale, etc.) and one that includes the best and brightest not limited to schools of education but including arts and sciences graduates. (4) If we are not going to pursue links to arts and sciences departments (e.g., providing our budding scientists with Ph.D. faculty mentors in chemistry or biology), why are we calling these university partnerships? (5) When it is widely understood that schools of education are lacking in rigor, why would you want to hitch your sails to such institutions? (6) Our kids will increasingly become guinea pigs for the latest theories and experiments coming out of schools of education, which, by design, aim their pedagogical ideas at the mass market of students, not at what is appropriate for select groups of students in Clayton or anywhere else."

How Do We Get Better Teachers?

The K-12 leadership wants to enhance the image of teachers as professionals. That's fine. Teachers deserve to be treated as professionals. Unfortunately, however, this has translated into the desire for precollegiate teachers not to have to get their hands dirty correcting spelling errors or engaging in other mundane tasks, not to have to teach facts, not to be constrained by scripted, sequenced lesson plans, in other words not to have to teach children. They should stop acting like college professor wannabes. They are being paid to teach lower-order skills—to insure that kids have a rock-solid foundation of basic skills and factual literacy so that they are ready to soar to the next level. Although some may find this a demeaning job description, that's their job. I can think of few more important callings in life. I also can think of few more challenging responsibilities. If they do not wish to do this, then they are in the wrong line of work. Our schools don't exist to serve the needs of teachers, to make them feel good about themselves or to spare them the drudgery of red ink; they exist to serve the needs of children. Educational reforms should be aimed mainly at improving school for the students, not for the teachers!

Admittedly, if one wants to attract higher quality talent to the K-12 teaching ranks, then it is necessary to improve working conditions and other factors that might now be discouraging those people from entering and remaining in the field. I agree it is important to improve the image and the reality of the teaching profession. This should be done by instituting such changes as merit pay and related personnel policies that are the basis for hiring, firing, and promotion in most professions, furnishing individual office space of the type college professors enjoy, permitting alternative certification, and reducing bureaucratization.

Ask yourself why it has been so difficult to entice top talent to enter and stay in the teaching profession. Certainly salaries are part of the problem. In this regard, schools cannot compete with business and other employment sectors. But it is not only salaries that are a deterrent. So are the following: the unwillingness of most school systems to offer differential pay to reward star teachers and to attract scarce instructors in fields like math and science, as well as their inability to get rid of deadwood, largely due to teacher union pressures; the unwillingness of administrators to support teachers in the area of discipline, where children's disruptive behavior can make classrooms totally unruly; the credentialing hurdles that state education departments erect as barriers to entering and moving up in the profession, including having to take numerous Mickey Mouse education courses; mounds of paperwork, including IEP "evals," and stifling administrative regulations. And that's only the beginning. The reason there is a surplus of qualified college professors, many of whom cannot find jobs, is not because it is such a lucrative profession; the pay in many cases is not substantially higher than that found in K-12. No, it's because the factors I have just mentioned are much less operative. It is said, in regard to the college professor, the classroom is your castle. In the case of the K-12 teacher, the classroom is often your dungeon.

That is particularly the case in public schools. Private schools, such as John Burroughs in St. Louis, are able to hire some of the best and the brightest teachers, even though those teachers could make more money working in Clayton or some other district. Many Burroughs instructors in English literature and other fields, including some with Ph.D.s, are hired out of Harvard or some comparable university, without having had a single education course. I know because I have had friends who have done so. They could not be employed by public schools without being state-certified, that is, graduating from an approved teacher-preparation program, either as part of or in addition to obtaining a bachelors degree. There is a strong movement nationwide to allow alternative certification so that qualified persons, either talented young arts and sciences graduates or retired chemists or engineers, can quickly fill teaching vacancies. Many of these are idealistic people, who are excited about the challenge of teaching children and who would be willing to work even in poor urban schools if they were given the chance and if they did not have to contend with the factors I mentioned above.

The "interlocking directorate" of ed schools, state agencies, unions, and other interest groups, works against alternative certification and other reforms that could improve K-12 education. Leo Botstein, the president of Bard College, has stated bluntly, "to make the teaching profession respectable" and "to improve [K-12] education, get rid of the education degree." One possible compromise has been suggested by many observers, including well-known columnist David Broder: "Require prospective teachers to take a four-year undergraduate major in their subject specialty, then add a fifth year of graduate education in teaching techniques and a period of practice-teaching with skilled mentors." Even the Holmes Group, a group of deans of leading U.S. schools of education, had endorsed this idea in the 1980s, but it went nowhere due to resistance from ed schools whose student enrollments would shrink and whose faculty would have to be downsized drastically.

Unfortunately, the new National Commission on Teaching and America's Future, headed by constructivist Linda Darling-Hammond, merely urges more of the same, more accumulation of education credits, as a solution to what ails our schools. There is no concrete evidence that the more education credits one has, the more likely one is to produce greater student achievement, and that teachers who follow an alternative certification route to the classroom perform any worse than teachers steeped in ed school coursework. In fact, what little data exist on this subject suggest that ed school training produces no value added whatsoever. Indeed, there is no evidence that teacher salaries are correlated with higher student performance either. For example, a Rand Study found in 2000 that "teacher salaries and the percentage of the teaching force with master's degrees appear to have little impact on student performance." As a taxpayer, I am willing to contribute more monies toward improving teacher remuneration and other benefits, but only—as a *quid pro quo*—if quality control measures can be added.

We need better data on student achievement, and thus increased student testing. Progressives contend that this will only add to the dreariness of our schools and further alienate talented people from the teaching profession. Others disagree. It is widely understood among practitioners that "you tend to teach what you test"—you cover in class whatever you will be held responsible for—and that whoever controls the shape of the tests controls the shape of the classroom. Hence, there are few more important subjects one could discuss in K-12 education than the "testing wars" now raging across the country.

The Testing Wars

What testing is about, in the view of K-12 critics, is accountability. K-12 apologists put a completely different spin on it. Note Ken Goodman, the whole-language advocate: "Even if it were true that there was scientific evidence that one method was superior to others, you can't force teachers to teach in ways that they don't believe in…. What we're doing is turning our schools into drill camps for testing. We've turned our teachers into test administrators." What Goodman is really saying is that you can't force teachers who are committed progressives to teach otherwise, even in the face of definitive scientific evidence.

As a college professor, I am somewhat sympathetic to the concern expressed by some more thoughtful progressives that the more pressure put on teachers to produce test results, the more they will merely "teach to the test," which is often what happens under edicts issued by superintendents. Teachers do need a certain amount of creative freedom to roam widely, beyond the prescribed curriculum. It is also true, however, that good teachers will find a way to be both creative and also meet the testing standards. Incompetent teachers, currently protected by teachers unions, will be exposed and, hopefully, fired. It would not seem too much to ask of schools that students, at least by the time they graduate from high school, show that they can write a grammatically correct, error-free sentence or two, that they can perform basic computations and solve simple math problems, that they know elemental facts about the U.S. Constitution and important historical events, and that they possess minimal understanding of scientific concepts. If that invites "teaching to the test," let's get to it.

Some of my K-12 friends ask me why they should be under the gun while I and other college professors face no such scrutiny to demonstrate what our graduates know or can do. I answer as follows. First, a twelfth-grade education is our national standard; college is optional. Secondly, although American higher education certainly can stand considerable improvement, the fact is that it enjoys public confidence in a way that K-12 does not; people around the world vote with their feet in support of American universities when they matriculate in droves not only to Harvard but to UM-St. Louis (we have over 1,000 foreign students). In contrast, as the *Nation At Risk* study and subsequent Public Agenda surveys have shown, there is widespread dissatisfaction with many aspects of precollegiate education, therefore putting the latter under greater scrutiny. Third, the K-12 establishment invites testing when it engages in constant faddism and makes wild claims touting its latest magic bullets; it has a reputation for snakeoil that higher education has avoided due to its basically conservative pedagogical culture. Finally, public and private universities have to compete equally in the marketplace, which represents a test of sorts that does not exist in K-12, where public schools enjoy a virtual monopoly.

In the end, I don't care what teaching methodology one uses as long as it works. As one Clayton official correctly put it, "we should be interested not so much in what is taught by the teacher but what is caught by the student." There's the rub. How do we properly *assess* what has been "caught"? How do we best measure student achievement to insure our school systems are functioning well? Here the testing methodology *is* key, since there can be no confidence in the results if there is no confidence in the tests.

High-Stakes vs. No-Stakes Tests

To the extent that Ken Goodman, Alfie Kohn, and other progressives are willing to tolerate testing, it is in a form other than standardized testing. What they call "authentic assessment," or "performance assessment," is inspired by the most common mode of evaluating students in the areas of art and music, where college admissions officers or other evaluators ordinarily ask for sample exhibits of one's work that demonstrate one's level of achievement. Progressives are especially high on the use of "portfolios," which are collections of student work. There is a reason why few college admissions officers use this mode in evaluating student achievement in history or math or most other subjects. It is incredibly burdensome and costly in terms of time, money, and labor-intensive administration. More importantly, portfolios do not measure ability in the same way that SAT I and II tests do. These tests are reliable, because they are objective and, hence, permit greater inter-scorer consistency and inter-student comparability. They are called standardized tests because they assume a clear standard all students must meet.

Progressives do not want clear standards. They understand that, without such standards, it is nearly impossible to engage in so-called "high-stakes" testing to enforce accountability, that is, to retain poor-performing students and to terminate poor-performing teachers and schools. Progressives prefer no-stakes, no "pain" testing. Kohn has said, "learning is threatened by specific, measurable, uniform standards." Better we should have loose, unmeasurable standards, because then we can avoid any consequences for failure. Kohn's attack on standardized tests, particularly the traditional fill-in-the-bubble multiple-choice tests used in large-scale evaluations, has been countered by a number of assessment experts. The Pacific Research Institute, relying on the testimony of Susan Phillips of Michigan State University, concludes: "Some people think that multiple-choice items can only measure factual knowledge and basic skills. That's not true. Well-written multiple-choice items can measure higher-order thinking skills. Likewise, performance assessments don't necessarily measure higher-order skills.... The bottom-line is that multiple-choice questions offer the best value in terms of cost, breadth, reliability, validity, and ability to generalize." Anthony Bryk of the University of Chicago adds: "States may lean toward portfolios and performance assessments. But those methods have troubling issues of reliability and validity that, for purposes of high-stakes testing, tend to drive you back to the multiple-choice format."

Despite all the problems inherent in performance assessments, progressives have succeeded in bad-mouthing multiple-choice examinations enough to prompt states to move at least partially away from such exams. The new performance assessments that many states have instituted, which are supposed to measure not only what students know but what they can do with their knowledge, look impressive until one sees how fuzzy the state standards are that are being tested. The problem is not that many performance assessments aren't demanding and challenging—they often do require students to perform very difficult intellectual tasks —but the standards are so vague for judging proficiency that they encourage, at best, chaotic grading and, at worst, grade inflation, especially in the age of the nonjudgmental, nonhierarchical, self-esteem-based classroom.

For example, Missouri recently has introduced an annual assessment called the Missouri Assessment Program (MAP, also called the "Show-Me Standards," named after the "Show-Me" state's reputation for stubborn, mule-like behavior). The MAP tests in several disciplines at several grade levels. The tests have three sections: a multiple-choice section that tests mainly for factual knowledge (something that was included over the objection of many progressive-minded consultants who said it would promote rote memorization); a short constructed-response section; and an essay component. Typical of the fluffy, semi-academic, almost ungradable nature of many of the "standards" embodied in the MAP tests is the following: "Students will demonstrate the ability to express one's emotions, concepts of beauty, and personal perceptions of works of the arts, humanities, and sciences." One can only imagine the potential inter-scorer inconsistency that could occur on the open-ended-answer portions of the test, depending upon who was grading your child's exam, for example a Jesse Helms or a Jesse Jackson. Not surprisingly, school districts have lodged complaints about scorer error on the MAP tests, with one critic noting that in a recent case "a 20 percent grading error was found on part of the Communication Arts portion of the test." This squares with the Pacific Research Institute report that "researchers have found that two trained scorers will agree only sixty to eighty percent of the time when grading an essay using a 1-to-5 scale."

Those states that have been misguided enough to rely on portfolios as the basis for their assessments, which are even more riddled with subjectivity than the MAP, have quickly abandoned them. In 1990, Kentucky passed education reform legislation that required portfolio assessment of students. Called the KIRIS assessment, the tests developed credibility problems when the inflated scores students were registering did not correspond with performance on the National Assessment of Educational Progress (NAEP) exam and the ACT (the sister exam to the SAT). By 1998, the entire system had been scrapped. Vermont's portfolio assessment experiment suffered a similar fate. According to Rand Corporation researchers, scorers were confused by the scoring rubrics, which added to problems of reliability and validity, even as the financial costs of the system were "astronomic." Maine, too, has been burned by heavy reliance on performance-based tests, recently restoring multiple-choice questions it previously had eliminated in favor of open-response items.

While some states are attempting to return to more traditional, more reliable testing formats that tap knowledge and skills based on clear standards, others, such as Maryland, persist in using performance assessments that have been the object of much criticism. In a critique prepared by the former head of the Maryland State Board of Education, supported by a study the state itself commissioned from the Abell Foundation, it was noted that "group practices [on the MSPAP] such as brainstorming, peer review, and cooperative learning cannot be reconciled with the reporting of individual scores," nor can the fact that "students answer too few questions to produce a score that accurately represents performance in a subject area." Despite the careful documentation of these and other problems presented by the evaluators, the Maryland state superintendent of education did what so many such functionaries do—she killed the messenger and refused to publish the report, contending that the consultants wanted to force the state "to go back to facts, facts, facts, memorization, and regurgitation."

I heard similar comments from the director of Clayton's assessent program in the 1990s, who greeted the MAP test as superior to its predecessor, which she characterized as big on "minute facts." Clayton and most other St. Louis area school districts would probably prefer portfolio assessment to the MAP, if they could convince the state to adopt it, since, even with the potential for grade inflation, the MAP often has produced low student achievement scores that have been widely reported in the local newspapers, causing great embarrassment to educators and threatening some school systems with state takeover.

In Missouri and elsewhere there are ongoing pressures either to dumb-down the state tests or devalue them, that is, reduce their high-stakes quality. Wisconsin, New York, Arizona, Virginia, Massachusetts, and California are among those states which, having trumpeted ambitious new tests, are now experiencing pressures to backpedal somewhat. Sometimes these pressures come from school administrators and teachers, who are so worried about adverse consequences that they resort to cheating, to literally teaching the test. In other cases, the pressures come from state officials and parents, who worry that high-stakes tests required for promotion or high school graduation may cause children to be held back. The result is that "nearly a third of the states that have drafted high-stakes graduation exams in recent years are scaling back or slowing their initial efforts. . . . These states have winnowed material to be tested, lowered passing grades or delayed the effective dates of those exams until as late as 2007, when many of the lawmakers responsible [for instituting the requirements] will be out of office."

The Politics of Testing

It is said that politics produces strange bedfellows. The testing wars truly have produced some strange coalitions. On the one side is an anti-testing camp, composed of (1) liberal, progressive educators who advocate essentially no control over the curriculum by anyone except educators, and who wish to substitute portfolios and performance assessment for standardized testing; (2) spokespersons for certain disadvantaged minority groups, who share the progressives' disdain for standardized tests because their membership tends to perform poorly on those tests relative to other groups; (3) conservative groups, including both religious and libertarian ones, who like the idea of rigorous standards but are fearful of the government at the state or national level imposing the wrong standards and, hence, are insistent on private schools maintaining their freedom from testing mandates and on public schools submitting only to local control; and (4) "soccer moms" and other parents, often from well-to-do suburban school districts, who worry that excessive testing may hurt their children, either because the tests are too hard and will prevent their kids from graduating or because they are too easy and may foster less creative learning environments.

This anti-testing camp is not really a coalition, in that the four elements, particularly the liberals and conservatives, barely talk to each other. Nonetheless, for different reasons, they all find themselves often making common cause. It is mainly the educationists, who potentially have the most to gain or lose, who have led the "growing revolt against the testers." Writing tracts with such titles as "Fighting the Tests: A Practical Guide to Rescuing Our Schools," "The Authentic Standards Movement and Its Evil Twin," and "News from the Test Resistance Trail," these folks portray themselves as crusaders standing between education heaven and hell. They have been joined by the leadership of the National Education Assocation (NEA) and the American Federation of Teachers (AFT), who claim they believe in standards but reject any testing that would effectively enforce standards. Albert Shanker, the late head of the AFT and a firm believer in rigorous standardized testing, would no doubt be appalled by the turn the AFT has taken. As for the NEA, an Associated Press report on its annual convention in July 2001 noted that "in its strongest stance yet against standardized testing, the NEA voted to support legislation giving parents the ability to let their children skip the tests." Here was the NEA, an outspoken opponent of parental choice when it came to vouchers, suddenly discovering parental choice when it applied to boycotting statewide tests! Only the most ardent unionist could fail to see the self-serving hypocrisy in this.

Some parents have taken up the call and participated with their children in boycotts of state assessments. In 2001, protests against testing occurred in a number of school districts around the country, the most visible cases being the 60 percent of the eighth graders in tony Scarsdale, New York and the over 20 percent of the students at two prestigious high schools in equally tony Marin County, California who stayed home or got their parents to sign waivers excusing them from examinations. Around the same time, at the other end of the socioeconomic spectrum, political pressure was brought to bear in New York and California to relax high school exit exam requirements since there was concern that too few African-Americans and Latinos would pass and that drop-out rates might soar. Add in middle-America parents who, for religious or other reasons, are wary of centralized control of education through statewide or nationwide tests, and one wonders who is left who supports a stricter testing regime.

At the same time, however, there is in fact a sizeable pro-testing camp composed of (1) traditionalist educators who believe so strongly in the *Nation at Risk* call for systemic change in K-12 education that they support a degree of national control, or at least guidance, in the form of national standards and national testing; (2) some leaders in inner city communities who believe that creating higher expectations for minority youngsters, backed by clearly measurable and testable standards, is the only way to improve urban schools; (3) corporate interests which, concerned about the lack of skills K-12 graduates are bringing to the workplace, also support a degree of national-level, federal oversight; and (4) concerned parents' groups which, unlike those in Scarsdale and Marin County, want greater assurances their kids are learning and, hence, support more rigorous testing at least at the state or local level.

My own school district is typical of the complex forces at work in the testing wars. One faction on the Clayton school board is concerned about testing overkill and how mandates from Jefferson City, Mo. might rigidify the curriculum and undermine progressive pedagogy, while another faction has the opposite concern, that the movement toward portfolio and other performance-based assessments may obfuscate and hide serious weaknesses in the curriculum, including the failure to teach basics. Few parents in the Clayton school district want a single test to determine their child's future—it is understood that any kid can have a bad day—but many would agree that a good standardized test is a sound basis for evaluating a school system as a whole, due to the unlikelihood of all kids having a bad day at once. Even the *New York Times*, normally supportive of progressive positions, has spoken out against Alfie Kohn and the anti-testing crusaders, editorializing that "Rod Paige, the secretary of education, was on the mark when he described those who opposed annual testing as apologists 'for a broken system of education that dismisses certain children and classes of children as unteachable.'"

There is reason to believe that, despite widespread news reports of "testing backlash" (fueled by the anti-testing camp), most parents as well as other constituencies around the country ultimately support tougher standards and tests. For example, a recent poll taken by the Business Roundtable "showed overwhelming support for standards-based reform among all groups, regardless of race, income, or political party. When asked whether students should be required to pass state tests before graduating from high school,...65 percent of parents and 70 percent of the general public answered yes. Support was even higher (76 percent of parents and 81 percent of the public) if students were allowed to take the state exam several times, which in fact is the customary policy in most states." Similarly, the nonpartisan Public Agenda organization found that "countering recent news reports of a parental backlash against academic standards and standardized tests," polls reveal "scant evidence to substantiate a backlash." Among the specific findings: "Only 11 percent [of parents] say their child's school requires them to take too many standardized tests. Seventy-five percent agree that 'students pay more attention and study harder if they know they must pass a test to get promoted or to graduate.' Seventy-six percent agree that 'requiring schools to publicize their standardized test scores is a wake-up call and a good way to hold schools accountable.'"

It is clear that only through high-stakes tests can schools be held accountable. Having said that, there is room for healthy debate over whether accountability is best lodged at the national, state, or local level. There is something to be said for national standards and national tests, so that children who move across state boundaries can readily adjust to their new schools and expect roughly equal quality of education. To the extent that they impose a common national curriculum on all public schools, however, they may promote lowest common denominator education. Statewide testing poses similar concerns; Clayton understandably has no more desire to have its curriculum dictated from Jefferson City than from Washington, D.C. Still, as the NAEP and SAT exams suggest, it is possible to have nationally developed standardized tests that are compatible with strong curricula to which all schools should aspire. Local control is probably best, since it enables citizens to exercise democratic governance through grass-roots involvement. But that assumes that school boards are responsive to their citizenry, are committed to high standards, are not intimidated or dominated by education lobbies, and do not allow pack pedagogy—in effect, a type of national control—to dictate what goes on in the classroom.

Throughout 2001, there was lively debate in Washington surrounding the Bush administration's plan to require annual testing of all public school children from third through eighth grades in the areas of reading and math and to inflict sanctions on failing schools. Sensitive to concerns about overly centralized control, the plan gave states considerable discretion in selecting the particular assessment vehicles they wished to use as long as they provided clear measures of progress and could be benchmarked against national standards such as those reflected in the NAEP. The plan aimed especially at closing the rich-poor gap in quality education by targeting improvements in urban schools, which receive much of the more than $100 billion a year spent by the federal government on K-12 education. There was bipartisan support behind the proposition that K-12 could not expect increased federal funds for new school construction or other purposes without adequate accountability, although differences existed over precisely how often tests should be administered and how severe the penalties should be for failure (the Democrats tending toward more lenient rules than the Republicans). The "No Child Left Behind Act" passed both houses of Congress and was signed into law by the President in January 2002, with battles still to be fought out over implementation. Some Republicans, such as Todd Akin of Missouri, have been most concerned about insuring that whatever tests are used tap cognitive knowledge and skills rather than affective feelings and opinions, and that Washington not usurp state and local perogatives. In the end, we probably will never have to worry about the imposition of national standards, since, as one education warrior has noted, "the conservatives don't like national, and the liberals don't like standards."

8

A Modest Proposal for a Cease-fire

The "closed alliance" that is the education establishment permits little dissent within its ranks and often stonewalls dissenters outside its ranks, making it hard to conduct a serious dialogue on K-12 issues. An example of "groupthink" within the K-12 ranks is a friend of mine who works as a leading professional development specialist in the St. Louis area, with strong ties to ed schools, state education agencies, and school administrators. Being privy to the inside workings of the establishment, this person has served as a mole, feeding me information that is often embarrassing, often unavailable to the outside world, and often confirming my worst fears about the latest fads being purveyed by K-12 gurus. This intelligence-gathering has been an important source of material for this book. Early on in this project, I took to thinking of my source as "Deep Rote," wanting to protect my friend's anonymity out of fear that he/she might be chastised for sharing information with "outsiders." Although this person disagrees with me on many issues, there is also some grudging acknowledgment that my criticism at times is on the mark. I have encountered teachers as well who are sympathetic with the concerns I have raised and are reluctant to voice their true feelings publicly for fear of ostracism or worse. Such is the lack of openness in the current K-12 culture.

Pitted against this powerful, almost monolithic alliance are a few ed school mavericks (in addition to well-known figures such as Diane Ravitch, some lesser known professors, such as the self-described "contrarians" Lucien Ellington at the University of Tennessee-Chattanooga and Mark Schug at the University of Wisconsin-Milwaukee, who have tried to wage guerrilla warfare within the National Council for the Social Studies), along with a rag-tag band of parents such as myself and others described in the previous pages. Parent protesters generally have proven no match for The Blob, which is adept at silencing critics through the artful manipulation of jargon, state-of-the-art dissembling, and well-produced PR campaigns aimed at local media whose idea of a good education story invariably involves the unveiling of the most recent nationwide school reform craze couched in catchy slogans. The forces of revolution—or counterrevolution—that are trying to buck the establishment have made headway only when they have been able to enlist the help of business and political leaders, although even the latter have also been frustrated in their efforts to shake up the system.

The tide of battle, however, may be turning. The disconnect between the Thoughtworld and the rest of us on such issues as teaching of basics, discipline, and ability-grouping has been widening to the point where there are growing pressures for accountability of the sort described in the last chapter. Public Agenda has characterized the gulf between ed schools and parents/citizens as follows: "Professors of education hold a vision of public education that seems fundamentally at odds with that of...the public. Seventy-nine percent of these teachers of teachers say 'the general public has outmoded and mistaken beliefs about what good teaching means.'...The disconnect between what the professors want and what most parents, teachers, and students say they need is often staggering. It seems ironic that so many of those who profess to believe that 'the real endeavor' is about questioning and learning how to learn are seemingly entrapped in a mind-set that is unquestioning in its conviction of its own rightness."

What ultimately is responsible for this huge gulf? The answer is found partly in the historical development of American education—there is a long record of insularity and arrogance on the part of a progressive movement that has never had to face up to its failures. But it is found, also, in the more recent developments I have cited here, best summarized in an excerpt from the testimony I gave before the Missouri Senate in 1996. I had been invited to address the legislature by some senators who shared my misgivings about the new "Show-Me Standards" developed by the Department of Elementary and Secondary Education (DESE). The Senate Education Committee was chaired by a five-term senator who was known to be a no-nonsense, relatively conservative Democrat from a small rural town who, though legally blind, could see through the slightest air of pedantry on the part of witnesses. I was careful not to adopt too professorial a tone:

Senators, you need to understand the current K-12 culture that DESE lives in and that informs the entire standards project. It is clear that what has happened is that educators around a decade or so ago made a wonderful discovery; they discovered that our schools were not giving much of an education to slow learners and children with learning disabilities. This was essentially a valid observation and a situation that needed correcting, and in fact some progress has been made. That is the upside of recent trends. But there is a downside. As educators tend to do, they take a good idea, such as "all kids can learn," and—like a child with a new toy—they go berserk with it, to the point where today there is absolutely no question that the bottom is driving the curriculum almost everywhere.

Virtually all of the latest fashions in K-12 education that I have surveyed—multiple intelligences, whole language, fuzzy math, self-esteem-building, multiage classrooms, block scheduling, etc.—are rooted not in concern for the highest achieving student, or even the average student, but the most educationally "disadvantaged" student. This is now the *sine qua non* of school reform in America, although these disadvantaged students are often among the main casualties of progressive faddism. Defining the problem as closing the gap between *groups* of students (academic haves and have-nots, whites vs. blacks), noble as the intentions are, merely invites bringing the top down to the level of the bottom. What we should be aiming for, instead, is improving *each individual child's* performance, in which case a persistence of "the gap" becomes more benign. We should not rule out eventually closing the gap, but such a desire should not be driving K-12 education.

Consider the ongoing debates over rich-poor gaps in world politics. If the rich nations are getting richer and the poor nations are getting richer, and their populations are all improving in terms of life expectancy, which has been the general long-term trend since World War II, shouldn't that be considered progress? This does not mean we shouldn't try to alleviate the worst poverty, only that it should not be done by making everyone equally poor. Some communist societies have tried that, with dismal results. In 1820, the richest country in the world had only three times as much income per person as the poorest; today the wealthiest country has 30 times the income. There is an argument to be made that the haves today could do more to help the have-nots—that there are moral and practical reasons why it makes sense to reduce wealth gaps within and between nations—but surely any objective observer would conclude that the vast majority of people on the globe are better off today on almost every measure of human well-being than in 1820. Indeed, there has been a steady narrowing of the life-expectancy gap between the most developed and least developed countries (the recent setbacks in Africa, due to the AIDS epidemic, aside). It is likely but not certain that, in America, a rising tide in public education will lift all boats. What is beyond question is that, under the current dumbing-down regime, most students are sinking.

Providing opportunities for extraordinary academic excellence should be among the first priorities of public schools, not the last. Regarding the attacks on honors courses, Public Agenda has reported that "the public is highly skeptical of...mixed-ability grouping.... Ideas such as grouping students with different skills together in one class don't make intuitive sense to most Americans." Although more than half of the ed school academics surveyed recently by Public Agenda favored mixed groupings (echoing the head of Columbia Teachers College, who was quoted as saying that "research shows that putting students of varying abilities in the same classes does not hurt fast learners and can help slow learners"), only a third of the public and 40 percent of teachers supported such reforms.

Populist pressures remain relentless, not on the part of "the people" but on the part of K-12 elites. Instead of trying so hard to narrow achievement gaps, we should be working to narrow the gulf between the educational establishment and the rest of society. Although the progressive-traditionalist divide is not the only one that separates the combatants who fight over education issues, it is the main front. Progressives need to be more open-minded, particularly open to addressing the concerns of traditionalists. Traditionalists, for their part, should be respectful of those progressives willing to engage them in serious conversation. If I have seemed disrespectful, it is not out of spite but out of frustration in getting a fair hearing from the other side. The British Prime Minister Winston Churchill once observed, in responding to criticisms about the United Nations being a mere "talk shop," that jaw-jaw is better than war-war. The current battles being waged in K-12 education do not serve the interests of anybody, least of all our children. It is worth asking what it would take to declare a cease-fire in the Great American Education War, to reach a rapprochement among adults on behalf of kids.

The Elements of a Peace

I realize it is not a profound idea to call for a dialogue among parties to a conflict. Nonetheless, a real dialogue between progressives and traditionalists would be a major breakthrough. Progressives have felt little need to reach out, since they are in control. Traditionalists at times have tried, but they are painfully aware that they deal from a position of weakness.

Game theorists, who study the dynamics of conflict and how win-win outcomes can be attained by competing players, often speak of a "prominent solution," that is, a compromise settlement package whose ingredients so self-evidently promise a mutually agreeable ending to a conflict that they are likely ultimately to be the basis for striking a final bargain; even though one side may win more than the other, both can achieve some gains. For example, the prominent solution in the "game" played between the big states and the small states at the Constitutional Convention in 1787 was a bicameral legislature featuring seating in the House of Representatives based on state population size and seating in the Senate based on state equality regardless of size, a bargain embodied in the famous Connecticut Compromise. The prominent solution to the Great American Education War is within reach. Less obvious is whether the players in this case are as up to the challenge of statesmanship as were the Founding Fathers. Granted, in 1787, the decision essentially rested with only fifty-five men who were present in Philadelphia, representing only thirteen jurisdictions. Decisions about the future shape of K-12 schooling in the United States rests today with many more people—members of boards and administrations representing some 15,000 local school systems, along with individuals found in state education departments and other parts of the education establishment, as well as in the independent sector of American education. The search for compromise need not be a hopeless task, however, since, despite the myriad number of players ostensibly to be accommodated at the bargaining table, we have seen how pack pedagogy reduces the problem considerably.

The outlines of a prominent solution seem as plain as day.

They revolve around acceptance of a more *balanced* pedagogical paradigm. We simply need to celebrate *both* the targeting of resources at low-achievers *and* the gifted (along with the middle); discovery learning *and* direct instruction; the development of higher-order skills (critical thinking, problem-solving, and the like) *and* basic skills (grammar, punctuation, computation, and the like); process *and* content; creativity *and* rigor; new performance assessments *and* old-fashioned standardized testing; and similar sorts of perfectly compatible emphases that wrongly have been portrayed as mutually exclusive.

To those, particularly in the progressive camp, who would say they already are committed to balance, I say, coming from Missouri, *show me.* Stop bashing traditional ideas about education, and maybe folks like me will stop retaliating in kind. Having identified legitimate educational concerns that needed addressing (e.g., draconian tracking and inadequate attention to struggling youngsters), but having *overcorrected* (e.g., stretching the notion of "all kids can learn" to "all kids are gifted"), bring the pendulum back to a more moderate position. When you talk about "full inclusion," include the likes of Hirsch and Ravitch on your ed school syllabi and professional development calendars rather than exposing future and present teachers only to the likes of Gardner and Sizer. Encourage faculty to upgrade their subject-matter knowledge in graduate-level arts and sciences courses and not limit themselves to honing their coaching techniques under the tutelage of PDC constructivists.

The following anecdote illumines the current imbalance. Recently, Deep Rote informed me he/she was attempting to get the powers-that-be in his/her professional development shop to invite E.D. Hirsch to come to St. Louis to speak to teachers and administrators. The response? "If we invite Hirsch, who is controversial, we will need to get somebody to balance him." It's okay to bring in Thomas "Seven Kinds of Smart" Armstrong's one-man show on multiple intelligences, but Hirsch is banned unless accompanied by a balancing act. Since he is generally persona non grata among that leadership, Hirsch has had to resort to establishing his own Core Knowledge Foundation in order to disseminate his "controversial" views about kids learning basic facts by the time they graduate from high school.

In my own attempts at dialogue with progressives, I have been struck by how often they are the ones who feel aggrieved, who feel they are tilting at windmills in trying to undo what they see as decades of decadence in K-12 education, reflected by the same old rows of desks, blackboards, and other atavistic features that they claim continue to dominate schooling. They seem to ignore the extent to which their jargon and their ideas have become the new orthodoxy among curriculum leaders and have created a new inertia. It is true that sometimes the latest theories do not get fully translated into practice and that there can be more talk than action. Indeed, the usual excuse progressives give for K-12 education not living up to the hype that attends their announcements of the latest best practices is that the reforms "have not been implemented." In schools across America, however, it is almost impossible today to have a conversation with a teacher, or at least the teacher's boss, in which the words "cooperative, hands-on, and active learning" do not pop up, as if on cue. It is almost impossible to find schools that are not seriously considering moving to a block schedule, if they have not already done so. And it is almost impossible to find a K-12 language arts program that is not heavily dominated by whole-language. As two iconoclastic ed school professors have said about their profession, "the first step needed [to improve it] is to acknowledge the ubiquity of Muzak Progressivism."

What Diane Ravitch calls "the powerful middle ground" may have raised its voice over the past decade, but there is no evidence it has dislodged constructivism in the minds of education professors and other key K-12 agenda-setters and change agents. Despite a flurry of recent articles calling for blending the best of traditional pedagogy with the the best of progressive pedagogy, there has been no synthesis, as the two sides continue for the most part to talk past each other. To quote a St. Louis area middle school principal who has searched vainly for evidence of a cease-fire, "common sense" remains "elusive," and "balance and moderation" remain "out of favor." To the extent that any balance is occurring, it is being imposed on K-12 by external forces, through the testing movement, which is being vigorously contested by the progressive leadership. There is no détente.

One is left wondering, if détente seems as yet unattainable and if the elements of a peace are not fully in place, where do we go from here? Perhaps we shouldn't bother to declare a truce in the Great American Education War. Rather than engineering a grand compromise from above, perhaps we should allow change to percolate up from below, in true democratic fashion.

Fixing the Disconnect Between Parents and Schools

How might consumer sovereignty work in the education sector? We may want to rethink whether we should be aiming for the pendulum to reside at a certain balance point, since it may be impossible to find that angle of repose that satisfies everybody and meets the needs of every child. Some parents of high-achieving children will always prefer progressive pedagogy and heterogeneous grouping, while others prefer more traditional pedagogy and ability-grouping. Parents of average and low-achieving kids will also be similarly divided. In addition, some teachers may feel more comfortable and may be more effective using one type of pedagogy rather than another. Rather than squabbling over who is right, we can avoid this by maximizing freedom of choice. This means not settling for the currently fashionable formula of "differentiating" or "individualizing" instruction within a given classroom, which is merely a top-down rationalization for squeezing in one-size-fits-all education, but rather providing a far larger menu of alternatives. The range of choices that ought to be more readily available to parents are (1) a variety of options within the public schools themselves, (2) charters, (3) vouchers (or tuition tax credits) usable at private schools, and (4) homeschooling. Today's educators are big on letting kids do their own thing. How about adults—parents, who have the main responsibility for those kids? Why not empower *them*?

Options Within the Public Schools

We certainly should not write off the public schools. They are likely to remain the primary educational service provider in America for years to come. We need to make them more responsive to parents. The director of governmental relations for the National PTA has stated that parental involvement is "mostly just rhetoric. Parents are out of the decision-making loop." The president of the Institute for Responsive Education says similarly, "It's common for school districts to plunge ahead with change efforts with no prior discussion with the community about the need for—or goals of—change." There is "a need for public *engagement*, a much closer relationship between schools and community members than in the past, with fuller communication and more public input at all stages of reform."

The conventional mode of parental involvement in schools is

the PTA, where it is generally expected one will not get immersed in curriculum matters and, in any event, will not make waves. As a parent activist in Greenwich, Connecticut says, "The issues addressed by the PTA have nothing to do with the academic performance of children. They are more concerned about funding for the playground and computers and the social aspects of children.... They [the administration] don't really want parents involved in the way I want to be involved, which is knowing the details of the curriculum, knowing what is being tested, and questioning the new standards."

I can vouch for the fact that any parent who seeks to become involved in his or her child's school will not necessarily be welcomed, especially if you dare to disagree with the curriculum leaders and others shaping the direction of the school district, which these days usually means questioning progressive, constructivist ideas. When I tried to organize Parents Against Average Schools, to protest the movement away from ability-grouping, I was not given quite the deferential, enthusiastic backing from the administration that characterized their treatment of Parents of African-American Students. The two groups shared the same acronym but not the ear of the administration. When another parent, a lawyer who had taken the time to write a fifty-page analysis supporting the 2000 National Reading Panel study's call for more balanced reading instruction, requested to be added to the Clayton Literacy Committee, she was refused, the only possible explanation being that she was out of synch with the whole-language orientation of the committee. I have witnessed similar treatment of parents in many other area school districts, only some of which I have reported on here.

My sense is that the Clayton school district is fairly typical, in terms of the real action on curriculum matters occurring behind the scenes, on committees led by staff versed in the latest fads and populated by token parent representatives chosen mainly for their conformity to the latter views, with committee proposals ultimately presented as faits accomplis at school board meetings, where the discussion is ordinarily rehearsed and tightly controlled. Some proposals, such as the Core-Plus "fuzzy math" program, have literally been rammed through with virtually no opportunity for public input, other than the three-to-five minute sound-bite permitted parents during the "public comment" segment of board meetings. Other curriculum proposals have been reviewed more carefully and deliberately, with more parent involvement, although in most cases the outcome has been just as predictable, since rarely have both pros and cons been presented along with all the relevant research that included data at odds with the committee's recommendation.

In fairness to the Clayton administration, and to school district administrations generally, the job of superintendent is not an easy one. In fact, it is so difficult and unattractive a position that in many metropolitan areas the same names get recycled in musical chairs fashion from one district to another. In St. Louis, for example, school districts usually hire firms to do "national searches," only to end up selecting a local figure who has either worn out his welcome in a nearby district or done such a good job that a raiding party is sent to get him.

Clayton's current superintendent, when he was recruited in 1995, was in the latter category, a highly respected leader who had done an excellent job in his previous tour of duty, in Parkway. (To show you how small a world K-12 is, his successor in Parkway was a former principal at Clayton's Wydown Middle School.) Like superintendents everywhere, he has had to be the ultimate politician, confronted with satisfying multiple constituencies, including Clayton parents of high-achievers demanding high-powered curricula, parents of learning-disabled students demanding special accommodations, parents of "the middle" kids demanding they not be overlooked, parents of the deseg kids demanding "the gap" be closed, local, state and federal government officials making testing and other demands, and teachers unions and faculty with their own agendas. Given these competing pressures, I suppose I should be thankful for whatever attention our superintendent has given the concerns I and like-minded parents have raised. He and I have met for coffee from time to time, which has usually produced a momentary détente between us, until I aired my next complaint in a memo to the school board, whereupon he would find my criticism offensive and I would find his response defensive. The administration actually has tried to be more responsive of late, having agreed to allow people like me, who have been frozen out of the curriculum committee process, to have input through the new Citizens Advisory Curriculum Council that meets periodically to discuss various academic issues. The current assistant superintendent for curriculum, who replaced my nemesis in 2000, has been the chair of the Council and has tried hard to run it in a fair fashion, although it remains to be seen whether this body will have any real impact in opening up the decision-making process.

The creation of the Citizens Curriculum Council was made possible only because the Clayton school board at present is evenly split between progressives and traditionalists, and the latter succeeded in persuading the administration to accept such a forum. Mark Twain is reputed to have said, "First God made idiots. That was just for practice. Then He created school boards." That's unfair. The fact is that one of the worst positions to occupy other than school superintendent is school board member. If one takes the job seriously, one must be prepared to donate hundreds of hours poring over documents, attending meetings, and doing other official business. It is hard for anyone who has a full-time job to carry out board duties except in the most perfunctory fashion. Even the most conscientious board member can easily be confused or intimidated by the technical jargon that inevitably dominates substantive curriculum discussions. There are strong pressures to go along and routinely accept staff proposals, since few wish to alienate the faculty and administration, if only because any resultant bad press in the local media may well depress property values. When board members are elected who refuse to be co-opted, and boldly question the direction the district is going in, as in the case of the present traditionalist faction on the Clayton board, they are portrayed by their opponents as bad people who wish to harm the district.

More parents should be willing to question their school district's board and administration. Parents certainly have a right to request information and raise concerns. Hopefully, this can be done in a civil, polite way rather than combatively, but that will depend on how willing the authorities are to engage in conversation. There would be less need for confrontation if public schools offered parents an array of choices. Some do, in the form of magnet schools that play to different students' interests and strengths, although these are threatened by the growing constructivist call for "integrated curricula." Others are experimenting with providing both traditional and progressive options, such as in Cincinnati, where (under a former Clayton superintendent) parents can now choose between a Core Knowledge school for their child or a more trendy alternative. Most districts, however, such as Clayton, do not allow parents to choose between traditional and trendy. There tends to be one party line.

Although I chose to stay and fight in the public schools, keeping my children there until they graduated (and continuing the fight as a taxpayer ever since), unhappy parents should not have to fight if they don't want to. You should be allowed simply to exit the system and place your child in an alternative setting more to your liking. The greater availability of options that would allow a parent to move a child, short of selling your house and relocating to another district or using the proceeds to pay private tuition, would not only help individual parents but would provide an important systemic benefit to K-12 education as a whole.

Public schools have continued to exist in a cocoon of controversy and dissatisfaction because the absence of consumer alternatives has left them alive and, if not well, still in business. So, despite constantly shooting themselves in the foot, they just keep firing away. A 2001 Public Broadcasting System documentary on the history of American schooling intimated that anybody who abandons public schools for private schools is contributing to the undermining of an indispensable American institution. I personally have been committed to the public schools, but I have no less respect for those parents who for their own reasons have decided otherwise. Their departure, or threat of departure, might in the long run help improve our schools by prompting them to be more responsive.

Charter Schools

Not very far removed from the public school system are charter schools, such as the Princeton Charter School established at the urging of the Princeton, N.J. parents who were "hungry for ABC's." These institutions are described as follows: "Charter schools are public schools. They agree to produce results—that is, meet the state's academic standards—in exchange for autonomy. They get a real budget and real decision-making power; they can hire and terminate their staff, for example.... They span the philosophical gamut, from progressive to traditional, but they have in common small class size, a strong sense of mission, and a keen sense of community. If they don't perform, they lose their charter, usually granted by a state agency.... If they don't attract students, they don't survive.... [Their] operating budgets depend on enrollment, as public funding follows the student."

There are now more than 2,000 charter schools in the United

States, serving over half-a-million students in thirty-eight states. In some cities, as many as 15 to 20 percent of the school-age population is in charters. Arizona leads the country in sheer numbers (416), followed by California (302) and Michigan (185); together these three states account for 44 percent of all charters nationwide, with states like Texas (165) and Florida (149) gaining ground. Missouri, in contrast, has only twenty-one. Thus far, charters have had mixed success in improving on the record of regular schools, although it is too soon to draw any conclusions about their overall effectiveness.

Although they have increased the range of choices provided by public schools, the problem is that in many communities charters are Potemkin villages, insofar as they only give the appearance of being independent of the existing K-12 establishment. Almost half of all the charters in the United States have had to get approval, under state law, from local school boards, putting them at the mercy of those boards. In St. Louis, it has proven difficult to start up many charters, since the state of Missouri has given the School of Education at UM-St. Louis the prime authority to determine which applicants qualify. Giving a school of education oversight power over charter schools is truly a case of putting the fox in charge of the hen house. In addition, public schools, through their links to state agencies, often throw up bureaucratic and other obstacles to the operation of charters, even where they are permitted to open under the sponsorship of parents' groups. In some cases, as in Ohio, teachers' unions and other threatened interests have mounted lawsuits against charters. Moreover, requiring charter schools to meet the very same standards that have resulted from curriculum processes regulated by the status quo can defeat the whole purpose of creating "break the mold" schools. The main quality control, in terms of a check on whether these schools are competent in meeting educational needs, should come from their ability or inability to attract a clientele willing to send their children voluntarily to those institutions.

Typical of the constraints and roadblocks faced by charters is the experience of the Thomas Jefferson Charter School, located in a suburb of Chicago. As described in a 1999 *Chicago Tribune* editorial, "parents and children in Elk Grove Township are being given a choice in public education. If they are happy with the schooling they receive, they can stay the course. If they would like something different, they can sign up for a new back-to-basics education program, the Thomas Jefferson Charter School. It's a choice, an option. But from the way the school board in District 59 responded, you'd think this was the Saddam Hussein Charter School.... District 59 declared war to prevent its own parents and children from having the chance to choose a back-to-basics education. The board filed suit to stop the opening...[and] sent home with every child a letter designed to scare the dickens out of their parents [regarding safety and other concerns]."

Thomas Jefferson was eventually permitted to open its doors, aided in part by the newspaper's whistle-blowing. Its initial intent was to be, in the words of the school principal, a "junior Princeton Academy" dedicated to "serious academics." As it happens, the school has found itself catering especially to immigrant families hungering for their kids to get a traditional education taught in English, as opposed to the bilingual or English as a second language (ESL) programs they feared they would be subjected to in the public schools. Two-thirds of the children come from ESL homes, posing a challenge to the teaching staff, but one the school embraces. The school is an example of how, contrary to the arguments made by anti-choice spokespersons, school choice programs do not necessarily entail "creaming off" the best kids from the best families. Granted, they do tend to attract families extremely concerned about education. Since when is this anti-democratic? I should add that, according to the principal, the local school district has yet to cooperate fully in supporting the charter.

Vouchers

To the extent the education establishment tolerates charter schools, it is to defuse the voucher issue. The dream of free-market economists, first conceived by the Nobelist Milton Friedman, is an education system in which parents have relatively equal economic incentives to use government schools or private schools, so that their decision will rest purely on educational grounds—what is best for their children—rather than on financial grounds. Such a system is roughly approximated in higher education, where, even though private universities tend to be more expensive than state universities, parents, if they so choose, can take advantage of a variety of federal and state grants and loans to help make up the difference and utilize the private school option for their kids, including possibly enrolling them in religious schools, such as

Notre Dame or Georgetown. In the K-12 sector, public schools have opposed publicly funded vouchers, that is, private-school transfer payments derived from state monies that go to parents who prefer to send their children to independent schools rather than to their local public schools. Their opposition has applied to secular and parochial schools alike. In other words, whereas in higher education the money follows the child, in K-12 the opposite is the case.

Only a few K-12 publicly funded voucher experiments have been attempted, notably in Milwaukee, Cleveland, and some Florida communities. (In New York City, Dayton, Ohio, and a few other places, voucher programs have been funded by private philanthropists.) The Milwaukee and Cleveland programs are specifically targeted at low-income students, who may choose among private, parochial, and other public schools, while the Florida program offers choice to any students in "failing schools." Although some studies have suggested positive benefits accruing to the students who left their public schools for private schools in these cases, the future of these programs is in doubt due to litigation brought by the defenders of the establishment. Voucher supporters received a huge boost in June 2002, when the U.S. Supreme Court ruled in the Cleveland case that parental use of vouchers to send their children to religious schools was not a violation of the First Amendment's constitutional separation of church and state.

The voucher movement has stalled somewhat politically in the face of massive anti-voucher campaigns organized by unions and other opponents, reflected in referendum defeats in Michigan and California and in the Bush administration's retreat on the issue in its handling of the recent federal education legislation. Polls taken in 2001 showed public support for vouchers at 34 percent, compared to 44 percent in the late nineties. There remains intense support, however, among a cross-section of conservatives, libertarians, and liberals, who have converged especially around vouchers as a partial solution to the problems experienced by minority families served by substandard urban schools. Among the African-Americans who have strongly supported vouchers are former U.S. Congressman Floyd Flake and former Milwaukee schools superintendent Howard Fuller, the head of the Black Alliance for Educational Options. Interestingly, even Arthur Levine, the head of Columbia University Teachers College, in a recent op-ed piece, grudgingly came out in favor of vouchers as a last-ditch remedy limited to the "poorest Americans attending the worst public schools."

There would seem no rational argument for confining vouchers in K-12 to low-income families. It's not as if all other families are happy with public schools and, hence, don't need alternatives. Even without vouchers to defray costs, private school enrollments have been increasing nationwide, jumping 19 percent over the past decade. I mentioned that St. Louis has the highest percentage of school-age students attending private institutions of any major metropolitan area in the country. In Hawaii, which has the highest pecercentage of any state, one in five children matriculate at private schools. All kinds of parents enroll their children in private schools—some have special needs kids with learning disabilities, who enroll at places like Churchill School in St. Louis, while others have special needs kids at the opposite end seeking extra academic challenge, who enroll at places like nearby John Burroughs School. Admittedly, public schools face herculean challenges in trying to be all things to all people. That's part of their problem—in insisting on one-size-fits-all education in full inclusion classrooms, they risk fitting nobody. Vouchers may hasten flight from the public schools, but they may also force public schools to respond by rededicating themselves to the highest level of academic integrity.

Homeschooling

I have noted that private schools are not immune from pack pedagogy and that many, in fact, have been constructivist trendsetters. If pack pedagogy continues to reach into private schools as it has public schools, with the teacher-as-coach model taking hold, then there may be a dramatic increase in homeschooling.

Already, there are an estimated 1.5 to 1.9 million children being taught at home, with the homeschooled population growing by 15 to 20 percent a year. It may not yet be a "juggernaut," but more and more children are following the path once traveled by Thomas Edison, Sandra Day O'Connor, and William Buckley. Although closely associated with the Christian Coalition, homeschooling now attracts a diverse set of families ranging from the very religious to the agnostic, particularly those agnostic about the educational prescriptions offered by the K-12 establishment.

Whatever their motives for pursuing this option, here, too, parents often are harassed by the watchpeople of the status quo. Half of all states require homeschoolers to be tested annually, in an effort to insure that they are not being deprived of an education. But the concerns of state authorities may be misplaced. There is no evidence that the education received by homeschoolers is inferior to the one they would have gotten in a normal school. To the contrary, homeschoolers have bettered the national averages on the ACT and SAT.

Homeschoolers are thinking outside the box, something you would assume progressives would admire rather than condemn. If parents are to be the final arbiter in The Great American Education War, and consumer sovereignty is to triumph, it is important for more parents to think intently about education, to become better informed so that they can be advocates for their children. Public schools can only help themselves by connecting better with parents, sharing information with them, and listening attentively to their concerns. If they do that, they have a chance to retain their current 90 percent share of the nation's children who use government schools. If they are unwilling, then they will deserve whatever further hemorrhaging might occur.

Is A K-16 System Possible?

One hears faintly utopian calls today for the creation of a "K-16 system," that is, a seamless web of educational training, proceeding smoothly from pre-school and kindergarten through undergraduate university education and beyond, each stage building cumulatively on the other. The problem with this vision is that constructivists don't believe in the concept of grade-level expectations. We can't even get the transitions right *within* K-12—it is generally acknowledged that the laid-back "middle school philosophy" advanced by progressives has caused problematical linkages with elementary and high school—yet somehow we are supposed to forge a single coherent order from cradle to college. The question is whether, in trying to make a mesh of things, we may instead make a mess of things. Will we bring our higher education institutions down to the level of K-12, a system that has been characterized mostly by mediocrity, or will we raise our K-12 institutions to the level of academia, a system that, up to now, has been recognized as the best in the world?

I have noted that the education "disease" that has afflicted K-12 is beginning to infect colleges and universities. American higher education recently has been going down its own slippery slope, with a declining commitment to academic rigor. Witness the grade inflation at Harvard and other universities. Witness the lowered admissions standards at the elite universities (both state institutions, such as UCLA, Cal-Berkeley, and Michigan, as well as the Ivys), where affirmative action now allows "life experiences" to trump SAT scores and class rank. Witness the fluff that now passes for "general education" requirements ("students from Dartmouth to Stanford are getting academic credit for studying Star Trek, vampires, and Looney Toons"; at Stanford, students even can enroll in "How Tasty Were My French Sisters," while at Michigan, coursework is offered on "diva-worship, drag, and muscle culture"; and at the University of Chicago, long known for its demanding core curriculum, there are pressures to "lighten up"). Witness the growing "Let Us Edutain You" pressures felt at even the best universities, where an instructor must remember to "select texts with plenty of cartoons, illustrations, and multi-colored inserts to break up the monotony of the printed page." And witness the flow of beer, estimated at fifteen cases consumed per student per year, as well as the skewing of priorities toward college sports as "pigskin and sheepskin collide."

It is hard to say which is declining faster, academic standards or ethical standards. Plagiarism and cheating generally have reached epidemic proportions on American campuses, even touching the military academies and threatening to destroy the 160-year-old honor code at the University of Virginia. I noted earlier that technology is only exacerbating the problem. We now have videotaped lectures that are institutionalizing the cutting of classes, and distance-learning that may one day make homeschooling the norm even in graduate education. The University of Phoenix, a "virtual university" which offers all courses on-line, is a glorified, high-tech correspondence school that gives new meaning to the phrase "diploma mill."

A University of Illinois professor recently expressed the concern about the direction in which colleges are headed, as follows:

> That the university is exceedingly "user friendly" is beyond any reasonable doubt.... While Chancellors reaffirm their commitment to inclusiveness sans intellectual boundaries, lowly teaching assistants award gentleperson C's to functional illiterates.... University administrations now overflow with specialists assigned to rescue

the academically lame and halt.... I, myself, am known for strict classroom decorum—if a student must read the school newspaper during lectures, I insist that he or she not obstruct the view of those seated behind. My grading standard is brutal—A's are given only those with opposed thumbs able to walk upright.

The professor is exaggerating, only slightly. Things aren't quite this bad, but this could be the future if present trends persist. Notwithstanding the slippery slope my colleagues and I have been going down, there still remain at least some pockets of excellence in the form of honors colleges, and at least some commitment to academic rigor at most places, in terms of rejecting self-esteem and multiple intelligences theory as pedagogical lodestars, continuing to rely mainly on the teacher-as-teacher (rather than the teacher-as-coach) model, preserving highly demanding faculty tenure and promotion guidelines, and still expecting, or at least hoping, that students are able to demonstrate that they know "stuff" and that they can communicate this using complete sentences. Given what we inherit these days from K-12, however, it is unclear how long we can maintain these standards.

In a recent survey of high-achieving kids listed in "Who's Who Among American High School Students," "89 percent said cheating was common at their schools, and 76 percent admitted to cheating on tests themselves.... Fifty-four percent of those surveyed said they spend seven hours a week or less studying." Those are the better students. A recent study of nine high schools in California and Wisconsin found that "less than 5 percent of all students are members of a high-achieving crowd that defines itself mainly on the basis of academic excellence," while another study found that "62 percent of 10th graders agreed with the statement 'I don't like to do any more school work than I have to.'" The latest national surveys of incoming college freshmen compiled annually by UCLA's Higher Education Research Institute show students "increasingly disengaged from the academic experience."

It is not surprising that, as reported by the National Commission on the High-School Senior Year, "while 70 percent of today's high-school graduates go on to enroll in some form of postsecondary education, only half of those who enroll at four-year institutions leave with a degree. The main reason for this? They weren't prepared in high school." Maybe we in higher education should feel good about the drop-out rates, since it seems to suggest we still are enforcing standards, despite the distractions of beer, football, and other nonacademic fare. The more proper interpretation, though, is that there is a dangerous disconnect between K-12 and 13-16, one that is making the entire system dysfunctional.

At UM-St. Louis, for example, our English Department just this year finally was impelled to require that all English majors pass a course in Traditional Grammar, based on the fact that the faculty "noticed the quality of writing had declined in the last five years. There have been problems with basic concepts, such as subject-verb agreement and other basic issues." Apparently, non-English majors have been written off as hopeless. We also have to teach students basic work and study habits, such as my having to attach a "writing caution" to all my course syllabi reminding students that plagiarism is unacceptable and that their papers should be "proof-read before prof-read." I resent the fact that this is necessary, that my students did not get this message sooner over the past twelve years of their lives. Is it really a good use of our country's educational resources to have Ph.D.s teaching subject-verb agreement and kindergarten teachers teaching critical thinking? The downward pressures are such that undergraduate education may soon be the equivalent of what used to be high school, while master's degree programs may be the equivalent of baccalaureate education. The dumbing down pressures are even being felt in doctoral education, as there are calls for elimination of the dissertation requirement, traditionally the main hurdle to completion of the Ph.D.

A dialogue is needed here, also, if we are to repair the breach between K-12 and higher education and create a well-functioning K-16 system. University faculty, at research universities especially, could stand to give more serious attention to their teaching and to experiment with a variety of pedagogical methods in addition to lecturing. I have seen K-12 classroom teachers who could serve as role models for college professors, in terms of going the extra mile to enhance their students' learning. The inattention to teaching has reached scandalous proportions at some universities, where faculty, being reasonably smart and recognizing that the reward system favors research and publication, barely put in six hours a week instructing, when they are not on leave in a tropical rainforest or some other remote locale mining data for their next book. Its popular television major aside, Syracuse epitomizes what institutions of higher education should aspire to, as it has taken steps recently to become a "student-centered research university," with a focus on improving the undergraduate experience through involving students in faculty research and through better mentoring generally.

So, yes, higher education needs to put its own house in order. Beyond the tensions between the teaching and research missions, academia is also struggling with the issue of what exactly constitutes an "educated" person these days. As the former president of Cornell University has said, "As we enter the new century, society's agreement on what defines an educated person, what constitutes essential knowledge and common discourse, has essentially collapsed. As a result, universities in the United States have a problem in the area of curriculum.... Curriculum means, literally, a running track; but, in recent years, it has been called 'a cafeteria with little indication of which are the entrées and which the desserts' and 'Dante's definition of hell, where nothing connects with nothing.'"

Sandra Stotsky has suggested the makings of "an alliance between alert parents and university professors in the academic disciplines," aimed at getting K-12 to do a better job of preparing kids for the next level. Such an alliance, if it could be mobilized, might well make a difference in the Great American Education War. However, instead of the conflict being decided by opposing alliances, it would be preferable if it ended through joint cooperation. A possible way out of the disconnect between K-12 and higher education is to develop ways of bringing together the subject matter expertise, which is the forte of academia, with the commitment to pedagogy, which is the forte of the precollegiate realm. On my own campus, we have made a few strides in this direction, by creating joint faculty appointments in arts and sciences and the school of education, establishing a new Center for Teaching and Learning that features monthly discussions between education professors and colleagues in other disciplines, and instituting courses for future teachers that are team-taught by content experts along with pedagogical specialists, including current K-12 practitioners. More has to be done here and elsewhere, in the way of real cooperative learning, if a meaningful K-16 system for the twenty-first century is to emerge.

Education in the Twenty-first Century

Perhaps it is a quixotic quest to aim to resolve debates that have gone on for centuries. As we begin a new millennium, however, we owe it to our children to try. I come back to the themes I stated at the start. First, parents need to become more involved in their children's education, and taxpayers more vigilant about how their tax dollars are being spent. By my count, there have been some 280 school board meetings in Clayton since I arrived in 1988. I have attended 275 of these, give or take a couple. These were the meetings open to the public. I would have loved to attend, in addition, the executive sessions that were closed to the public, and been the fly on the wall listening in on the frank conversations one rarely hears in the public settings. I cannot begin to count the reams of paper I have handled in the innumerable curriculum documents that have been cranked out by the district staff which I asked to see. Even less countable are the hours spent simply thinking about these issues and chatting with fellow parents and others about them. I can be accused of a lot of things, but one I cannot be charged with is failing to invest time and effort to become informed. The more you put forth that effort, the more you have a right to be heard as a citizen.

Second, one should be wary of a false sense of accomplishment on the part of your child or your school. The number of "My child is an honors student" bumper stickers and "We are a blue-ribbon school" banners is multiplying in inverse proportion to NAEP achievement scores in math and other subject areas. The problems with K-12 education in America are not confined to merely the lowest-achieving students in the lowest-achieving schools. Your child may be bringing home A's, and you may therefore find yourself satisfied. But you need to ask how authentic is that A, how much learning does it really represent, and how much work did your child really have to expend to earn it? In many ways, the best students are the very ones being harmed the most by current trends in K-12, which are impacting equally Clayton, University City, and all the other districts into which pack pedagogy reaches, from Beverly Hills, Missouri (one of the poorest communities in the St. Louis region, next door to my university) to Beverly Hills, California. While we need to be concerned, of course, about *all* students, if we do not maintain the highest standards of excellence at the top, how can we have any faith in the academic integrity of what is happening below? The war of attrition that is being waged against honors courses and other forms of ability-grouping can only ultimately produce mass mediocrity, not mass excellence. Hence, we all have a stake in sustaining true academic exceptionalism. Those schools that promote it, whether public or private, should be celebrated rather than vilified.

Third, all parties—parents, teachers, administrators, professional development consultants, professors in schools of education and other parts of academia, state agency officials, and political and business leaders—need to engage in a genuine conversation about improving our education systems. The onus to provide leadership in engaging these various educational stakeholders in a full, honest discussion falls particularly on the members of the K-12 establishment, since they currently control the system that is primarily responsible for providing the foundation of all learning our children will receive.

We have no way of knowing for sure what the future holds for education, anymore than we could have predicted with certainty the events of September 11, 2001, when the terrorist bombing of the World Trade Center and the Pentagon changed our national psyche probably forever. It was on that very morning that President Bush happened to be speaking to an elementary school class in Sarasota, Florida, symbolizing the fact that education had been ranked in every public opinion poll as the number one public policy concern, domestic or foreign, facing the United States and had been preoccupying Congress for months. The Florida trip had been scheduled to kick-off a weeklong "Putting Reading First" campaign and to call attention to the administration's education reform proposals. Just as the President's classroom visit was abruptly cut short by his having to leave for Washington, so also the national conversation that had been occurring over education was suddenly put on hold. Hopefully, the national security threats stemming from September 11 can be put behind us, so that education and other pressing matters can be addressed. There is reason to believe that education will remain high on the nation's agenda, since the issues will not go away and since, arguably, they remain as vital to our national security and well-being as more visible military concerns. As a people, it is more important than ever for us to come together and work toward improving the education of America's children.

Notes

Chapter 1

page

1   reported in the news: Media attention to education mirrors polls showing education as a hot-button issue among the general public. A *Newsweek* public opinion poll taken during the 2000 presidential election campaign (on June 24) asked "Which should be the highest priority of the government in Washington?" Almost one-third (32 percent) of the respondents said education, compared to 24 percent for social security and 23 percent for health care. A poll taken subsequently by the Public Education Network in conjunction with *Education Week* continued to show that "Americans rank education as their highest public-policy priority," with 37 percent rating education above Social Security and Medicare. *Education Week*, April 18, 2001. Although the terrorist bombings of the World Trade Center and the Pentagon on September 11, 2001 elevated national security ahead of education, education has remained a top domestic policy concern.

1   The Great American Education War: I owe an intellectual debt to a number of "combatants" who have preceded me in sounding the alarm about the decline of American education. See, in particular, E.D. Hirsch, Jr., *The Schools We Need And Why We Don't Have Them* (New York: Doubleday, 1996), Diane Ravitch, *The Troubled Crusade* (New York: Basic Books, 1983) and *Left Back: A Century of Failed School Reforms* (New York: Simon and Schuster, 2000), and the numerous editorial columns in the *New York Times* written by Albert Shanker during the 1990s while he was head of the American Federation of Teachers.

6   Conant Report: James Bryant Conant, *The American High School Today* (New York: McGraw-Hill, 1959).

8   jazz band: The jazz band incident captured in microcosm the total folly of the progressive agenda. William Martin, a viola player in the St. Louis Symphony Orchestra and the father of a successful pianist produced by the U. City jazz program, many years later reminisced in a local news article that "you had to have kids who, by the time the program started, were already well-versed on their instruments. And in U. City, there are so many...people who are interested in their kids having a well-rounded arts education...that a lot of kids had already studied an instrument by the time they're playing in high school. So by the time they're playing in band, the band director doesn't have to go back and teach them their instruments. They can jump right into the music. And then if you have a creative person like John Brophy [the band director], who is bringing in new material that...challenges the band, it's just like a garden. You've got the good soil, and you plant everything right, and you get the rain and the sun at the right time—it's going to flower." Quoted in Paul Harris, "Coming Home in Triumph," *St. Louis Post-Dispatch*, June 10, 1999. As simple a formula as this would seem for growing exceptional minds and talents, the latest crop of educators coming out of schools of education, with their hang-ups about bluebirds not flying higher than redbirds, appeared unable to fathom it. They appear content to cultivate same-size, dwarf-variety seedlings.

11   upper-middle-class suburban locale: In 2001, Clayton was ranked 204th among the richest cities in America, as reported in *Worth*; cited in *St. Louis Post-Dispatch*, May 23, 2001.

Chapter 2

12   *Anatomy of Revolution*: Crane Brinton, *The Anatomy of Revolution* (New York: Random House, 1938).

13   field of dreams: David Tyack and Larry Cuban, *Tinkering Toward Utopia: A Century of Public School Reform* (Cambridge: Harvard University Press, 1995), and Diane Ravitch, *Left Back: A Century of Failed School Reforms* (New York: Simon and Schuster, 2000).

13   "bawl words into [the pupil's] ears": Cited in Jacques Barzun, *From Dawn to Decadence* (New York: Harper Collins, 2000), p. 138.

13   "guide on the side": Linda Darling-Hammond, a professor of education at Stanford University, typifies today's progressives, voicing the common refrain that teachers should be "in more of

a coaching role...—a 'guide on the side,' helping students find answers online, rather than a 'sage on the stage.'" *Newsweek* (October 29, 2001), p. 61. I am indebted to an unknown source for the "Socrates" quote, which I came across at a public forum on education. For the particulars of this debate, see Williamson M. Evers, "From Progressive Education to Discovery Learning," in Evers, ed., *What's Gone Wrong in America's Classrooms* (Stanford, Calif.: Hoover Institution Press, 1998), pp. 1-21.

14   "Criticisms of Public Education": I listed only some of the "Ten Criticisms of Public Education." See *NEA Research Bulletin*, XXXV, no. 4 (December 1957), cited in Benjamin Levin, "Criticizing the Schools: Then and Now," *Education Policy Analysis Archives*, 16, no. 16 (August 20, 1998).

14   "It's the education disease": Cited in Peter Applebome, "Buzzwords for Failure," *New York Times*, December 17, 1995. See Sykes' *Dumbing Down Our Kids: Why America's Children Feel Good About Themselves But Can't Read, Write or Add* (New York: St. Martin's Press, 1995). Also see Wade A. Carpenter, "Ten Years of Silver Bullets," *Phi Delta Kappan* (January 2000), pp. 383-388.

15   hundreds of billions of dollars: Figures on education spending can be found in Robert Samuelson, "The Wastage in Education," *Newsweek*, August 10, 1998, p. 49; Marci Kanstoroom and Chester E. Finn, Jr., eds., *New Directions: Federal Education Policy in the 21st Century* (Washington, D.C.: Thomas B. Fordham Foundation, 1999), p. 4; Martin Gross, *A Conspiracy of Ignorance* (New York: Harper Collins, 1999), p. 9; and Richard Rothstein and Karen Miles Hawley, "Where's The Money Gone? Changes in the Level and Composition of Education Spending," http://ericae.net/ericdb/ED396422.htm.

15      $2,235 in 1960 to $7,591 by 2000: Cited in Russell Roberts, "More Money Hasn't Made Public Schools Better," *St. Louis Post-Dispatch*, July 11, 2002.

16   apologists: See "The 10th Bracey Report on the Condition of Public Education," *Phi Delta Kappan* (October 2000), pp. 133-144, and Bracey's *The War Against America's Public Schools* (New York: Allyn and Bacon, 2002). The Berliner and Biddle book was published by Addison-Wesley in 1995. Another book in this genre is Richard Rothstein, *The Way We Were?* (New York: The Century Foundation Press, 1998).

16   "38 percent of fourth grade students": Kanstoroom and Finn, *op. cit.*, p. 2. These data are 1999 results. In 2000, "37 percent

of U.S. 4th graders ranked 'below basic' in reading [on the NAEP]—i.e., they cannot actually read." Similar problems have persisted in math and other areas. Chester E. Finn, Jr. and Kelly Amis, *Making It Count* (Washington, D.C.: Thomas B. Fordham Foundation, 2001), pp. 11-13.

16   "12th grade achievement has dropped from...309 to 296": Gross, *op. cit.*, p. 33.

16   "Nine year olds' 1999 scores": Tom Loveless, *How Well Are American Students Learning?* (Washington, D.C.: Brookings Institution, 2000), p. 6.

17   "In the Third International Math and Science Study": Gross, *op. cit.*, p. 3.

17   "In December 2000": Finn and Amis, *op. cit.*, p. 11. The 1999 follow-up TIMMS study found that American eighth-graders did better than American twelfth-graders but worse than American fourth-graders, confirming the conclusion that American students do worse relative to foreign students as they progress through the K-12 system. See the report in the *Christian Science Monitor*, December 5, 2000.

17   "The annual [bipartisan] Public Agenda poll for 1998": Elaine K. McEwan, *Angry Parents, Failing Schools* (Wheaton, Ill.: Shaw Publishers, 1998), p. 14.

17   "In 1995, 78 percent": Karen W. Arenson, "Classes Are Full At Catch-Up U.," *New York Times*, May 10, 1996.

17   "From 1967 to 1997": Richard Vedder, *Can Teachers Own Their Own Schools?* (Oakland, Calif.: The Independent Institute, 2000), p. 5.

19   "the leveller's axe": The reference here is to how the Bronx High School of Science, Stuyvesant High School, and Brooklyn Technical High School in New York City have struggled to remain elite schools with tough admissions tests and strong academic products, fighting efforts to make them more "egalitarian." The author notes they "are everything the public school system has mistakenly tried to eradicate." Heather Mac Donald, "How Gotham's Elite High Schools Escaped the Leveller's Ax," *City Journal* (Spring 1999). Also see "Elite High School Is A Grueling Exam Away," *New York Times*, April 2, 1998, describing the "nonnegotiable meritocracy" that is Stuyvesant High School.

19   "what had begun": Ravitch, *op. cit.*, p. 330.

21   harkens back to Woodstock: This argument is nicely developed by Robert Bork, *Slouching Towards Gomorrah: Modern Liberalism and The American Decline* (New York: Regan, 1996).

21   postmodernism: Among the critiques of postmodernism in acad-
       emia, see Allan Bloom, *The Closing of the American Mind* (New
       York: Simon and Schuster, 1987) and Peter Shaw, *The War
       Against the Intellect* (Iowa City: University of Iowa Press, 1989).

21   rigor and merit are now four-letter words: For a discussion of
       the attack on knowledge in K-12, see E.D. Hirsch, Jr., *The
       Schools We Need and Why We Don't Have Them* (New York:
       Doubleday, 1996). In *Cultural Literacy* (Boston: Houghton
       Mifflin, 1987), Hirsch made the case for a common core of basic
       facts and information all American students should share. His
       Core Knowledge Foundation is an effort to promote cultural lit-
       eracy through the development and dissemination of rich
       fact-based curricula.

21   "Mad has become mainstream": Cited in Chris Hedges, "For
       Mad, A Reason to Worry," *New York Times*, March 28, 2001.

21   "generational blur": Todd Purdum, "Behind the Wheel Driving
       the Nation's Culture," *New York Times*, September 17, 2000.

22   F. Scott Fitzgerald: It was the progressive-minded assistant
       superintendent for curriculum in Clayton who first brought this
       quote to my attention, in her annual "State of the Curriculum"
       report in 1999. I told her she should take her own good advice.

Chapter 3

25   "educational populism": E.D. Hirsch, Jr., "An Address to the
       California State Board of Education," April 10, 1997, cited in
       Common Knowledge (Winter/Spring 1997), p. 4.

25   academic haves vs. academic have-nots: An example of this sort
       of analysis of K-12 education is Jay Mathews, *Class Struggle:
       What's Wrong (and Right) with America's Best Public High
       Schools* (New York: Times Books, 1998), which attacks as elitist
       the practice of selective honors courses at the high school level.
       Mathews is the lead education writer for the *Washington Post*.
       Although his writings tend to have a populist edge, he has
       recently argued that the gap between high and low achievers
       should not be closed at the expense of the former. See "Ignoring
       the Gap and Raising the Bar on Test Scores," *Washington Post*,
       October 23, 2001.

28   4,000 public schools Blue Ribbons: See Debra Saunders, "A Blue
       Ribbon for Everything But Education," *San Francisco
       Chronicle*, October 1, 2000, commenting on the findings of a
       recent Brookings Institution study.

28   "only nineteen of these seventy": Tom Loveless, *How Well Are*

American Students Learning? (Washington, D.C.: Brookings Institution, 2000), pp. 27-28. "In the current BRSP application packet for elementary schools, academic achievement is the last criterion discussed, eighth on the list of eight characteristics." *Ibid.*, p. 30.

28   "It's a feel-good program": Cited in Saunders, *op. cit.*

29   "Only for My Kid": Alfie Kohn, "Only For My Kid: How Privileged Parents Undermine School Reform," *Phi Delta Kappan* (April 1998), pp. 569-577.

30   "I am one of those 'privileged' parents": J. Martin Rochester, "What's It All About, Alfie?: A Parent-Educator's Response to Alfie Kohn," *Phi Delta Kappan* (October 1998), pp. 167-168.

31   "serious critical and original thinking": Quoted in *U.S. News and World Report* (April 28, 1997), p. 12.

32   I expressed outrage: The Clayton *Cliff Notes* project was publicized in the *St. Louis Post-Dispatch*, May 13, 1996, in an article with the headline "Students' Cliff Notes Praised by Teacher, Editor."

32   "sole purpose": The quote is from a statement by Nelson Canton, an NEA official, reported in the *St. Louis Post-Dispatch*, June 19, 1996.

34   how math could be made fun and interesting: See Harold L. Schoen, et al., "Issues and Options in the Math Wars," *Phi Delta Kappan* (February 1999), p. 448. The authors of Core-Plus, a sister curriculum to Everyday Math and Connected Math, state that "using calculators removes the 'skill filter' that paper-and-pencil manipulation has become for some students." I discuss "fuzzy math" at greater length in Chapter 6.

35   there was talk of possibly eliminating at least a few of the honors courses: In the November 11, 1996 issue of *The Globe*, the high school newspaper, an article entitled "Students Get Caught in the Middle Between Honors and Non-Honors Classes" expressed concern that non-honors courses had been dumbed-down and hinted at the possibility that Freshman Honors English might be done away with in order to avoid the headaches caused by the elimination of the remedial curriculum. *The Globe* reported the chair of the English department as lending "credence" to the idea that "one way to fix the perceived gap between honors and non-honors freshman English is to eliminate Honors Freshman English," although no such step has yet been taken.

37   "they transition to CHS": This was reported on p. 2 of a Clayton 1999–2000 "Assessment Study."

37   "ironclad" policy: In a *Globe* editorial in February 1995, the B-policy was characterized as "ironclad." In a phone conversation I had with the English department chair on October 25, 2000, she indicated that an "elastic clause" had been amended to the original policy, whereby a sub par student could conceivably remain in the course depending on the outcome of a conversation between student, parents, and teacher. Out of sixty students in Freshman Honors English in 2001, one-third were overrides, as reported by the district superintendent at a meeting of the Citizens Advisory Curriculum Council in December 2001.

37   "end to honors classes": The headline in the *St. Louis Post-Dispatch* at the time read "Parkway South's End to Honors Classes, Talk of More Change Worrying Parents." Curiously, it was this same principal who was to succeed our assistant superintendent for curriculum after she left the Clayton district in 2000; to his credit, he had moderated his views about honors courses by the time he arrived in Clayton.

37   "The Dumbing Down of American Education": *St. Louis Post-Dispatch*, May 19, 1994.

38   "We're trying to be politically correct": *St. Louis Post-Dispatch*, December 4, 1997.

38   "the following are non-negotiable": Comment by David Hornbeck, cited in Peter Kinder, "Missouri Follows Kentucky Reform," *Southeast Missourian*, April 6, 1995. Hornbeck was with the New Standards Project, which was influencing many of the school reform efforts states were undertaking in the 1990s.

38   "we must cast aside old notions": Richard Andrews, "Implementing Missouri's Educational Agenda," draft, January 7, 1993, pp. 3 and 9.

38   "the demanding academic expectations": Patrick Bassett, "Science Academy: Excellence Need Not Apply," *St. Louis Post-Dispatch*, May 19, 1994. Students at Avery Coonley were allowed to continue to compete for individual awards, but the school awards were discontinued.

39   "New Trier Township High School": Carol Innerst, *Washington Times*, October 20, 1997.

39   "it took twenty people": Based on a phone call I made to a New Trier parent on October 31, 2000. The parent, in addition to having a child at the high school, was on the board of the elementary school which was a feeder to New Trier High School. She herself had graduated from New Trier many years earlier and noted how "since 1964 the school had declined academically."

39   "racial segregation": One of the consultants was quoted as saying that "ability grouping in Montgomery County looks more like racial segregation." Cited in Blair Lee, "Let's Quit Blaming the Schools and Teachers for Low Test Scores," *Montgomery County Journal*, October 4, 2000.

39   "fiction in concluding that tracking": Tom Loveless, "Searching for a Way to Close the Achievement Gap," *Washington Post*, October 22, 2000. Loveless is the director of the Brown Center on American Education at the Brookings Institution.

40   "Once again, we are faced": Beverly Jennison, letter to the editor, *Montgomery County Journal*, October 2, 2000.

40   Mathematically Correct: The Internet website maintained by the organization is http://www.mathematicallycorrect.com.

40   "John Adams students": Erica Zeitlin, "District Divided Over Whole Math," *Our Times* (Santa Monica), July 27, 2000.

41   "through AP courses": *AP Program Guide (2000-2001)*, pp. 4 and 41, published by the College Board.

41   I will leave to the reader to ponder: Some progressive voices have expressed concern that too many schools are still dragging their feet in opening up AP courses to a wider number of students. They argue that the AP test, taken at the end of the course, provides a safeguard against dumbing down, since the exam hypothetically is pitched to the college level and students must normally get a score of at least a 3 on a 5-point scale in order for most colleges to accept credit. See Jay Mathews, "Motivated Students Miss AP, IB Opportunities," *Washington Post*, October 30, 2001. Unfortunately, this begs the question of whether, with growing waves of students taking AP courses, high grading standards can be maintained in the future and whether, regardless of passing rates on the AP exams, the weakening of admission criteria for entrance into AP courses will lower the quality of the educational experience in those classes for high-achieving students.

41   A Jeffersonian Aristocracy of Merit, or A Democracy of Dunces: On the concept of an "aristocracy of merit," see Jefferson's Query XIV in *Notes on the State of Virginia*, written in 1787. The phrase "democracy of dunces" is borrowed from Andrew Ferguson, "A Democracy of Dunces?," *Washington Magazine* (1993), cited in *St. Louis Post-Dispatch*, November 10, 1993.

41   "the best twenty geniuses": Cited in Ken Colston, "Jefferson As the Nation's Schoolmaster," *St. Louis Post-Dispatch*, April 10, 1994.

42   lowest-common-denominator education: A good treatment of the current anti-merit mindset is William Henry, "In Defense of Elitism," *Time* (August 20, 1994), pp. 63-65.

42   "large public universities are the megamalls": "Best Colleges," *U.S. News and World Report* (September 16, 1996), p. 108.

42   "the most selective public college in America": Richard Moll, *The Public Ivys: A Guide to America's Best Public Undergraduate Colleges and Universities*, cited at the College of William and Mary homepage.

43   "the United States is squandering": Cited in "School Bored," *St. Louis Post-Dispatch*, November 5, 1993.

43   "the quiet crisis": Joseph S. Renzulli and Sally M. Reis, "The Reform Movement and the Quiet Crisis in Gifted Education" (Storrs, Conn.: National Research Center on the Gifted and Talented, 1990), mimeo.

43   "The post-Sputnik concerns": Sandra Stotsky, *Losing Our Language* (New York: The Free Press, 1999), pp. 36-37.

43   "in the least restrictive environment": The legislation, when first passed in 1975, was called the Education for All Handicapped Children Act. It was renamed IDEA in 1992.

43   A 1988 Supreme Court ruling: Anne P. Dupre, a former law clerk to U.S. Supreme Court Justice Harry Blackmun and also a former teacher, questions the legal, moral, and other assumptions behind full inclusion in "Disability and the Public Schools: The Case Against 'Inclusion,'" *Washington Law Review*, 72 (July 1997), pp. 775-858.

44   "Educationists now find themselves": Charles Sykes, *Dumbing Down Our Kids: Why America's Children Feel Good About Themselves But Can't Read, Write or Add* (New York: St. Martin's Press, 1995), p. 185.

44   "Nothing prepared Debbie Masnik": *Ibid.*, p. 183.

44   Jimmy...is described as": John Leo, "Mainstreaming's 'Jimmy Problem,'" *U.S. News and World Report* (June 27, 1994).

44   "repeatedly jingles a set of keys": Sarah Lubman, "More Schools Embrace 'Full Inclusion' of the Disabled," *Wall Street Journal*, April 13, 1994.

44   "my five-foot-two son": *Ibid.*

46   "I don't apologize for our high expectations": Jere Hochman, "Successful Teaching in Parkway Schools," *St. Louis Post-Dispatch*, November 1, 1997.

46   "The [NASBE study group] has looked": "Winners All: A Call

for Inclusive Schools," a report of the NASBE Study Group on Special Education," published by the National Association of State Boards of Education, October 1992.

47   "several leading education reformers": *Ibid.*

47   "inappropriate diagnoses of 'learning disabilities'": Jon Westling, "The Tale of Dozy Samantha," *Electronic Telegraph*, September 29, 1995; also discussed in Ruth Shalit, "Defining Disability Down," *The New Republic* (August 25, 1997), pp. 16-22.

48   "The basket of benefits": Robert J. Sternberg, "Extra Credit for Doing Poorly," *New York Times*, August 15, 1997.

48   Conant Report did nothing to improve the inferior education: Ravitch is very critical of the Conant report for "whitewashing" the failure of American schools to challenge large numbers of students. Diane Ravitch, *Left Back: A Century of Failed School Reforms* (New York: Simon and Schuster, 2000), p. 363.

50   St. Louis Career Academy: See a series of articles on the St. Louis Career Academy that appeared in the *St. Louis Post-Dispatch* on September 4, 1996, December 3, 1996, and July 13, 1997. The "innovative" pedagogy being implemented by this vocational school was essentially a carbon copy of that prescribed by progressives for all schools.

50   "no group of students [high or low achievers]": Jeannie Oakes, *Keeping Track* (New Haven: Yale University Press, 1985), cited in Debra Viadero, "On the Wrong Track?," *Education Week* (October 14, 1998), p. 30.

50   1990 review of the literature: Robert Slavin, "Achievement Effects of Ability Grouping in Secondary Schools: A Best Evidence Synthesis," *Review of Educational Research* (1990).

50   "[ability] grouping is by its nature an elitist strategy": "To Group or Not To Group: Is That Really the Question?," *Johns Hopkins Magazine* (September 1995), p. 49. For other criticisms of ability-grouping, see the forum on "Tracking: Should It Be Derailed?," in the Education Life section of the *New York Times*, November 1, 1992.

51   "we have arrived at a moment in our cultural history": "To Group or Not To Group," *op. cit.*, p. 48. This article features a debate between Slavin and Durden.

51   "detracking boosts the test scores": Laura M. Argys, Daniel I. Rees, and Dominic J. Brewer, "Detracking America's Schools: Equity at Zero Cost?," *Journal of Policy Analysis and Management* (1996).

51   "Somebody's going to pay": Statement by Laura Argys; quoted in Viadero, *op. cit.*, p. 30.

51   "the homogeneous grouping of slow-learning children": James J. Gallagher, "When Ability Grouping Makes Good Sense," accessed on the Internet on November 1, 1999. Gallagher, the Kenan Professor of Education at the University of North Carolina-Chapel Hill, was criticizing articles such as "Tracking Found to Hurt Prospects of Low Achievers," *Education Week* (September 16, 1992). Also see Gallagher, "Ability Grouping: A Tool for Educational Excellence," *College Board Review* (Summer 1993), pp. 21-27.

51   "students who are academically or intellectually gifted": Karen B. Rogers, *The Relationship of Grouping Practices to the Education of the Gifted and Talented Learner* (Storrs, Conn.: National Research Center on the Gifted and Talented, October 1991), p. xii.

51   "could greatly damage American education": James A. Kulik, "An Analysis of the Research on Ability Grouping: Historical and Contemporary Perspectives" (Storrs, Conn.: National Research Center on the Gifted and Talented, February 1992), p. 6. Also see John F. Feldhusen and Sidney M. Moon, "Grouping Gifted Students: Issues and Concerns," *Gifted Child Quarterly*, 36 (Spring 1992), pp. 63-67; and Feldhusen, "Synthesis of Research on Gifted Youth," *Educational Leadership*, 46 (March 1989), pp. 6-10.

51   "gospel [among progressives] that tracking is a bad thing": Viadero, *op. cit.*, p. 27.

51   "generally speaking, research fails to support the indictment": Tom Loveless, *The Tracking and Ability Grouping Debate* (Washington, D.C.: Fordham Foundation, July 1998); obtained from the Internet on November 6, 1998 at http://www.edexcellence.net/library/track.html. See also Tom Loveless, *The Tracking Wars: State Reform Meets School Policy* (Washington, D.C.: Brookings Institution, 1999) and "Will Tracking Reform Promote Social Equity?," *Educational Leadership* (April 1999).

51   "our children will be the losers": John F. Feldhusen, "Susan Allan Sets the Record Straight: Response to Allan," *Educational Leadership* (March 1991), p. 66, and James A. Kulik, "Findings on Grouping Are Often Distorted: Response to Allan," *Educational Leadership* (March 1991), p. 67.

52   John Dewey, the godfather of progressive education: John Dewey, *Democracy and Education* (New York: Macmillan, 1916).

52   "teachers should deliberately reach for power": George Counts, *Dare the School Build a New Social Order?* (Carbondale, Ill.: Southern Illinois University Press, 1978), p. 58. See Ravitch, *op. cit.*, chapter 6, especially pp. 210-214 on Counts.

52   "Where is the active contestation": This was a training session given by Peter Murrell of Northeastern University in St. Louis in the mid-1990s, on the subject of "New Directions for Professional Development Schools."

52   "the [K-12] paradigm needs to shift from competition": John L. Mahoney, "Winners and Losers in the School Game," *Education Week* (December 16, 1992), p. 36.

53   "adequacy": Cited in Charles Sykes, "The Attack on Excellence," *Chicago Tribune Sunday Magazine*, August 27, 1995.

53   "the Pol Pot of education": See Dennis Farney, "For Peggy McIntosh, 'Excellence Can Be A Dangerous Concept,'" *Wall Street Journal*, June 14, 1994.

53   "in 1969, 7 percent of all students": Arthur Levine and Jeannette Cureton, *When Hope and Fear Collide: A Portrait of Today's College Student* (San Francisco: Jossey-Bass, 1998), p. 125.

53   "since the Vietnam era, rampant grade inflation": Patrick Healy, "Harvard's Quiet Secret," *Boston Globe*, October 8, 2001. Also see the study by Ben Gose reported in *The Chronicle of Higher Education*, February 14, 1997 and July 25, 1997, cited by Bradford P. Wilson, "The Phenomenon of Grade Inflation in Higher Education," presented at the meeting of the Virginia Association of Scholars, Radford University, October 24, 1998.

54   At Princeton, 83 percent of the grades between 1992 and 1995: Randal C. Archibold, "Give Me an 'A' or Else," *New York Times*, May 24, 1998.

54   "at Stanford, an astonishing 93 percent": *New York Times* editorial, June 5, 1994. *The Times* was commenting on the fact that Stanford University, responding to criticisms about grade inflation, had just announced that "the failing grade will be restored and teachers will be encouraged to award C's and D's when deserved." Also see Valen Johnson, *College Grading: A National Crisis in Undergraduate Education*, forthcoming.

54   "studying 'Gunsmoke'": Russell Baker, "Idea for a Sitcom," *New York Times*, October 21, 1997.

55   "our absolutely myopic concern": Quoted in Wilson, *op. cit.* As an example of how an anti-competition ethos can be found in private schools and not just public schools, the headmaster of a

K-6 independent school in St. Louis (Tom Hoerr of New City School) has complained about a "King of the Hill" mentality.

55   Why not eliminate grades if they have become meaningless?: The College Board reported in 1998 that SAT "test-takers [college bound seniors] with A averages grew from 28 percent of the total to 38 percent in the last ten years"; this occurred as "the SAT scores of those students fell an average of 12 points on the verbal portion...and 3 points on the math." *New York Times*, September 2, 1998.

55   "The school board in Clark County": Albert Shanker, *New York Times*, June 16, 1996.

56   the best grade you could earn was a C+: Interview with Walter Ehrlich on October 25, 2000.

57   the score declined from 478 in 1963 to 424 in 1980: These statistics are cited in Robert J. Samuelson, "Merchants of Mediocrity," *Newsweek* (August 1, 1994), p. 44.

57   some 40 percent of high school seniors: Based on an extensive content analysis, one analyst found that, in the area of literacy in particular, schools in recent years had lowered the difficulty level of reading materials, with the result that students experienced increasing problems on the verbal portion of the SAT. "Baby-Boomer Books Faulted in SAT Drop," *New York Times*, November 3, 1993.

57   "it means every child in America": Charles Krauthammer, "Kids Look Brighter, By Decree," *Washington Post*, August 5, 1994.

57   "This is nationalized grade inflation": Bruno V. Manno, "The Real Score on the SATs," *Wall Street Journal*, September 13, 1995.

58   notoriously difficult analogies section: *Wall Street Journal*, June 28, 2002.

58   "trends in state results from the National Assessment": "New Practices May Jeopardize NAEP Statistics," *Education Week* (September 6, 2000).

58   suing state testing agencies: "Meet Edith, 16: She Plans to Spell-Check Her State Writing Test," *Wall Street Journal*, January 21, 2000. The article reports on an eighth-grade student in Oregon who has dyslexia. Also see "Dyslexic Would-Be Lawyer Sues Over Bar-Exam Timing," *New York Times*, October 23, 1997.

58   "in 1900, the...procedure set [forth by the state]": Steven Ehlmann, "Objective Criteria Will be Scrapped," *St. Louis Post-Dispatch*, January 2, 1996.

59   disparate impacts might be due to poor educational preparation and other variables: The famous Coleman Report noted a direct correlation between, on the one hand, academic achievement and, on the other hand, family support systems able and willing to reinforce homework and other regimens, concluding that there were limits to what schools could do to close gaps absent those socioeconomic factors. James S. Coleman, *Equality of Educational Opportunity* (Washington, D.C.: Department of Health, Education, and Welfare, 1966).

59   "The use of any educational test": Edward Blum and Marc Levin, "Washington's War on Standardized Tests," *Wall Street Journal*, May 26, 1999. Also see Abigail Thernstrom, "Testing, the Easy Target," *New York Times*, June 10, 1999. In 2002, under pressure from various groups claiming that the SAT was biased against minorities, plans were announced to revamp completely the core part of the test which assesses language and analytical ability. See "College Board to Revise SAT," *New York Times*, March 23, 2002.

59   "mounted a campaign in 1900": Ravitch, *op. cit.*, p. 90. Around the same time, *The Ladies Home Journal* also advocated against homework.

60   American students spend fewer hours on homework than foreign students: In 1999, a follow-up analysis of the Third International Mathematics and Science (TIMMS) Study that compared U.S. students with students from thirty-seven other nations showed that American students spend less time doing homework than their counterparts in other countries. "In both mathematics and science, U.S. students reported more often than students in other nations that they use class time to begin homework. Seventy-four percent of U.S. eighth-grade mathematics students reported often beginning homework in class compared to the international average of 42%; 57% of science students reported often beginning homework compared to the international average of 41%." U.S. Department of Education, "Pursuing Excellence: Comparisons of International Eighth-Grade Mathematics and Science Achievement from A U.S. Perspective, 1995 and 1999," December 5, 2000.

61   "Research really does not demonstrate": "Parkway Northeast Middle School Flyer," December 19, 1997, quoting Nella Conners, *Homework: A New Direction*, published by National Middle School Association, p. 37.

62   "an unpremeditated plot to destroy the students": Cited in Sykes, "The Attack on Excellence," *op. cit.*

62   "much to widen the educational gap": The quotation is from a book review of Etta Kralovec and John Buell, *The End of Homework* (Boston: Beacon Press, 2000), featured in the September 2000 *NEA Today* newsletter, p. 46. Similar thinking can be found in Richard Rothstein, "Easing the Family Burden of Homework," *New York Times,* May 23, 2001. Rothstein states that "it is unconscionable for educators to exacerbate inequality by assigning homework without first ensuring such [support services for poor households] are in place."

62   *Can We Be Equal and Excellent, Too?:* John Gardner, *Can We Be Equal and Excellent, Too?* (New York: Harper, 1961).

62   "creeping idolatry": Rory Ellinger, "Democracy Needs Public Schools," *St. Louis Post-Dispatch*, June 17, 1996.

62   "the egalitarianism of the American system": Michael W. Kirst, *Who Controls Our Schools?* (New York: Freeman, 1984), pp. 73-74. We certainly have come a long way since the beginning of the twentieth century, when formal education stopped for 95 percent of children at the end of eighth grade.

63   many high school students unprepared for college: Alex P. Kellogg, "Report Finds the Majority of U.S. Students Not Prepared for College," *Chronicle of Higher Education*, October 5, 2001.

Chapter 4

65   *Frames of Mind:* Howard Gardner, *Frames of Mind: The Theory of Multiple Intelligences* (New York: Basic Books, 1983). Also, see Gardner's *The Unschooled Mind: How Children Think and How Schools Should Teach* (New York: Basic Books, 1991) and *Multiple Intelligences: The Theory Into Practice* (New York: Basic Books, 1993).

66   "Multiple intelligences is not the name of a theory": James Traub, *Better by Design?* (Washington, D.C.: Thomas Fordham Foundation, 1999), p. 55.

66   seven "kinds of smart": The phrase "Seven Kinds of Smart" is taken from Thomas Armstrong, *7 Kinds of Smart: Identifying and Developing Your Many Intelligences* (New York: Dutton/Signet, 1993), one of the many books that owes its inspiration to Gardner. Armstrong has also written *Multiple Intelligences in the Classroom* (Alexandria, Va.: Association for Supervision and Curriculum Development, 1994).

66   "*Linguistic:* The capacity to use words": *Update* 36 (October 1994), p. 5; adapted from Armstrong, *Multiple Intelligences in the Classroom, op. cit.*

67   "spiritual" intelligence: See Traub, *op. cit.* On the eighth and ninth intelligences, see Howard Gardner, "The Meaning of Multiple Intelligence," a commentary in the *St. Louis Post-Dispatch*, December 26, 1995.

71   "I am a demon": Howard Gardner, *The Disciplined Mind* (New York: Simon and Schuster, 1999), p. 25.

72   "West End School Is Mecca": Samuel Autman, "West End School is Mecca for Intelligence Theory," *St. Louis Post-Dispatch*, December 3, 1997.

72   "Sixth-graders in small groups": Joan Little, "'Intelligences' Theory Applied in Local Schools," *St. Louis Post-Dispatch*, November 20, 1994.

73   "frowned and said": James Traub, "Multiple Intelligence Disorder," *The New Republic* (October 26, 1998), p. 22.

73   "explicitly political agenda": *Ibid.*

73   "Blacks and other groups are underrepresented": Carolyn Bower and Holly Hacker, "Some Minority Gifted Students Miss Out, Experts Say," *St. Louis Post-Dispatch*, December 3, 2000.

74   "MI pizza" pie chart: See Armstrong, *Multiple Intelligences in the Classroom, op. cit.*

75   "the only resistance we have had": *St. Louis Post-Dispatch*, June 4, 1998.

75   "using twists, turns, and pirouettes": *St. Louis Post-Dispatch*, November 23, 2000.

76   "I am a student at Villanova University": Posted at cathleen.gannon@villanova.edu on March 5, 2000; I obtained it through a listserve communication on November 24, 2000.

77   *"Adventure Tales of America"*: I received this in the mail from a colleague. The exact source is unknown. A related ad can be found at http.//www.adventuretales.com/features.htm.

77   "Michele Zuckerman's": Elaine K. McEwan, *Angry Parents, Failing Schools* (Wheaton, Ill.: Harold Shaw Publishers, 1998), p. 22.

77   "Andrea was an eighth grader": Charles Sykes, *Dumbing Down Our Kids: Why America's Children Feel Good About Themselves But Can't Read, Write, or Add* (New York: St. Martin's Press, 1995), pp. 5-6.

78   "programmers and polo players": Marge Scherer, "Perspectives/Martian Chronicles," *Educational Leadership* 55 (September 1997), p. 1.

78   "physically pretend to be graphs": Linda Campbell, "How

Teachers Interpret MI Theory," *Educational Leadership* 55 (September 1997), p. 14.

78 "children have difficulties recalling the letter and number": Statement by Valeria Lovelace, an assistant vice-president of the Children's Television Workshop, cited in Ralph Blumenthal, "Curriculum Update for 'Sesame Street,'" *New York Times*, November 19, 1995.

79 "bodily kinesthetic intelligence [refers to] using one's body": Thomas Hoerr, "Different Strokes for Different Folks," *St. Louis Post-Dispatch*, September 6, 1994.

80 "sheer fraud": My op-ed piece, entitled "The Three Stooges As Geniuses," appeared in the *St. Louis Post-Dispatch*, November 27, 1995. Howard Gardner's rebuttal, entitled "The Meaning of Multiple Intelligence," appeared in the *St. Louis Post-Dispatch*, December 26, 1995. (I assume it was the head of New City School who alerted Gardner to my article, since I cannot imagine how else he would have known about my existence.)

81 The entire K-12 profession: There are, of course, exceptions. For example, in "Neither Freak Nor Geek: The Gifted Among Us," *Education Week* (October 27, 1999), p. 36, James Delisle, a professor of education at Kent State University, comments that "for the past decade, thanks to the myopic work of Howard Gardner, who wants us to believe that 'all children are gifted at something,' I was beginning to feel that gifted kids no longer existed in the make-believe world of multiple intelligences." It should be noted that *Education Week* is unusual among K-12 publications for its balanced coverage of developments in the field.

82 "If I had called them talents": The statement was made in an interview on public radio in Boston, cited in Will Fitzhugh, "Polonius Redux," *New England History Teachers Association Newsletter and Forum* (Fall 1999).

82 "you can't go from neuroscience": Quoted in Valerie Strauss, "Brain Research Oversold, Experts Say," *Washington Post*, March 13, 2001.

82 "educators are making a very big mistake": Bruer's book is *The Myth of the First Three Years* (New York: Free Press, 1999). Quoted in *ibid.*

82 "MI theory has received an extremely mixed reception": Traub, *Better by Design?*, *op. cit.*, p. 56.

82 "Most people who study intelligence": Traub, "Multiple Intelligence Disorder," *op. cit.*, p. 21.

82 "is almost certainly wrong": Cited in E.D. Hirsch, Jr., *The*

Schools We Need and Why We Don't Have Them (New York: Doubleday, 1996), p. 261.

82   "Since none of the work has been done": George Miller, "Varieties of Intelligence," *New York Times Review of Books*, December 25, 1983, Section 7, p. 1.

83   "stumble badly": Cited in James Collins, "Seven Kinds of Smarts," *Time* (October 19, 1998), p. 95.

83   "at best useful fictions" and "there is not even one empirical test": These remarks are cited in Mary Eberstadt, "The Schools They Deserve," *Policy Review* (1999). Sternberg has developed the concept of "successful intelligence," which points to the existence of three categories of intelligence—analytical, creative, and practical. See Robert J. Sternberg, *The Triarchic Mind: A New Theory of Human Intelligence* (New York: Viking, 1988), and *Successful Intelligence* (New York: Plume, 1997). George Johnson, a biologist at Washington University in St. Louis, argues that the latest medical research confirms the traditional view that "one surprisingly small region of the brain is responsible for humans' general intelligence" and that "environment and education play a role in how intelligence develops—but not much." George Johnson, "One Surprisingly Small Region of the Brain is Responsible for Humans' General Intelligence," *St. Louis Post-Dispatch*, July 28, 2000.

83   "evidence for the specifics of Gardner's theory": Collins, *op. cit.*, p. 95. Denis Doyle, senior fellow at the Hudson Institute, bluntly says the theory is "not only wrong, it's dangerous." *Update, op. cit.*, p. 7.

83   "gives her fifth-graders": Traub, *Better By Design?, op. cit.*, p. 57.

84   nonliterate culture is driving out the literate culture: For statistical evidence on the decline of literacy, see Sandra Stotsky, *Losing Our Language* (New York: Free Press, 1999), and "Baby-Boomer Books Faulted in S.A.T. Drop," *New York Times*, November 3, 1993. Some of the discussion below is taken from my "The Decline of Literacy" article in *Education Week* (May 15, 1996), p. 34. I will discuss literacy at greater length in Chapter 6.

84   "elevate media-viewing": *Education Week* (November 29, 1995), p. 11.

84   television and films: On the rigors of movie-going, one commentator notes he "learned the hard way that a three-hour movie requires at least a tub of popcorn." Quoted in Michael Marriott,

"Films Face the Squirm Factor," *New York Times*, January 9, 1996.

84   "amusing ourselves to death": Neil Postman, *Amusing Ourselves to Death* (New York: Penguin Books, 1986).

85   Library of Congress reshelving: Joel Achenbach, "The Too-Much-Information Age," *Washington Post*, March 12, 1999.

85   reports of condensed versions of literary classics: Joan Little, "Littler Women," *St. Louis Post-Dispatch*, February 24, 1995.

85   leading undergraduate international relations text: John T. Rourke, *International Politics on the World Stage*, 7th ed. (New York: Dushkin/McGraw-Hill, 1999).

85   "What's next—pop-ups?": Comment made by Professor Neil Richardson of the University of Wisconsin, at the annual meeting of the International Studies Association, Washington, D.C., February 20, 1999.

85   "As survivors of aging print": Benjamin Barber, *Jihad vs. McWorld* (New York: Times Books, 1995), pp. 118 and 127.

86   "If they [students] still have not passed": "Why Johnny Can't Fail," *Harper's* (September 1999), p. 22, based on an essay by Jerry Jesness in *Reason* (July 1999).

86   "in the last four years of American schooling": Leo Botstein, "We Waste Our Children's Time," *New York Times*, January 25, 2001.

88   "Paying Attention Intelligence": Will Fitzhugh, "Multiple Alternatives," *New England History Teachers Association Newsletter and Forum* (Fall 1998).

88   "spousal intelligence": Steven Kirsh, "The Theory of SPURIOUS Intelligence," *Psychoillogical Bulletin* (Summer 1997), pp. 5-8.

89   "academic intelligence offers virtually no preparation": Daniel Goleman, *Emotional Intelligence* (New York: Bantam Books, 1995), p. 36. Goleman acknowledges his debt to Gardner, calling him "the guiding visionary" behind schools beginning to offer "education in life skills" (p. 37). Gardner himself has questioned whether emotional intelligence can properly be called an "intelligence." Richard Rothstein, in "A School District Refuses to Worship Scores Alone," *New York Times*, February 14, 2001, notes how the school district of Park Ridge, Illinois has tried to teach and assess emotional intelligence; a math teacher is described as "weaving emotional skills explicitly into academic lessons." Also, see Robert Coles, *The Moral Intelligence of Children* (New York: Random House, 1997).

89   "In May 1994": Sykes, *op. cit.*, pp. 39-40.

Chapter 5

91   "the *McGuffey Readers*": Michael Kirst, *Who Controls Our Schools?* (New York: W.H. Freeman, 1984), pp. 28-30.

92   rejection of Committee of Ten's recommendations: Ravitch notes that the twentieth century saw increasing efforts by progressives to utilize schools to impart certain "values" and "life skills" (moral and practical education for participation in civic life), aimed especially at the masses of newly arrived immigrant children and other "disadvantaged" children. Diane Ravitch, *Left Back: A Century of Failed School Reforms* (New York: Simon and Schuster, 2000).

92   "Hutchins disapproved": *Ibid.*, pp. 300-302.

92   "teachers were now being told": This was Ravitch's description of what Riesman had to say in *The Lonely Crowd*; cited in *ibid.*, p. 342. The argument that there is a strong strain of anti-intellectualism in American culture is most forcefully made in Richard Hofstadter, *Anti-Intellectualism in American Life* (New York: Knopf, 1963).

93   "Nurturing the Life of the Mind": Kathleen Vail, "Nurturing the Life of the Mind: If Schools Don't Value Intellect, Who Will?," *American School Board Journal* (January 2001), pp. 19-23.

93   schooling as social work: These criticisms are discussed in Martin Gross, *The Conspiracy of Ignorance* (New York: HarperCollins, 1999).

93   "to pour 60 gallons of education": Comment made in a conversation with Walter Ehrlich, a former University City teacher who later became a professor of history at the University of Missouri-St. Louis.

94   "an inclusive system for education of *all* children": "Winners All: A Call for Inclusive Schools," a report of the NASBE Study Group on Special Education, published by the National Association of State Boards of Education, October 1992.

94   "Everywhere, I found idealistic people": Rita Kramer, *Ed School Follies: The Miseducation of America's Teachers* (New York: The Free Press, 1991), pp. 209-210.

95   Goodlad: John Goodlad, *A Place Called School* (New York: McGraw-Hill, 1984), cited in Kirst, *op. cit.*, p. 53.

96   cooperative learning as repackaged nostrums: Although self-esteem building and community building are part of the same progressive project, there can be a tension between a preoccupation with self and a preoccupation with others. Diane Ravitch notes how Dewey and his contemporaries struggled with trying

to "integrate child-centered education with social reform." Ravitch, *op. cit.*, pp. 203-204.

97 "student centered and designed to unleash students' creativity": Reported by Mark Walsh in "High Court Turns Down Mo. Teacher's Appeal Over Firing," *Education Week* (March 17, 1999).

97 *Post-Dispatch* editorial supporting Lacks: A *Post* editorial writer did write a follow-up op-ed article expressing second thoughts about Lacks' teaching. Christine Bertelson, "Lacks Was Wrong: School Isn't Place to Hone Profanity," *St. Louis Post-Dispatch*, April 8, 1995.

98 "It is not so much Cissy Lacks who has been on trial": J. Martin Rochester, "Standards in the Classroom," *St. Louis Post-Dispatch*, March 26, 1995.

99 "Educating the Whole Child": News release by the Clayton School District, November 16, 2000.

99 "We felt it was time to eliminate long term, homogeneous grouping": The anti-ability grouping language was contained in "Clayton's Language Literacy Curriculum" report, p. 1, presented to the Citizens Curriculum Council, February 15, 2001. The wording created confusion among parents at the February meeting. One parent of a learning-disabled child, reading the report to mean that all ability-grouping had been eliminated in K-12 grades, was upset to learn that the high school still had honors courses. At my request, the head of the high school English department asked the committee chair to revise the report so as to clarify the fact that the district still had honors courses. The report was never revised to reflect this fact.

100 "a nationally recognized motivational speaker": News release by the Clayton School District, November 15, 1994.

101 "children in multiage classrooms do better": District Multiage Curriculum Study Group, "Multiage Curriculum Information," April 1997, pp. 1-2.

101 Meramec tops other schools in state assessments: The 1997 report also buried Meramec's resistance to multiage classrooms in the back of the document, rather than directly addressing the school's reservations about that practice. In the Clayton School District's 2000 Annual Report, *Milestones of Excellence*, the district reports that Meramec third- and fourth-graders scored higher than their counterparts at Glenridge and Captain schools across the board, in all academic subject areas. This tended to follow an annual pattern.

102   "I want our schools to mirror the real world": Conversation with Phyllis Stoecklein on March 15, 1995.

102   eliminating the multiage vs. traditional options: Technically, Captain also had "looped" classrooms, where students were not necessarily placed in multiage settings but nonetheless stayed with the same teacher for more than one year.

103   "violence prevention" curriculum: "Violence Prevention Curriculum," Clayton School District, 1996, p. 1.

104   "increase enrollment of African American students": "Academic Achievement Update for Clayton African American Students," a report to the Clayton School Board on March 7, 2001.

105   "The soft bigotry of low expectations": Taken from John McWhorter, *Losing The Race: Self-Sabotage in Black America* (New York: Free Press, 2000).

105   "we are giving special treatment to one group": *St. Louis Post-Dispatch*, July 17, 1995.

106   Clayton Advocates for Abilities Awareness and Parents of African-American Students: On October 16, 1992, the *Clayton Clipboard*, a district-wide newsletter, announced the formation of these groups.

106   Clayton is also big on character education: In fact, the current principal of Clayton's Glenridge Elementary School (who succeeded the retired multiage classroom advocate) was recently a proud graduate of the Leadership Academy for Character Education, "an intensive yearlong professional program taught by the nation's top experts on students' moral development." *West End-Clayton Word*, March 22, 2001, p. 2.

108   "progressive ed banished competition": Janet Daley, "Progressive Ed's War on Boys," *City Journal* (Winter 1999), p. 26.

108   "study, study, study": An Education Ministry official recently commented that "now we are going to try the sunshine approach, giving [kids] more chances to play sports.... We would like to give them some free time and the psychological freedom to do things they are interested in." Howard W. French, "More Sunshine for Japan's Overworked Students," *New York Times*, February 25, 2001. Japan is in the process of moving away from a six-day school week; see K.C. Myers, "More to Life Than Math Scores, *Cape Cod Times*, March 20, 2002.

108   "called the police—for a little teaching help": *St. Louis Post-Dispatch*, June 1, 1998.

109   "marching taught students to work together": *St. Louis Post-Dispatch*, February 28, 2000.

109   "the St. Louis Career Academy isn't": *St. Louis Post-Dispatch*, September 4, 1996. On the growing "school-to-work" curricula found in not only vocational schools but public schools generally, see Carol Innerst, "School-to-Work: Right Problem, Wrong Solution," in Marci Kanstoroom and Chester E. Finn, *New Directions in Federal Education Policy in the 21st Century* (Washington, D.C.: Fordham Foundation, March 1999), p. 101. The historical context of vocational education is discussed by Ravitch, *op. cit.*, pp. 78-81 and 323-327, and Kirst, *op. cit.*, pp. 34-38. A good critique is offered by Lynne Cheney, "Limited Horizons," *New York Times*, February 3, 1998.

109   "Today the purpose of schools": From a memo "to the faculty" in the Francis Howell School District, dated October 25, 1993.

110   "Within days of assuming office [in 2001]": Linda McKay, "Teaching Values Should Not be Out of Character for Our Schools," *St. Louis Post-Dispatch*, March 14, 2001. For various views on character education, see Thomas Lickona, *Educating for Character: How Our Schools Can Teach Respect and Responsibility* (New York: Bantam, 1991), Denis P. Doyle, "Education and Character," *Phi Delta Kappan* (February 1997), pp. 440-443, and William Damon, *The Moral Child* (New York: Free Press, 1988).

111   "were queuing up": Douglas Frantz, "Trouble at the Happiest School on Earth," *New York Times*, August 1, 1999.

111   "In the late 1930s" and "By the 1980s": Ravitch, *op. cit.*, pp. 273 and 427.

112   "The big theory": *Ibid.*, p. 426.

112   Few question the importance of self-esteem: The work of Abraham Maslow and Carl Rogers in the 1960s was especially influential in affecting popular thinking about "self-actualization."

112   "violent and criminal individuals": Roy F. Baumeister, Laura Smart, and Joseph M. Boden, "Relation of Threatened Egotism to Violence and Aggression: The Dark Side of High Self-Esteem," *Psychological Review* 103 (January 1996), p. 26.

112   related study on exaggerated self-image: Brad J. Bushman and Roy F. Baumeister, "Threatened Egotism, Narcissism, Self-Esteem, and Direct and Misplaced Aggression: Does Self-Love or Self-Hate Lead to Violence?," *Journal of Personality and Social Psychology* 75 (July 1998), pp. 219-228.

113   "one of the most disappointing aspects": Remarks by Neil Smelser of the University of California-Berkeley; cited in Ravitch, *op. cit.*, p. 428.

113   "self-esteem theorists have it backward": Harold W. Stevenson, "Oscars Made of Tin," *New York Times*, October 11, 1994.

113   "I believe that self-esteem comes": Cited in Cal Thomas, "Competition Is Key to Education Reform," *St. Louis Post-Dispatch*, September 27, 1996.

114   *Punished by Rewards*: Alfie Kohn, *Punished by Rewards: The Trouble with Gold Stars, Incentive Plans, A's, Praise, and Other Bribes* (Boston: Houghton Mifflin, 1993).

114   body of research that refutes Kohn: For an excellent analysis of the utility of external rewards, such as high-stakes external exit-exams, as a motivational tool encouraging improved student academic performance, see the work of John Bishop of Cornell University, who reports his and other research refuting Kohn. See especially John H. Bishop, Ferran Mane, Michael Bishop, and Rovira Virgili, "Secondary Education in the United States: What Can Others Learn from Our Mistakes," 2001; John H. Bishop and Ferran Mane, "The New York State Reform Strategy: Incentive Effects of Raising the Bar Above Minimum Competency," 1998; and John H. Bishop, "Do Curriculum-Based External Exit Exam Systems Enhance Student Achievement?," 1997. These papers are available from the Center for Advanced Human Resource Studies at Cornell.

114   pendulum is swinging back: For example, see Janine Bempechat, *Getting Our Kids Back on Track* (San Francisco: Jossey-Bass, 2000), Maureen Stout, *The Feel-Good Curriculum: The Dumbing Down of America's Kids in the Name of Self-Esteem* (New York: Perseus Books, 2000), "The Curse of Self-Esteem," cover story in *Newsweek* (February 17, 1992), and William Celis, "Down From the Self-Esteem High," *New York Times*, August 10, 1993.

114   "in a sea change from the gestalt": *New York Times*, October 18, 2000.

114   "thirty years after districts": Ann Bradley, "Muddle in the Middle," *Education Week* (April 15, 1998), p. 1.

114   "sacrificed academic excellence": The quotes relating to Howard County are taken from Peter Maass, "Study of Howard Middle Schools Criticizes Focus on Self-Esteem," *Washington Post*, October 11, 1996.

115   "an instructional method in which small groups": Elaine K. McEwan, *Angry Parents, Failing Schools* (Wheaton, Ill.: Harold Shaw Publishers, 1998), p. 147.

115   parents resent how cooperative learning exploits high-achieving

children: On the potential problems cooperative learning in heterogeneous groups poses for gifted students, see Marian Matthews, "Gifted Students Talk About Cooperative Learning," *Educational Leadership* (October 1992), pp. 48-50.

116 "the marvelous development of progressive educational ideas": Cited in Ravitch, *op. cit.*, p. 205.

116 "Among the means for developing attitudes": *Ibid.*, p. 125.

116 "A great many more firms talk": Adam Bryant, "All For One, One For All and Every Man for Himself," *New York Times*, February 22, 1998.

117 "these classes are simply no worse": Simon Veenman's study was published in the Winter 1995 issue of *Review of Educational Research*. The summary of the study, including the quotation, appeared in *Education Week* (March 20, 1996).

117 1,500 distinct ethnic groups: James N. Rosenau, *Turbulence in World Politics* (Princeton: Princeton University Press, 1990), p. 406. Another study counts as many as 5,000 distinct ethnic communities; see Bruce Russett and Harvey Starr, *World Politics: The Menu for Choice*, 5th ed. (New York: W.H. Freeman, 1996), p. 48.

118 7,000 distinct languages: Rosenau, *op. cit.*, p. 407.

118 "The new ethnic gospel": Arthur M. Schlesinger, *The Disuniting of America* (New York: W.W. Norton, 1992). Also see Ravitch, *op. cit.*, pp. 420-425.

119 "American education is no longer": William Pfaff, "Canada's Lesson in Multiculturalism," *St. Louis Post-Dispatch*, November 2, 1995. Interestingly, however, growing numbers of Americans, due to intermarriage and other factors, are refusing to identify themselves as belonging to a specific racial or ethnic category, thereby complicating the work of multiculturalists. Eric Schmitt, "For 7 Million People in Census, One Race Isn't Enough," *New York Times*, March 13, 2001.

119 multicultural studies on college campuses: See David O. Sacks and Peter A. Thiel, *The Diversity Myth* (Oakland: The Independent Institute, 1998). The odd result of a commitment to increased diversity on campus is often increased separatism, in terms of separate dorms for blacks and other minorities as well as separate graduation ceremonies and other segregated practices. For example, note Michigan State University's "first Black Celebratory" commencement exercise conducted in 2002, reported in "At MSU, Plans for Pomp Create Friction," *Detroit Free Press*, April 5, 2002.

119   "The critical question is": Lucien Ellington, "Multicultural Theorists and the Social Studies," *The Social Studies*, March/April 1998, pp. 57-59.

120   charges of female discrimination in K-12 education in math and science: Myra and David Sadker, *Failing at Fairness: How America's Schools Cheat Girls* (New York: Scribner's, 1994), and Peggy Orenstein, *Schoolgirls: Young Women, Self-Esteem, and the Confidence Gap* (New York: Doubleday, 1994).

120   girls may be doing better than boys: See Tamar Lewin, "How Boys Lost Out to Girl Power," *New York Times*, December 13, 1998, and Christina Hoff Sommers, *The War Against Boys* (New York: Simon and Schuster, 2000). Also see Daley, *op. cit.*

120   women outnumber men in law school admissions: Reported in *New York Times*, March 26, 2001, p. 1. Also see "Degrees of Separation: Gender Gap Among College Graduates Has Educators Wondering Where the Men Are," *Washington Post*, June 25, 2002.

120   "This we think we know": Christina Hoff Sommers, "The War Against Boys," *The Atlantic Monthly* (May 2000), p. 59.

120   cooperative learning thought to favor girls: The portrayal of girls as noncompetitive and nonaggressive relative to boys can be seen in Carol Gilligan, *In a Different Voice: Psychological Theory and Women's Development* (Cambridge: Harvard University Press, 1982), and Dennis Farney, "For Peggy McIntosh, 'Excellence' Can Be a Dangerous Concept," *Wall Street Journal*, June 14, 1994.

121   "distinctions by race are so evil": Cited in Ward H. Connerly, *Creating Equal* (San Francisco: Encounter Books, 2000), p. 3.

121   "African-Americans come from an oral tradition": "Teachers Are Urged to Connect With Pupils," *St. Louis Post-Dispatch*, July 16, 1998.

121   "Research about the African-American culture": Pat Guild, "The Culture/Learning Style Connection," *Educational Leadership* (1994), p. 17. Katherine Kersten, a critic of progressivism, describes the recent makeover of a gifted and talented magnet school in St. Paul, Minnesota, where the school board "is turning the school upside down in the name of racial and socioeconomic 'equity.'" She notes the district no longer seeks "to identify children of high intellectual ability [but instead] looks for superior 'problem solvers' gifted in the 'multiple intelligences.' *Never Mind the Facts*, published by the Center of the American Experiment, November 2000.

121   "dinosaurs or lost civilizations": Ravitch, *op. cit.*, p. 36.

121   Beethoven and his mother: This is suggested by Peggy McIntosh of Wellesley College. See Farney, *op. cit.*

122   "[Young people] need to learn": Edwin Yoder, "Civilization's Legacy of Riches from Dead White Males," *St. Louis Post-Dispatch*, January 10, 1996. For example, on the impact of the European state system on the evolution of the doctrine of sovereignty around which international relations has been built over the past 400 years, see Hedley Bull and Adam Watson, eds., *The Expansion of International Society* (Oxford: Oxford University Press, 1985).

122   "jigsaw classroom": Elliot Aronson, "Jigsaw Classroom Could Help Prevent Plague of Violence," *St. Louis Post-Dispatch*, April 8, 2001. Aronson is the author of *Nobody Left to Hate: Teaching Compassion After Columbine* (New York: Worth/Freeman, 2000).

123   "was a school that did basically everything": *New York Times*, March 11, 2001.

123   "Names can really hurt us": *St. Louis Post-Dispatch*, March 9, 2001.

123   increase in school health clinics: *New York Times*, March 11, 2001.

123   forty-five hours of community service: *Newsweek* (May 3, 1999), pp. 26-27, and *St. Louis Post-Dispatch*, April 24, 1999.

123   Littleton, Colorado "educational faddists": *Wall Street Journal*, October 29, 1993. The newspaper reported on a recent school board election in which the progressive candidates had been defeated by traditionalists.

123   "Hundreds of millions of dollars": Matthew Rees, "Can We Buy Safer Schools?," *New York Times*, April 27, 1999.

124   dodgeball "is something that should not be used": "Moves to Restrict Dodgeball on Increase in U.S. Schools," *New York Times*, May 6, 2001.

124   end to "elimination sports": A 1986 journal article entitled "Premeditated Murder: Let's Bump Off Killer Ball" was published in *Physical Education, Recreation, and Dance*. See *ibid.*

124   "parent, social worker, doctor": "Study Says Schools Should Stress Academics," *New York Times*, September 23, 1994.

124   "recent education reform efforts have fallen short": *St. Louis Post-Dispatch*, September 27, 1994.

124   "CED's insistence": This was one of his "Where We Stand" columns, in the *New York Times,* September 25, 1994.

125   "Traditionally the elementary school": The text was Edward

Thorndike and Arthur Gates, *Elementary Principles of Education* cited by McEwan, *op. cit.*, p. 57.

Chapter 6

126   recycled theories traced to Dewey: This point is made most clearly by Diane Ravitch, *Left Back: A Century of Failed School Reforms* (New York: Simon and Schuster, 2000), pp. 441ff.

126   "we must overcome the fetichism": Cited in *ibid.*, p. 73.

127   twenty-nine percent of incoming freshmen enroll in remedial courses: These statistics are found in Karen W. Arenson, "Classes Are Full At Catch-Up U.," *New York Times*, May 10, 1996, and Martin Gross, *A Conspiracy of Ignorance* (New York: Harper Collins, 1999), p. 21.

127   remedial courses in New York, Georgia and Kentucky state universities: Robert J. Samuelson, "The Wastage in Education," *Newsweek* (August 10, 1998), p. 49.

127   "the California State University system": Kenneth Weiss, "Cal State Expels 2,009 Students for Lack of Skills," *Los Angeles Times*, January 24, 2001.

128   writing deficiencies "very serious": Remarks in a letter to me, written in response to my letter of August 14, 1996.

129   "is not a theory about teaching": Richard L. Andrews, et al., *Implementing Missouri's Educational Agenda*, January 7, 1993, pp. 15-16.

129   constructivism and postmodern thought: To show how postmodern thought invited baloney-type thinking, Professor Alan Sokal, a New York University physicist, submitted an article to *Social Text*, a prominent postmodern journal, which the editors accepted for publication and which he later admitted was a "prank," an elaborate hoax consisting of completely made-up ideas designed to expose the silliness of constructivist theory. The editors did not find the prank very funny. See Stanley Fish, "Professor Sokal's Bad Joke," *New York Times*, May 21, 1996.

129   "The policy presents formal English": Tom Loveless, "The Academic Fad That Gave Us Ebonics," *Wall Street Journal*, January 22, 1997.

130   barely half of the public knows each state has two U.S. Senators: Thomas Dye, *Politics in America*, 4th ed. (Upper Saddle River, N.J.: Prentice-Hall, 2001), p. 120.

131   Piaget and constructivists: Jean Piaget, *The Psychology of Intelligence*, trans. Malcolm Piercy and D. E. Berlyne (New York:

Harcourt, Brace, 1950). G. Stanley Hall, writing before Piaget, advocated delaying instruction in reading and writing, based on notions of "developmental appropriateness." See G.E. Partridge, *Genetic Philosophy of Education: An Epitome of the Published Educational Writings of President G. Stanley Hall of Clark University* (New York: Sturgis and Walton, 1912).

131   "Our schools are in crisis": David Gelernter, "No—Learn First, Surf Later," *Time* (May 25, 1998), p. 35.

131   "that learning requires effort is another myth": Frank Smith, *Insult to Intelligence* (New York: Arbor House, 1986); cited in Nicholas Lemann, "The Reading Wars," *Atlantic Monthly* (November 1997), p. 129.

131   "The criticism of practice": J.R. Anderson, H.A. Simon, and L.M. Reder, "Applications and Misapplications of Cognitive Psychology to Mathematics Education" (unpublished paper) accessed on the Internet at http://act.psy.cmu.edu/ACT/-papers/misapplied-abs-ja.html.

132   "I learned to multiply": George Johnson, "Simple Repetition Can Have a Powerful Impact on Learning," *St. Louis Post-Dispatch*, June 30, 2000.

133   "We read a list of possible programs": This appeared to be a ringing endorsement for focusing on the basics, yet ARC then tried to dismiss the finding with the comment that "when evaluating this question, it is important to remember that work done by Public Agenda [the well-known bipartisan research organization that has uncovered vast public support for traditional education] has shown that the public tends to regard 'computers' as a fourth basic—reading, writing, arithmetic, and computers." ARC Executive Summary, June 9, 1999, p. 5.

134   "it's time to recognize that, for many students": Steven Leinwand, "It's Time to Abandon Computational Algorithms," *Education Week* (February 9, 1994).

135   "using calculators removes the 'skill filter'": Harold L. Schoen, et al., "Issues and Options in the Math Wars," *Phi Delta Kappan* (February 1999), pp. 445 and 448.

135   signers of *Washington Post* letter: See Debra Viadero, "Academics Urge Riley to Reconsider Math Endorsements," *Education Week* (November 24, 1999), and Julianne Basinger, "Scholars Weigh in Against Education Dept.'s Endorsement of 10 Math Programs for Children," *Chronicle of Higher Education* (November 1999). In addition to the four Nobel laureates (one of whom, Leon Lederman, later withdrew his signature), two

winners of the Fields Medal, the most prestigious prize in the field of mathematics, signed the letter.

135 "teach to the lowest common denominator": Cited in Viadero, *op. cit.*

136 "You would be doing your students": The letter was dated February 25, 2000.

136 Clayton board votes on Core-Plus curriculum: "Program Approved Despite Protests," *Suburban Journal* (West County), March 5, 2000.

137 "teaching and communicating science": *St. Louis Post-Dispatch*, January 18, 2001.

137 "I felt compelled to let you know": The op-ed piece, entitled "Trendy K-12 Math Curricula Don't Add Up," appeared in the *St. Louis Post-Dispatch*, May 16, 2000. The e-mail was from Professor Ray Balbes, on May 17, 2000.

138 "proposed that children read literature": Ravitch, *op. cit.*, p. 443.

139 "was a successful one-man army": James S. Hirsch, "The Grammarian Who Lost a War of Words," *Wall Street Journal*, December 29, 1994.

139 "superficial concerns": This was a comment made by at least one member of the Clayton Language Literacy Committee, in response to concerns raised by the school board when the new language arts curriculum was under discussion in 1994. At a board meeting on December 7, 1994, one board member rightly called such a response "insulting." The committee included in its membership a new elementary school teacher who had been on the faculty of the school of education at a local university, where, according to one colleague, she had developed a reputation as a "whole-language fanatic"; I was not at all surprised to learn she was on the board of the National Council of Teachers of English. Another committee member was known to suggest to her middle school students that they should not worry much about perfecting their spelling or grammar; this was reported to me by a neighbor's child.

139 "You are paying less and less attention": Remarks at the Clayton Board of Education meeting on May 11, 1994.

139 "I am enclosing a copy": Letter dated June 1, 1994.

141 "the holistic hustle": See Richard Mitchell, *The Graves of Academe* (Boston: Little, Brown, 1981), pp. 167-169 and 178-182.

141 "We started [in 1992]": Report of the Clayton Language Literacy Committee on February 15, 2001, p. 1.

141   National Reading Panel report released in April 2000: *Teaching Children to Read: An Evidenced-Based Assessment of the Scientific Research Literature on Reading and Its Implications for Reading Instruction* (Washington, D.C.: NIH, 2000).

141   "in the largest, most comprehensive evidenced-based review": "National Reading Panel Reports Combination of Teaching Phonics, Word Sounds, Giving Feedback on Oral Reading Most Effective Way to Teach Reading," NIH News Alert, April 13, 2000.

142   "The report suggests": "Reading Panel Urges Phonics for All in K-6," *Education Week* (April 19, 2000).

142   NIH/National Reading Panel's conclusions disputed: See E. Garan, "Beyond the Smoke and Mirrors: A Critique of the National Reading Panel Report on Phonics," *Phi Delta Kappan* (March 2001), pp. 500-506.

142   "pedagogical molasses": See Ravitch, *op. cit.*, pp. 437-438.

142   "right-wingers": Steve Zemelman, et al., "Sixty Years of Reading Research—But Who's Listening?," *Phi Delta Kappan* (March 1999), p. 515.

142   "illusion of balanced instruction": Louisa Cook Moats, *Whole Language Lives On: The Illusion of "Balanced" Reading Instruction* (Washington, D.C.: Thomas Fordham Foundation, 2000).

142   "flawed": Clayton Language Literacy Curriculum Framework, April 11, 2001, p. 23. It was presented at a school board meeting on May 16.

143   "Clayton's Language Literacy Document": *Ibid.*, p. 20.

143   "worshipper of conservative thinkers": One of the chief administrators of the school district called me that.

143   "the world's leading medical research organization": "Johns Hopkins Scientist Picked to Head NIH," *USA Today*, March 27, 2002.

144   "developing student writers": "Developing Accountability for Spelling in Writing," Rockwood School District, 1997, p. 34.

144   "spelling expectations for student writers": *Ibid.*, p. 35.

144   "invented spellings need to be phased out": *Ibid.*, p. 50.

145   "teachers need a plan": *Ibid.*

145   "Polls and surveys": Ann Bradley, "Public Agenda Captures Voice of the People," *Education Week* (October 11, 1995), p. 12.

146   "Signs of quiet revolt": Kate Zernike, "Parents Hungry for

ABC's Lead New School Movement," *New York Times*, April 28, 2001.

146   "In the past year, well-educated parents": Meg Sommerfeld, "Calif. Parents Target Math Frameworks," *Education Week* (April 24, 1996), pp. 1ff.

147   California in 1997 votes to restore basic skills: "California Board Approves Set of Math Standards," *New York Times*, December 3, 1997, and "In Math Standards, California Stresses Skills Over Analysis," *New York Times*, December 14, 1997. Also see Barbara Kantrowitz and Andrew Murr, "Subtracting the New Math: California Chooses a Back-to-Basics Approach," *Newsweek* (December 15, 1997), p. 62.

147   Mathematically Correct website: The website is www.mathematicallycorrect.com. It has spawned a competing website manned by the reformers, www.mathematicallysane.com.

147   "though the voices are loudest in California": Sommerfeld, *op. cit.* Tom Loveless has written about "the second great math rebellion," as "from coast to coast, articles in newspapers and magazines report parents organizing against their districts' math programs"; reminding me of my Clayton experiences, he observes that "across the country, disillusioned parents...report a response to their objections that reveals a breathtaking arrogance on the part of administrators implementing these reforms." Tom Loveless, "The Second Great Math Rebellion," *Education Week* (October 15, 1997).

147   "the new curriculum has enraged many parents": Anemona Hartocollis, "The New, Flexible Math Meets Parental Rebellion," *New York Times*, April 27, 2000. Also see "Levy Naming Panel To See if Math Classes Add Up," *New York Daily News*, October 3, 2000.

148   "I can tell you that I teach": Received March 15, 2001.

148   "He's one of these very evangelical supporters": *New York Post*, June 4, 2001.

149   "the 14th largest school district in the country": *Washington Post*, May 14, 2001.

149   Midwestern "firestorms": *Milwaukee Journal Sentinel*, May 27, 2001; *Detroit News*, June 17, 1998.

149   "A plaque in Andover High School": Mark Clayton, "How a New Math Program Rose to the Top," *Christian Science Monitor*, June 3, 2000.

149   Wayne State University mathematician: *Ibid.* The professor, Gre-

gory Bachelis, was accused of producing a flawed study and was threatened with a lawsuit.

150 "If medical doctors experimented": Reported in a November 27, 2000 news release prepared by NYC Honest Open Logical Debate, a protest group led by parent-activist Elizabeth Carson.

150 readings wars started in California: For a survey of reading wars around the country, see Gross, *op. cit.*, chapter 4, and Charles Sykes, *Dumbing Down Our Kids* (New York: St. Martin's Press, 1995), chapter 8.

150 "Honig...wanted not merely": Nicholas Lemann, "The Reading Wars," *Atlantic Monthly* (November 1997), pp. 128-129. For Honig's "recanted view," see "Preventing Failure in Early Reading Programs," in Williamson M. Evers, *What's Gone Wrong in America's Classrooms* (Stanford: Hoover Institution Press, 1998), pp. 91-116.

151 "good people do believe in alchemy": *Ibid.*, p. 133.

151 "whole language [had] been isolated": *Ibid.*, p. 134.

151 "most research backs the need for lots of phonics": "If You Can Read This...," *Newsweek* (May 13, 1996), p. 7.

151 "We want to alert the educational authorities of Massachusetts": Letter dated July 12, 1995, sent to Commissioner Michael Antonucci, with a copy to Governor William Weld.

152 Massachusetts state education department sympathetic to views expressed by the forty scholars: The deputy commissioner is Sandra Stotsky, whose *Losing Our Language* (to be discussed below) documents the decline of language skills in America and is highly critical of whole-language instruction. Stotsky has encountered stiff resistance to her efforts to toughen standards in language arts and other areas.

152 "has proved both popular and controversial": Jay Mathews, "Teaching History As a Matter of Fact: Va. Emphasis on Dates and Data Gaining National Recognition," *Washington Post*, March 11, 1997.

153 "a good education teaches": Cited in Randal C. Archibold, "What Is Good Education?," *New York Times*, January 14, 2001.

153 "The two great points": I am indebted to Robert Bliss, the Dean of the Pierre Laclede Honors College at UM-St. Louis, for calling my attention to this quote, which appears in the Honors College Handbook (Fall 2000), p. 1.

153 "educational objectives": Benjamin Bloom, ed., *Taxonomy of*

Educational Objectives (New York: Longmans, 1956). Bloom was later criticized by traditionalists for his association with Outcome-Based Education (OBE) and his emphasis on the affective rather than cognitive domain. He wrote that "the purpose of education and the schools is to change the thoughts, feelings, and actions of students." See *All Our Children Learning. A Primer for Parents, Teachers, and Other Educators* (New York: McGraw-Hill, 1981), p. 180.

153   statement from Eastman Kodak scientist: David Ross, received on an e-mail listserve on May 30, 2001.

154   1895 Salina, Kansas exam: Taken from an original document on file at the Smoky Valley Genealogical Society and Library in Salina, Kansas and reprinted by the *Salina Journal*; accessed at http://skyways.lib.ks.us/kansas/genweb/ottawa/exam.html.

155   "consisted of [several] vacuous statements": Diane Ravitch, "Higher, But Hollow, Academic Standards," *New York Times*, May 16, 1999.

155   "Wouldn't it be nice": Unsigned editorial, *The New Criterion* (May 2001).

156   Constructivism and early progressives: Ravitch, *op. cit.*, chapter 7.

157   "Gramsci saw that it was a serious error": E.D. Hirsch, Jr., "Why Traditional Education is Progressive," *The American Enterprise* (March/April 1997), p. 1.

157   "the school has again but one way": Cited in Ravitch, *op. cit.*, p. 223.

157   *Cultural Literacy*: E.D. Hirsch, *Cultural Literacy and the Idea of General Education* (Chicago: University of Chicago Press, 1988). This was preceded a year earlier by his *Cultural Literacy: What Every American Needs to Know* (Boston: Houghton Mifflin, 1987).

158   "progressive education works best": Cited in Louisa C. Spencer, "Progressivism's Hidden Failure," *Education Week* (February 28, 2001).

158   "13 innovators who changed education": *New York Times*, Sunday Education Supplement, November 2, 1997. A few traditionalists were also cited.

158   "lead to more creativity": Drew Lindsay, "Against the Establishment," *Washington Post*, November 11, 2001.

158   "distinctly old-fashioned program": "Teaching the Old-Fashioned Way," editorial in *Baltimore Sun*, January 15, 1995. Also

see Albert Shanker, "A Baltimore Success Story," *New York Times*, August 20, 1995.

159   Casey Carter: Casey S. Carter, *No Excuses: Lessons From 21 High-Performing, High-Poverty Schools* (Washington, D.C.: Heritage Foundation, 2000). Also see Michael Marshall, "Core Schools Outperform State Test Averages in Maryland," *Common Knowledge* 11 (Winter/Spring 1998); the newsletter is published by the Core Knowledge Foundation.

159   controversy over 1994 history standards: Ravitch, *op. cit.*, pp. 433-437 offers an account of the conflict over the history standards, as does Karen Diegmueller and Debra Viadero, "Playing Games with History," *Education Week* (November 15, 1995).

160   "authors tend to save their unqualified admiration": Lynne V. Cheney, "The End of History," *Wall Street Journal*, October 20, 1994. Also see her subsequent op-ed essay, "The National (Sub)Standards," *Wall Street Journal*, October 23, 1995.

160   "lies somewhere between comedy and farce": Diggins' book is *On Hallowed Ground: Abraham Lincoln and the Foundations of American History* (New Haven: Yale University Press, 2000). The quotation is cited in a review of the book by Edward Rothstein in the *New York Times*, October 28, 2000.

160   "If Europeans braved": Cited in Ravitch, *op. cit.*, p. 436.

161   "portray American history in a bad light": Cited in Diegmueller and Viadero, *op. cit.*, p. 34.

161   "Admittedly, the history standards": Albert Shanker, "The History Standards," *The New Republic* (November 28, 1994), p. 39.

162   "was to bring about": Cited in Ravitch, *op. cit.*, p. 434. Sam Wineburg, in *Historical Thinking and Other Unnatural Acts* (Philadelphia: Temple University Press, 2001), takes a more balanced approach toward content and process.

162   "like to pose as courageous progressives": Sean Wilentz, "The Past Is Not A 'Process,'" *New York Times*, April 20, 1998.

162   "Knowledge Still Counts": Albert Shanker. "Knowledge Still Counts," *New York Times*, January 14, 1996.

162   "Bill Gates is": E.D. Hirsch, Jr., "Why General Knowledge Should Be a Goal of Education in a Democracy," *Common Knowledge* 11 (Winter/Spring 1998), p. 14.

163   "widely lamented historical illiteracy": Ravitch, *op. cit.*, pp. 127-128, traces the deprecation of facts in the study of history to progressive ideas found in the "Cardinal Principles of Sec-

ondary Education" issued by the Commission on the Reorganization of Secondary Education in 1918, which created a new subject called "social studies."

163   "fourth-graders were asked": "Don't Know Much About History," editorial in *St. Louis Post-Dispatch*, November 3, 1995.

163   "can be read as a coroner's report": Lewis Lapham, "Ignorance Passes the Point of No Return," *New York Times*, December 2, 1995.

163   "Two out of three seventeen-year-olds": Gross, *op. cit.*, pp. 3-4.

163   "a nation of nitwits": Bob Herbert, "A Nation of Nitwits," *New York Times*, March 1, 1995. It may be small solace to note that the British public seems equally ignorant. A recent *Guardian* newspaper poll found that young people are especially so, as "young 18- to 24-year-old British adults are measurably 'dumber' than older age groups. British youth emerge consistently as knowing less...than older people about many of the main events and personalities of British history and culture. Fewer than a third of them can name Winston Churchill, Britain's war-time hero, as a prime minister who served before 1945." John Ezard, "Poll Finds Young Brits 'Dumber' Than Oldsters," *The Guardian*, October 28, 2000.

164   "young people are in danger": David Broder, "Young People Are in Danger of Losing America's Civic Memory," *St. Louis Post-Dispatch*, July 4, 2000.

164   "there are no real-world examples": Carter, *op. cit.*, p. 28.

164   "writing process" model: The history of the "writing process" model and how it came to dominate English composition is traced in Heather Mac Donald, "Why Johnny Can't Write," *The Public Interest* (Summer 1995), pp. 3-13. Also, see John Simon, *Paradigms Lost: Reflections on Literacy and Its Decline* (Baltimore: Penguin Books, 1976).

165   "it doesn't even tell you": Remark by John Mayher of New York University, quoted in *Education Week* (November 29, 1995), p. 11. The absurdity of this comment is captured by the famed Harvard paleontologist Stephen Jay Gould, who, expressing bewilderment over the absence of important content in the science curriculum of some school districts, remarked, "It's like saying, 'we're going to continue to teach English, but you don't have to teach grammar anymore.'" Interview by Claudia Dreifus, *New York Times*, December 21, 1999.

165   "out of some 340 sessions": Martha Kollin, in "The Great Debate (Again): Teaching Grammar and Usage," a special issue

of *English Journal* (November 1996), p. 27. See also the article by Ed Vavra in the same volume. The Assembly has succeeded recently in getting NCTE to pay at least a modicum of attention to grammar.

165   Stotsky blows the whistle: Sandra Stotsky, *Losing Our Language* (New York: The Free Press, 1999).

165   "writers should be encouraged": Cited in *ibid.*, pp. 212-213.

166   "With the new English standards": "The Decline of Literacy," *Education Week* (May 15, 1996), p. 34. The article by the NCTE director, Miles Myers, was "Where the Debate About English Standards Goes Wrong," p. 48.

166   "From kindergarten through secondary education": "Grammar Slammer," *Insights* (Spring 1997), p. 1.

166   "I learned about grammar": David Mulroy, "The War Against Grammar," *Wisconsin Interest* (Fall/Winter 1999), p. 12.

167   Flesch and Chall: Rudolf Flesch, *Why Johnny Can't Read* (New York: Harper and Row, 1955), and Jeanne Chall, *Learning to Read: The Great Debate* (New York: MGraw-Hill, 1967). For more recent confirmation of Flesch and Chall, see Jack M. Fletcher and G. Reid Lyon, "Reading: A Research-Based Approach," in Williamson Evers, ed., *What's Gone Wrong in America's Classrooms* (Stanford: Hoover Institution Press, 1998), pp. 49-90.

167   reading wars in 1980s: For a brief history of the reading wars, see Ravitch, *op. cit.*, pp. 443-450, Lemann, *op. cit.*, pp. 129-130, Elaine K. McEwan, *Angry Parents, Failing Schools* (Wheaton, Ill.: Shaw Publishers, 1998), pp.86-92, and Art Levine, "The Great Debate Revisited," *Atlantic Monthly* (December 1994), pp. 38-44.

167   "reject negative, elitist, racist views": Quoted in Ravitch, *op. cit.*, p. 444. See Goodman, *What's Whole in Whole Language?* (Exeter, N.H.: Heinemann, 1986).

167   "despite the efforts of the defenders": Stotsky, *op. cit.*, p. 268.

167   "need to take a close look": *Ibid.*, pp. 3 and 13-14.

168   "long-term use of simplified texts": Donald P. Hayes and Loreen T. Wolfer, "Was the Decline in SAT Verbal Scores Caused by Simplified Textbooks?," unpublished manuscript prepared for the *Journal of Educational Research* (1993).

168   "the nationwide decline in verbal [SAT] scores": "Baby-Boomer Books Faulted in SAT Drop," *New York Times*, November 3, 1993.

168   "the latest dismal NAEP scores": E.D. Hirsch, Jr., "The Latest Dismal NAEP Scores," *Education Week* (May 2, 2001).

168   "two-thirds of students tested": Kate Zernike, "Gap Widens Between Best and Worst on U.S. Reading Test," *New York Times*, April 7, 2001. Also see *New York Times*, November 9, 1997, reporting "12th graders are losing reading skills."

169   "are so remarkably vague": Quoted in the *Wall Street Journal*, May 26, 1996. Also, see Albert Shanker, "What Standards?," *New York Times*, April 7, 1996.

169   "ebonics with an equals sign": Tony Snow, "Save Us from the 'New-New Math,'" *Boston Globe*, April 21, 2001.

169   Kline: Morris Kline, *Why Johnny Can't Add: The Failure of the New Math* (New York: St. Martin's Press, 1973).

169   "Like the new math of the 1960s": Ravitch, *op. cit.*, p. 439.

170   "Heap praise on kids": Snow, *op. cit.*

170   "So you've got thirteen": Cited in "Math Wars," a *Wall Street Journal* editorial on January 4, 2000.

170   making math fun for girls and minorities: The debate over computation skills has been cast as a "struggle for economic and social justice," with many progressive educators believing that "traditional instruction dooms most students to failure." Barry Simon, a professor at Cal-Tech and an opponent of constructivist math, questions this view, arguing that "if anyone is racist or sexist, it is those who claim that women and minorities are unable to deal with traditional mathematics." See Richard Colvin, "Debate Over How to Teach Math Takes Cultural Turn," *Los Angeles Times*, March 17, 2000.

170   "psychic toll": Leinwand, *op. cit.*

170   calculator dependency harms inner-city children: Daniel Golden, "Calculators May Be Wrong Answer as 'Digital Divide' Widens in Schools: Low-Income, Minority Students More Likely to Use Them," *Wall Street Journal*, December 15, 2000. Also see Jay Mathews, "Some Educators Say Saxon Math Books Are Great Teaching Tools, But Many School Systems Refuse to Use Them," *Washington Post*, June 19, 2001.

171   "According to the Third TIMSS": David Klein, "Math Problems: Why the U.S. Department of Education's Recommended Math Programs Don't Add Up," *American School Board Journal* 187 (April 2000), p. 54. Also, see Jamie Campbell and Qilin Xue, "Cognitive Arithmetic Across Cultures," *Journal of Experimental Psychology* (June 2001), which found that "better performance on the complex arithmetic was associated with

lower reported calculator use in elementary and secondary school."

171   "Japanese and Chinese teachers": Accessed through the Mathematically Correct website at http://mathematicallycorrect.com in an on-line discussion of the NCTM standards. Also see Wayne Bishop, "Mathematics Education: Where Are We Now?," paper delivered at the Core Knowledge Foundation Annual Conference, March 12, 1998.

171   "The reason for the New Math": Cited in "Math Wars," *op. cit.*

171   "the [U.S.] Department of Education's expert panel": Mark Clayton, "Flaws in the Evaluation Process," *Christian Science Monitor*, June 3, 2000. For example, Harold Schoen, who was a co-director of Core-Plus, also was responsible for some evaluative studies used as a basis for the panel's decisions. Schoen and his colleagues present their case in Harold L. Schoen, et al., "Issues and Options in the Math Wars," *Phi Delta Kappan* (February 1999), pp. 444-453.

172   Leinwand seat on advisory boards: Mark Clayton, "How a New Math Program Rose to the Top," *Christian Science Monitor*, May 23, 2000.

172   "second great math rebellion": Loveless, "The Second Great Math Rebellion," *op. cit.*

172   "in my view, a test of eighth-grade students": Quoted in *Education Week* (October 1, 1997), p. 27.

172   "wrote a vivid critique": The description is taken from Ravitch, *op. cit.*, p. 440.

172   "wacko math": Quoted in McEwan, *op. cit.*, pp. 125-126.

172   "The new results": Louis V. Gerstner and Tommy Thompson, "The Problem Isn't Kids," *New York Times*, December 8, 2000. Also see Diana Jean Schemo, "8th Graders Fall Off from 4th Grade," *New York Times*, December 6, 2000.

173   "the most comprehensive and rigorous": Ethan Bronner, "U.S. High School Seniors Among Worst in Math and Science," *New York Times*, February 25, 1998.

173   American vs. Asian students: For the view that the TIMSS data provide valid comparisons between American and foreign students, see Harold W. Stevenson, "Mathematics Achievement: First in the World by the Year 2000?," in Williamson Evers, ed., *What's Gone Wrong in America's Classrooms?* (Stanford: Hoover Institution Press, 1998), pp. 137-154.

173   NAEP tests show little progress: See Tom Loveless, *How Well*

Are American Students Learning? (Washington, D.C.: Brookings Institution, 2000).

173   13,000 Ph.D.s: Gross, *op. cit.*, p. 7.

173   "While not abandoning": Anemona Hartocollis, "Math Teachers Back Return of Education in Basic Skills," *New York Times*, April 13, 2000. The NCTM president stated, "Teachers shouldn't say the correct answer doesn't matter. In our zeal to make sure we're focusing on understanding, we cannot forget correct answers matter." This statement was made at the time a preliminary draft of the revised standards appeared; quoted in David J. Hoff, "Math Council Again Mulling Standards," *Education Week* (November 4, 1998).

173   "Now school districts throughout the country": Bill Evers and Jim Milgram, "The New Consensus in Math: Skills Matter," *Education Week* (May 24, 2000), p. 56. In the words of the Johns Hopkins mathematician Stephen Wilson, directed toward parents, "When you send your kids to college, send them with basic mathematics skills down pat or I and my colleagues nationwide will flunk them." "What You Must Learn in School for Success in Math," *Montgomery Gazette*, December 22, 2000.

174   "my students are always pushed": Quoted in *St. Louis Post-Dispatch*, May 31, 2001.

Chapter 7

175   "He was another in the long line": Jacques Barzun, *From Dawn to Decadence: 1500 to the Present* (New York: Harper Collins, 2000), pp. 180-181. Two other seventeenth-century thinkers who presaged constructivism, and were instrumental in bringing Comenius to Oxford University, were John Drury and Samuel Hartlib. Where many of these early progressive thinkers differed from today's counterparts is that they believed in "streaming," or ability-grouping.

176   "children can and should learn": Williamson M. Evers, "From Progressive Education to Discovery Learning," in Evers, ed., *What's Gone Wrong in America's Classrooms* (Stanford: Hoover Institution Press, 1998), p. 2. An extensive criticism of Rousseau and his Romantic vision of education is found in E.D. Hirsch, Jr., *The Schools We Need and Why We Don't Have Them* (New York: Doubleday, 1996).

176   "do nothing": Cited in Diane Ravitch, *Left Back: A Century of Failed School Reforms* (New York: Simon and Schuster, 2000), p. 170.

176 Rousseau abandoned his children: Paul Johnson, *Intellectuals* (New York: Harper and Row, 1988), p. 21. Johnson calls Rousseau "an interesting madman."

176 "Ellen Key": Barzun, *op. cit.*, pp. 608-609.

176 Dewey as pivotal figure in child-centered education: Oddly, for someone who believed so much in learning by doing, Dewey did not set a particularly good example. As Ravitch points out, "despite Dewey's gospel of learning by doing, the great philosopher taught by standing in front of class and lecturing." Ravitch, *op. cit.*, p. 178. Ravitch discusses the influence of Dewey on the "activity movement" and other twentieth-century educational fads throughout her book.

177 "[It was] the perfect book": *Ibid.*, p. 387.

177 "Neill's paean to student freedom": *Ibid.*

178 "something akin to a secular religion": *Ibid.*, p. 442. Ravitch here was quoting Paul Cobb of Vanderbilt University.

178 "generation of absentee parents": The quotation is attributed to Leonard Steinhord of American University.

178 "chaperons": Ravitch, *op. cit.*, p. 302.

178 "It's like going to a golf pro": Cited in Carol Innerst, "Students Fall Behind All Along the Way," *Washington Times*, October 20, 1997, p. A-12.

180 "large person": Expeditionary Learning Informational Packet, May 6, 1998. The document indicated that "Expeditionary Learning is a comprehensive school design for grades K-12 based on principles that grow from the experience of Outward Bound, founded in Great Britain."

181 House of Tots: Barzun, p. 609.

182 Reggio devalues alphabet charts: See "Reggio Technique Builds Thinking Skills," *St. Louis Suburban Journal*, October 12, 1997.

182 average Clayton teacher salary: The Clayton data are from the Clayton School District's 2000 annual report, *Milestones of Excellence*, p. 3. The national data are from Martin Gross, *A Conspiracy of Ignorance* (New York: Harper Collins, 1999), p. 9. Also, data on the St. Louis area as a whole are provided by the Cooperating School Districts, *Teacher Salaries/Benefits, 1999-2000*.

182 "Listening to a story or a speech": Bill Mendelsohn, "In Defense of the Lecture," *Clayton Curriculum Quarterly* (May 1999).

184 "Open enrollment, no testing required": *Mindwonders* 12 (Fall 2000).

184   "the idea is to learn by doing": "Ordinary Tasks Best Demonstrate Science Concepts, Wellston Teacher Says," *St. Louis Post-Dispatch*, November 10, 1997.

185   "the school board has approved": "Area Schools Turn Learning into an Expedition," *St. Louis Post-Dispatch*, June 7, 2001.

185   "Before Matt leaves": "Getting Down and Dirty," *St. Louis Post-Dispatch*, May 25, 2001.

185   "reduce the sage on the stage": Parkway Northeast Middle School, Friday Flyer, February 13, 1998.

185   "rows of quiet well-disciplined children": Interview in the *West End-Clayton Word*, August 14, 1997.

186   "Alpine Valley": Albert Shanker, "What's New?," *New York Times*, December 3, 1995.

186   "No one contests": Gilbert Sewall, "Lost in Action: Are Time-Consuming, Trivializing Activities Displacing the Cultivation of Active *Minds*?," *American Educator* (Summer 2000), pp. 4-6.

186   "Activities expand exponentially": *Ibid.*, p. 6.

187   "This content needs no dressing up": *Ibid.*, pp. 7-9.

187   "It is an enigma": John Hoven, "Let's Readjust This 'Fuzzy' Math Picture," *The Montgomery County Gazette*, August 8, 1999. Hoven quotes Richard Hofstadter, the intellectual historian: "The new education [urged by progressives like John Dewey] prided itself on the realism of recognizing and accepting the intellectual limitations of the masses, and yet on the idealism of accepting, encouraging, and providing for the least able members of the student body. It was founded upon a primary regard for the child, and avoided making large claims upon his abilities."

187   "a student who is doing and experiencing": *St. Louis Post-Dispatch*, April 30, 1998.

188   "when you ask a black male": "Teachers Are Urged to Connect With Pupils," *St. Louis Post Dispatch*, July 16, 1998. On the successful use of direct instruction with African-American students, male and female, see William Raspberry, "Tried, True, and Ignored," *Washington Times*, February 2, 1998.

188   Sizer's Dewey-like learning principles: Theodore Sizer, *Horace's Compromise—The Dilemma of the American High School* (Boston: Houghton Mifflin, 1984).

188   "research challenging the effectiveness": "Acclaimed Reforms of U.S. Education Are Popular but Unproved," *Wall Street Journal*, December 28, 1994. Also see James Traub, *Better by Design?*

(Washington, D.C.: Thomas B. Fordham Foundation, 1999), pp. 25-29.

190   "a certain noise level": Ravitch, *op. cit.*, p. 396. The open education movement is discussed on pp. 395-397.

191   "It reduces the overall amount of time": Elaine K. McEwan, *Angry Parents, Failing Schools* (Wheaton, Ill.: Harold Shaw Publishers, 1998), p. 145. McEwan cites two websites containing useful information on block scheduling. One is "Block Scheduling Sources and Connections" (http://www.jbit.com/bs2.htm) and "The Case Against Block Scheduling" (http://athnet.net/~jlindsay/Block.shtml#wronko).

192   "Recently I helped form": The letter was written by Jan Knape on May 19, 1994.

192   Ladue High School has not resisted fad: "Board Backs Block Schedule," *St. Louis Suburban Journal*, April 21, 1999. The article noted that "a controversial block schedule for Ladue High School was approved despite pleas from some parents and students."

192   "it brings equity": "New School Schedules Aim to Make Time, Money Count," *St. Louis Post-Dispatch*, October 21, 1997.

192   "Some teachers are ending their lectures": "Kids' Homework May Be Going the Way of the Dinosaur," *Wall Street Journal*, October 11, 1993.

193   "having longer classes": The principal of Parkway North High School was quoted in "High Schools Plan Schedule Changes to Aid Students," *St. Louis Post-Dispatch*, February 13, 1997.

193   "interest in alternative forms of scheduling": Meg Sommerfeld, "More and More Schools Putting Block Scheduling to Test of Time," *Education Week* (May 22, 1996).

193   "But does block scheduling help": Meg Sommerfeld, "Research Spans Spectrum on Block Scheduling," *Education Week* (May 22, 1996).

194   I am not a Luddite: I headed the National Science Foundation-sponsored Learning Package Project as executive director of the International Studies Association's Consortium for International Studies Education, a network of universities involved in the development and dissemination of innovative undergraduate pedagogical materials.

194   Faustian bargain: Clifford Stoll has called computers in the classroom "the filmstrips of the 1990s." Recalling his own school days in the 1960s, the astrophysicist notes, "We loved them because we didn't have to think for an hour." Quoted in

Todd Oppenheimer, "The Computer Delusion," *The Atlantic Monthly* (July 1997), p. 48. Also see Clifford Stoll, *High-Tech Heretic: Why Computers Don't Belong in the Classroom and Other Reflections by a Computer Contrarian* (New York: Doubleday, 1999).

194   "Undoubtedly, computers will": Hirsch, *op. cit.*, p. 265.

195   "learn first, surf later": David Gelernter, "No—Learn First, Surf Later," *Time* (May 25, 1998), p. 35. Interestingly, Gelernter recently has teamed with another well-known critic of technology-based education, former U.S. Secretary of Education William Bennett, to explore ways of improving on-line education in K-12, particularly aimed at homeschoolers. See *New York Times*, December 28, 2000.

195   "search engines are closer": David Rothenberg, "How the Web Destroys the Quality of Students' Research Papers," *The Chronicle of Higher Education* (August 15, 1997). Also see Steven Knowlton, "How Students Get Lost in Cyberspace," *New York Times*, November 2, 1997.

195   "I noticed a disturbing decline": *Ibid.*

196   "Slacker.com": *New York Times*, September 22, 1999.

196   A-1 Termpapers: "Boston U. Sues Those Selling Term Papers on Internet," *New York Times*, October 22, 1997.

197   "students become independent learners": *NEA Magazine* (November 1996).

197   "Pupils Who Can't Even Spell Power Point": *New York Times*, May 31, 2001, D1.

197   "It's what I call the romance": Quoted in Amy Harmon, "Internet's Value in U.S. Schools Still in Question," *New York Times*, October 25, 1997. See Larry Cuban, *Teachers and Machines: The Classroom Use of Technology Since 1920* (New York: Teachers University Press, 1986).

197   "most of it is akin to glorified video": Ethan Bronner, "High-Tech Teaching Is Losing Its Gloss," *New York Times*, November 30, 1997. Also see Edward Rothstein, "Educational Value of Computers May Be Highly Overrated," *New York Times*, July 7, 1997.

197   "there is no good evidence": Oppenheimer, *op. cit.*, p. 45.

198   "the reality is we haven't": Harmon, *op. cit.*

198   "unfortunately, many of these studies": Oppenheimer, *op. cit.*, p. 47.

198   "The research is set up": *Ibid.* Oppenheimer states that even the

much-publicized "Classrooms of Tomorrow" study done by Apple Computers showed "scant evidence of greater student achievement" tied to computer use.

198   all educational research can be criticized: E.D. Hirsch offered an excellent critique of educational research in his April 10, 1997 address to the California State Board of Education. See *Common Knowledge* (Winter/Spring 1997).

198   "The complaint of the fair-minded critics": Williamson Evers, "How Progressive Education Gets It Wrong," *Hoover Digest*, no. 4 (1998).

198   constructing constructivist classrooms: For example, see *Colorado Teacher Education 2000: A Review of Four Institutions*, a report prepared by David Saxe, who was commissioned by the Colorado Commission on Higher Education to examine the state's education schools and who found them dominated by progressivism and constructivism. The findings are summarized in the June 7, 2001 edition of *The Education Gadfly* (the electronic newsletter of the Thomas B. Fordham Foundation found on the web at www.edexcellence.net/gadfly/). Also, see the second note for p. 199.

199   "If I were seriously ill": Cited in Ravitch, *op. cit.*, p. 290. See, also, "Why Education Experts Resist Effective Practices (And What It Would Take to Make Education More Like Medicine)," published by the Thomas B. Fordham Foundation in April 2000, written by Douglas Carmine, Director of the National Center to Improve the Tools of Educators. In contrast, Arthur Levine, the current head of Teachers College, proclaims that "we are heading to an era in which schooling will change profoundly. The teacher will not be the talking head at the front of the classroom, but the expert on students' learning styles, the educational equivalent of a medical doctor." Arthur Levine, "Tomorrow's Education, Made to Measure," *New York Times*, December 22, 2000.

199   constructivist bias against knowledge: See Lawrence A. Baines and Gregory Stanley, "'We Want to See the Teacher': Constructivism and the Rage Against Expertise," *Phi Delta Kappan* (December 2000), pp. 327-330, and Paul Regnier, "The Illusion of Technique and the Intellectual Life of Schools," *Phi Delta Kappan* (September 1994), pp. 223-226. I have exchanged numerous communications with Lucien Ellington, a professor in the school of education at the University of Tennessee-Chattanooga, who has railed against the obsession with method over content and who has launched an "anti-panacea," "contrarian"

campaign against the rush to innovation that he sees characterizing most ed schools.

199 "share an important quality": Albert Shanker, "Remembering
Teachers," *New York Times*, December 29, 1996.

199 "the scores of students": "New York State Regulators Toughen
Standards for Teachers," *New York Times*, September 18,
1999). See a number of studies reported by John H. Bishop, et
al., at Cornell University, including "Secondary Education in the
United States: What Can Others Learn from Our Mistakes?,"
which concludes that "the teacher's general academic ability and
subject knowledge are the characteristics that most consistently
predict student learning."

200 "U.S. eighth-grade students": *Christian Science Monitor*,
December 5, 2000.

200 teachers who major in science and other fields: A publication of
the Woodrow Wilson Center in Washington, based on U.S.
Department of Education data, points out that "34 percent of
U.S. mathematics teachers at the 12th-grade level and 53 percent
of all secondary-level history teachers neither majored nor
minored in their subject in college. Forty percent of public
school students are likewise without a competent science
teacher." Chiarra R. Nappi, "Local Illusions," *Wilson Quarterly*
(Autumn 1999), p. 48. In 1996, a blue-ribbon commission
headed by North Carolina Governor James Hunt reported that
roughly a quarter of all teachers do not even have enough college credits to minor in the subjects they teach.

201 "that many students in America": "Harsh Critique of Teachers
Urges Attention to Training," *New York Times*, October 25,
1999.

201 "why is teacher certification": Diane Ravitch, "Why Students
Don't Know Much About History," *Education Week* (March 4,
1998).

201 statistics on out-of-field instructors: Cited in Diane Ravitch,
"Lesson Plan for Teachers," *Washington Post*, August 10, 1998,
and Ravitch, "Put Teachers to the Test," *Washington Post*, February 25, 1998.

201 K-12 unwilling to test teachers: A February 18, 1999 *USA
Today* editorial notes that "forty-four states demand teachers
pass pedagogy tests; only 21 require content tests. And the rigor
of those content tests is dubious." Diane Ravitch, in *Left Back*,
op. cit., p. 318, notes that the American Council on Education
tried as far back as 1939 to institute rigorous subject exams for

teacher certification, but was rebuffed by schools of education and other actors who had a stake in the existing licensing arrangements. Other countries require teachers to pass far stiffer subject tests. See Bishop, *op. cit.*

201 "the assumptions underlying those tests [in 1875]": Lee S. Shulman, "Those Who Understand: Knowledge Growth in Teaching," *Educational Researcher* (February 1986), p. 5.

201 U.S. Department of Education "Annual Report on Teacher Quality": *Washington Post,* June 12, 2002.

202 "a new examination for the licensing": Martin Gross, *A Conspiracy of Ignorance* (New York: Harper Collins, 1999), p. 4. For data on Illinois and Chicago schools, see the *Chicago Sun-Times* investigation of elementary, middle, and high school teachers who took at least one "Basic Skills" or subject matter test between 1998 and 2001. The findings were reported in the *Sun-Times* "Failing Teachers" series during 2001.

202 "thirty percent failed": John Silber, "Those Who Can't Teach," *New York Times,* July 7, 1998. So many aspiring teachers failed the reading and writing test in April 1998 that it was felt necessary to grade on a curve so as to avoid greater embarrassment. Another round of tests administered in August 1998 resulted in nearly half the test-takers failing. There have been pressures since to revise the tests so as to produce better results. "Nearly Half of Aspiring Teachers Fail Latest Massachusetts Test," *Washington Post,* August 13, 1998.

202 "regrettably, when compared": Michael Kirst, *Who Controls Our Schools?* (New York: W.H. Freeman, 1984). The 1990s saw little improvement. Silber, *op. cit.*, notes that "in 1997, the average combined SAT score for all students was 1,016. But those hoping to become teachers scored only 964, 5.1 percent below the national average."

203 "in one of my courses": The letter by Laurence C. Schwartz appeared in the July 24, 1998 issue of the *New York Times.*

203 "I recently began a Masters": The letter was dated October 5, 1997.

203 "if I ever see you on the street": The class was taught by Professor John Dinan. Why he wished to share such embarrassing comments with me that reflected so poorly on his students remains a mystery.

203 Kramer: Rita Kramer, *Ed School Follies: The Miseducation of America's Teachers* (New York: The Free Press, 1991). Also see Gross, *op. cit.*, Chapter 3, "The Making of a Modern Teacher."

204   UM-St. Louis Business and Education student grades: Robert Nauss, in a report dated January 12, 1995.

204   "reform after reform": Alan Kreuger, "But Does It Work?," *New York Times*, November 7, 1999.

204   humanities faculty and touch football: Richard Mitchell, *The Graves of Academe* (Boston: Little, Brown, 1981).

204   closing of education schools at Yale and elsewhere: See *New York Times*, September 16, 1997, and Joseph Horn, "A Critical Look at Texas Colleges of Education," accessed through the Internet at http://tppf.org/cltcc.html.

205   "mumbo-jumbo": This comment was made in an e-mail received on October 25, 1999. The source is confidential.

205   "teachers can claim professional development credits for gambling": Stephanie Banchero, "Teacher Reforms Veering Off Track: Massage Classes, Horse Betting Used for Recertification," *Chicago Tribune*, August 12, 2001.

206   "being and doing": This appeared on a document entitled "Middle School Curriculum of the Future" that was circulated by the Network for Educational Development on February 17, 1995.

206   "educators in professional learning communities": Rick DuFour, "Professional Learning Community," *The Leadership Academy Developer* (Winter 2000–2001), published by the Missouri Department of Elementary and Secondary Education.

206   statewide needs survey: "Network for Staff Development Needs Survey," prepared by the Missouri Department of Elementary and Secondary Education, April 1996.

206   "Thoughtworld": Hirsch, *The Schools We Need, op. cit.*

206   "deep-seated intellectual uniformity": See E.D. Hirsch, Jr., "Challenging the Intellectual Monopoly," *Education Week* (November 6, 1996).

208   attracting higher quality teaching talent: For two somewhat different takes on what these factors are and what might be done to alleviate them, see Kirst, *op. cit.*, pp. 142-148 and Chester E. Finn, Jr., et al., *The Quest for Better Teachers: Grading the States* (Washington, D.C.: Thomas B. Fordham Foundation, November 1999).

208   why it is hard to entice top talent to stay in the profession: Retention has been at least as serious a problem as recruitment. See Vartan Gregorian, "How to Train—and Retain—Teachers," *New York Times*, July 6, 2001.

208   differential pay: At times it has been the rank-and-file union

membership more than the leadership that has resisted perfor-
mance-based pay. In 2000, the delegates to the National
Education Association annual convention rejected the use of job
performance evaluations in paying bonuses. See "Teachers
Reject Linking Job Performance to Bonuses," *New York Times*,
July 6, 2000.

209   alternative certification: For example, Harold Levy, Chancellor
of the New York City Public Schools, recently unveiled a plan
"to hire as many as 3,000 aspiring or unlicensed teachers into
[a] program called New York City Teaching Fellows." Abby
Goodnough, "Fast Track Certification Program for Teachers to
Expand Tenfold," *New York Times*, October 14, 2000.

209   "interlocking directorate": This term is credited to Hirsch, *The
Schools We Need, op. cit.*

209   "to make the teaching profession respectable": Leo Botstein,
"Making the Teaching Profession Respectable Again," *New
York Times*, July 26, 1999. Botstein admittedly offers some
rather simplistic remedies at times. He also questions much traditional pedagogy.

209   "Require prospective teachers": David Broder, "Children's
Future Is at Stake," *St. Louis Post-Dispatch*, September 18,
1996. Although I have expressed reservations about university
partnerships, I credit Clayton with recently focusing such efforts
on one university in particular, Truman State (in Kirksville,
Mo.), which has developed exactly the kind of program Broder
describes, although it remains to be seen whether the postbac-
calaureate year will be consumed with learning the gospel of
constructivism.

209   Darling-Hammond is among the many progressives who have
ridiculed traditional teaching as the "sage on the stage" model.
Newsweek (October 29, 2001), p. 61.

210   ed school training produces no value added: See Chester E. Finn,
Jr., "How Necessary Is Ed School?," editorial in the August 23,
2001 edition of *The Education Gadfly*, published by the Thomas
B. Fordham Foundation; Finn reports on a Hoover Institution
study of "Teach for America," the teacher-volunteeer corps
aimed at attracting liberal arts graduates into public schools for
two-year stints. Also see "Teacher Certification Reconsidered:
Stumbling for Quality," a report of the Abell Foundation issued
in October 2001; the report is discussed in "Assessing
Certification of Teachers: Abell Foundation Says Academic
Requirements Should Be Dropped," *Baltimore Sun*, October 10,
2001.

210   "teacher salaries": "National Study Examines Reasons Why Pupils Excel," *New York Times*, July 26, 2000. Also, see Dale Ballou and Michael Podgursky, *Teacher Pay and Teacher Quality* (Kalamazoo, Mich.: W.E. Upjohn Institute for Employment Research, 1997), and Ballou and Podgursky, "Reforming Teacher Training and Recruitment," *Government Union Review* 17, no. 4 (1998), pp. 1-53.

210   "Even if it were true": Quoted in Charles Ornstein, "Reading Research Gets Respect," *Dallas Morning News*, June 17, 2001. This criticism has been articulated the loudest in Alfie Kohn, *The Schools Our Children Deserve* (Boston: Houghton Mifflin, 1999) and *The Case Against Standardized Testing* (Portsmouth, NH: Heinemann, 2000).

212   "portfolios": On the weaknesses of portfolio assessment, see Peter N. Berger, "Portfolio Folly," *Education Week* (January 14, 1998).

212   no "pain" testing: See "Educators Focus on 'Pain' of Standards," *New York Times*, September 30, 1999. On concern for how tests can hurt the confidence and self-esteem of struggling students, and how it is better to have students assess their own work rather than promote external evaluation, see Richard J. Stiggins, "Assessment, Student Confidence, and School Success," *Phi Delta Kappan* (November 1999), pp. 191-198.

212   "learning is threatened by": Alfie Kohn, "Beware of the Standards, Not Just the Tests," *Education Week* (September 26, 2001).

212   "Some people think that multiple-choice items": Quoted in "Developing and Implementing Academic Standards," a report of the Pacific Research Institute, accessed at http://www.pacificresearch.org/issues/edu/standards/main1.html. On the virtues of traditional multiple-choice tests, and how well-written ones can tap higher-order, critical thinking abilities, also see R. Lukhele, et al., "On the Relative Value of Multiple-Choice, Constructed Response, and Examinee-Selected Items on Two Achievement Tests," *Journal of Educational Measurement* 31 (1994), pp. 234-250, and Hirsch, *Address to the California State Board of Education, op. cit.* Hirsch states that "top scientists would probably advise you against using end-of-year performance tests, if your aim is to use assessments that are accurate, dependable, and reasonably priced. Specialists will also tell you that almost all the nasty things said about multiple choice tests are incorrect."

213   "States may lean toward": Quoted in *Education Week* (January

11, 1999). Nonetheless, FairTest and other groups have argued that exams such as the SAT are biased. As noted in Chapter 3, the SAT, particularly the SAT I which tests general verbal and quantitative ability, has been accused of exhibiting bias against minorities. For the latest attacks on the SAT, see Ben Gose and Jeffrey Selingo, "The SAT's Greatest Test," *The Chronicle of Higher Education* (October 26, 2001), and Peter Sacks, "Education's Bleak House," *Education Week* (October 24, 2001).

213   fuzzy state standards: In 1998, the Fordham Foundation published a report card on the quality of the new standards in each state which found most assessment programs flawed in the fields of English, history, math, and science due to the fact the standards were "extremely vague," "hostile to knowledge," "entranced by relevance," and "standards of teaching rather than standards of learning." See Chester E. Finn, Jr., et al., *The State of the Standards* (Washington, D.C.: Thomas B. Fordham Foundation, 1998), and Finn, et al., "Four Reasons Why Most State Academic Standards 'Don't Cut the Mustard,'" *Education Week* (November 11, 1998). Also, see Diane Ravitch, "Higher, but Hollow, Academic Standards," *New York Times*, September 16, 1999.

213   Missouri introduces new MAP assessment: The *St. Louis Post-Dispatch*, in a November 16, 2001 editorial, acknowledged that Missouri's Show-Me Standards were so weak that "a high school student can graduate with a straight-D average and the reading ability of an average fourth grader."

213   "Students will demonstrate": This was a standard contained in the Communication Arts area in a May 1994 draft of *Academic Performance Standards for Missouri Schools: An Interpretive Guide*, published by the Missouri Department of Elementary and Secondary Education. The New Standards Project, led by progressive educators Marc Tucker and Lauren Resnick, has heavily influenced the development of state standards and assessments in Missouri and across the country. See John O'Neil, "On the New Standards Project: A Conversation with Lauren Resnick and Warren Simmons," *Educational Leadership* (February 1993), pp. 17-21.

213   "a 20 percent grading error": Michael R. Clynch, "Does Testing Add Up? No," *St. Louis Post-Dispatch*, May 8, 2001. Districts that have requested regrading of MAP tests, such as the Ladue school system, sometimes have found markedly different results the second time around, raising further questions about the reliability of the evaluations.

214   "researchers have found that two trained scorers": Pacific Research Institute, "Developing and Implementing Academic Standards," *op. cit*. Even traditional, non-performance-based standardized tests can suffer from scorer error at times. See Jacques Steinberg and Diana B. Henriques, "When a Test Fails the Schools, Careers and Reputations Suffer," *New York Times*, May 21, 2001, and Steinberg and Henriques, "Right Answer, Wrong Score: Test Flaws Take Toll," *New York Times*, May 20, 2001. The error potential is greatly magnified with the newer performance assessments.

214   KIRIS assessment: See Ken Jones and Betty Lou Whitford, "Kentucky's Conflicting Reform Principles," *Phi Delta Kappan* (December 1997), pp. 276-281, "Revamped Kentucky Schools Are A Study in Pros and Cons," *New York Times*, March 25, 1996, and "New CATS Credibility Crisis: Inflated Scores, Deflated Goals," *KERA Update* (October 2001). The latter report was published by Richard Innes, a parent and airline pilot, who almost single-handedly has led the fight against performance assessment in Kentucky.

214   Vermont portfolio assessment: Pacific Research Institute, "Developing and Implementing Academic Standards," *op. cit*.

214   Maine portfolio assessment: Donna Garner, "The Fallacy of Performance-Based Assessments in Maine," accessed through the Internet on February 27, 1999. Like Innes in Kentucky, Garner, an English teacher, has led the fight against performance assessment in Texas and has monitored developments around the rest of the country as well.

214   some states returning to traditional testing: For some evidence of "state standards becoming more specific and measurable" and "content making a comeback," see Chester E. Finn and Michael J. Petrilli, eds., *The State of the Standards 2000* (Washington, D.C.: Thomas B. Fordham Foundation, 2000). The authors remain critical of many state standards, however. Missouri improved from a grade of D- in 1998 to a grade of D+ in 2000. On those states that have instituted stronger content standards, with mixed results, see "The Good News Behind the Good News in Massachusetts," *The Education Gadfly*, 1, October 24, 2001; and "Massive Failure Rates on New Tests Daze Va.," *Education Week* (January 20, 1999).

214   "group practices [on the MSPAP]": Memorandum from Robert Embry to Nancy Grasmick, Maryland State Superintendent of Education, dated December 24, 1996. Follow-up criticisms have been offered by two members of the Abell Foundation study

team that was commissioned to evaluate the Maryland assessment program. See the op-ed article by Williamson Evers in *Baltimore Sun*, January 3, 2000, and Ralph Raimi, "Poor Performance Review," *Washington Times*, April 1, 2001.

214 "to go back to facts, facts": Quoted in an article in *Baltimore Sun*, August 3, 2000. Grasmick's official reason for blocking the publication of the report was that it contained sensitive information on test questions, not that it contained a scathing condemnation of the testing program.

215 "minute facts": Presentation made to the Clayton Board of Education by Elizabeth Schmitz on October 16, 1996.

215 backpedalling on state tests: "Academic Standards Eased As a Fear of Failure Spreads," *New York Times*, December 3, 1999.

215 cheating on state tests: Cheating on a state test was discovered in 2000 at Potomac Elementary School in the Montgomery County, Maryland school district. See "Evidence of Cheating on Md. Test 'Substantial,'" *Washington Post*, June 2, 2000, and "Bitter Lessons," *Newsweek* (June 19, 2000), pp. 50-52. Also, see "Three Fresno Teachers Disciplined Over Cheating on Test," *Los Angeles Times*, July 28, 2000, and "Review Tests Go Too Far, Critics Say," *Washington Post*, July 10, 2001. In 2000, the Massachusetts Teachers Association launched a $600,000 ad campaign attacking the more rigorous assessments that the state education department was attempting to institute. "High Failure Rates Spur Teacher Protests," *USA Today*, November 28, 2000.

215 tests may hold children back: The news media have reported on widespread political pressures to relax standards. See, for example, Jacques Steinberg, "Student Failure Causes States to Retool Testing Progams," *New York Times*, December 22, 2000, "State Board of Education 'Rigged' End-of-Grade Test Scores," *Carolina Journal Weekly Report*, May 28, 2001, Kate Zernike, "Why Johnny Can't Read, Write, Multiply or Divide," *New York Times*, April 15, 2001, and "Los Angeles May Ease Up on School Promotion Policy," *New York Times*, December 2, 1999.

215 "nearly a third of the states": Steinberg, *op. cit.* Also, see James Traub, "The Test Mess," *New York Times Magazine*, April 7, 1992.

216 "growing revolt against the testers": Richard Rothstein, "The Growing Revolt Against the Testers," *New York Times*, May 30, 2001. Rothstein, whose articles reflect a clear progressive bent, supports testing that, by its nature, cannot be used for high-stakes purposes.

216   crusaders standing between education heaven and hell: The first article is by Alfie Kohn, the second by Scott Thompson, and the third by Susan Ohanian. They all appeared in the January 2001 issue of *Phi Delta Kappan*, pp. 348-366.

216   "in its strongest stance yet against": Quoted in an article by the AP reporter Greg Toppo, entitled "NEA: Let Kids Skip Standardized Tests," July 7, 2001, accessed on the Internet at www.contracostatimes.com/news/education/stories/. On both the NEA and AFT, see "Teachers Union Leaders Oppose Push to Testing," *New York Times*, July 4, 2000.

216   Scarsdale and Marin County boycott: See "In the Suburbs, Testing Meets a Backlash," *Washington Post National Weekly* edition, May 28-June 3, 2001, and "Marin Students Boycott State Test," *San Francisco Chronicle*, May 4, 2001. Also, Charles Sykes, "Soccer Moms vs. Standardized Tests," *New York Times*, December 6, 1999.

217   relaxation of high school exit exam requirements: Dan Walters, a columnist for the *Sacramento Bee*, notes that in 2001 "the results [of statewide testing] for African-American and Latino students were abysmally low. More than 90 percent would fail the mathematics portion and nearly three-fourths would flunk the language exam." "Worst Fears About Exit Exam Come True," accessed on the Internet on June 10, 2001, at www.dailybreeze.com/content/bop/nmwalters10.html. On the problems in New York, see "Holding Firm to State Standards," *New York Times*, May 14, 2001.

217   "Rod Paige": "How to Leave No Child Behind," *New York Times* editorial page, May 21, 2001.

218   "showed overwhelming support": This was an August 2000 survey, reported in Diane Ravitch, "Who Says Parents Oppose Standards-Based Reform?," *The Record* (Bergen County, N.J.), February 19, 2001.

218   "countering recent news reports": This was a September 2000 survey, reported in "Survey Results of National Poll of Parents of Public School Students Concerning Academic Standards," published by Public Agenda in September 2000. A 2002 Public Agenda survey indicated "the great majority of middle and high school students are comfortable with the increased testing." Louis Gerstner, Jr., "The Tests We Know We Need," *New York Times*, March 14, 2002. Gerstner, chairman of IBM and co-chairman of Achieve, Inc., noted that "at the National Education Summit of governors, educators, and business leaders in 1996, a consensus emerged that the United States had no shot at real public school reform without...rigorous testing."

219   "No Child Left Behind Act": For descriptions of the initial plan, see "Schoolbook Balancing Act," including excerpts of President Bush's statement announcing his education initiative, in *New York Times*, January 24, 2001. Also, see "In Reconciling School Bills, 2 Chambers Agree on Tests," *New York Times*, July 15, 2001. Details of the final bill passed by Congress and signed by President Bush in 2002 can be found in "Details of the Education Bill," Associated Press press release of January 8, 2002, and "With Fanfare, Bush Signs Education Bill," *Washington Post*, January 9, 2002.

219   Todd Akin: On May 23, 2001, Rep. Akin offered an amendment to HR 1 (No Child Left Behind Act of 2001) that all tests "be tests of objective knowledge, based on measurable, verifiable...standards, and shall not assess the personal opinions, attitudes, or beliefs of the student being assessed." Other conservatives, such as Chester Finn, have criticized what they see as excessive wiggle-room given to non-performing districts and the failure of the Bush administration to fight for vouchers and other such mechanisms to promote competition. Liberals have their own lingering concerns about inadequate budget expenditures. See Thomas Toch, "Bush's Big Test," *The Washington Monthly*, November 2001.

219   "the conservatives don't like national": This statement is credited to Arthur Levine, the head of Columbia University Teachers College.

Chapter 8

220   "closed alliance": Comes from a 1960 statement by James Conant, the then president of Harvard University; cited in Martin Gross, *A Conspiracy of Ignorance* (New York: HarperCollins, 1999), p. 10.

220   "groupthink": The term is taken from Irving L. Janis, *Groupthink*, 2nd ed. (Boston: Houghton Mifflin, 1982).

221   widening disconnect between the Thoughtworld and the rest of us: Poll after poll shows a huge gap between the idealized vision of schooling harbored by education professors and the more down-to-earth concerns felt by the general public. Scott Willis, "Responding to Public Opinion," *Education Update* 17 (June 1995), published by the Association for Supervision and Curriculum Development, pp. 1-5. Also, see the second note for p. 145.

221   "Professors of education hold a vision": Steve Farkas and Jean Johnson, with Ann Duffett, *Different Drummers: How Teachers*

of Teachers View Public Education, a Report from Public Agenda (1997), cited in Sandra Stotsky, *Losing Our Language* (New York: The Free Press, 1999), p. 201. Surveys show education professors are out of sync not only with parents but with classroom teachers as well. "Are Teachers of Teachers Out of Touch?," *New York Times*, October 22, 1997.

222   "Senators, you need": Testimony before the Missouri Senate, Jefferson City, Missouri, January 16, 1996.

222   worry less about closing the gap and more about improving individual performance: Jay Mathews makes this point in "Ignoring the Gap and Raising the Bar on Test Scores," *Washington Post*, October 23, 2001. He states that "I think focusing on ethnic gaps—particularly in education—is not a useful exercise."

222   rich-poor gap in 1820 vs. today: The data are from Jeff Madrick, "Rich Nations Have Been Too Insensitive to Poverty," *New York Times*, November 1, 2001.

223   "the public is highly skeptical of": Scott Willis, "Responding to Public Opinion," *Education Update* 17 (June 1995), p. 5. The willingness of the Association for Supervision and Curriculum Development, a key arm of the K-12 establishment, to publish this critique of educators shows that, on occasion, contrary views are aired (as with *Phi Delta Kappan*'s publishing my reply to Alfie Kohn). However, there is little question that a content analysis of ASCD publications or other K-12 publications would reveal an overwhelming endorsement of progressive, constructivist views.

223   "research shows that putting students": cited in "Are Teachers of Teachers Out of Touch?,"*op. cit.*

224   traditionalists have tried to reach out: I have in mind particularly the effort of Diane Ravitch, at the end of *Left Back*, where she offered some kind words about Howard Gardner and other progressives, only to be widely repudiated by the progressive community for her criticisms of progressive education earlier in the book.

226   theories do not get fully translated into practice: One of the better treatments of this issue is found in David Tyack and Larry Cuban, *Tinkering Toward Utopia: A Century of Public School Reform* (Cambridge: Harvard University Press, 1995).

226   "the first step needed [to improve it]": Mark C. Schug and Richard D. Western, "The Homeless Social Studies Teacher: How Muzak Progressivism Has Harmed Social Studies Education," unpublished paper, Center for Economic Education, University of Wisconsin-Milwaukee, 2001.

226 "the powerful middle ground": Diane Ravitch, *Left Back: A Century of Failed School Reforms* (New York: Simon and Schuster, 2000), p. 450.

226 calls to blend the best of traditional and progressive pedagogy: Examples of calls for balance are "The Great Debate" symposium in *Education Week* (April 21, 1999), Carl D. Glickman, "Dichotomizing Education: Why No One Wins and America Loses," *Phi Delta Kappan* (October 2001), pp. 147-152, Gary DeCoker, "Core Knowledge and Teacher Education: Time for a Cease-Fire," *Education Week* (April 25, 2001), and Jacques Steinberg, "Clashing Over Education's One True Faith," *New York Times*, December 14, 1997. The common sense benefits of drawing on the insights of both Hirsch and Sizer are nicely discussed in a series of 1996 book reviews coinciding with the publication of Hirsch's *The Schools We Need* and Sizer's *Horace's Hope*. See Sara Mosle, "Doing Our Homework," *New York Times*, September 29, 1996, Thomas Toch, "Two Titans of Education Square Off," *U.S. News and World Report* (October 7, 1996), and Barbara Kantrowitz, "The Jargon Jungle," *Newsweek* (October 7, 1996).

226 "common sense" remains "elusive": Jan Jacobi, "Balance, Moderation, and Time-Tested Quality Equal Success," *St. Louis Post-Dispatch*, January 3, 2000. He is the head of the middle school at Mary Institute and Country Day School, and also happens to be a Clayton parent.

227 "mostly just rhetoric": Statement by Arnold Fege, quoted in Willis, *op. cit.*, p. 3.

227 "It's common for school districts": Statement by Tony Wagner, quoted in *ibid.*, pp. 3-4.

227 "a need for public engagement": *Ibid.*, p. 3.

228 "The issues addressed by the PTA": Quoted in Ionnie Harp, "Who's Minding the Children?," *Education Week* (September 28, 1994).

228 parental involvement is unwelcome: One of the better accounts of a parent's experience in eagerly seeking involvement in the life of his child's school only to sour on the experience when, in raising criticisms, he was accused of "betraying" the school's philosophy and of being an "elitist," is Sol Stern, "My Public School Lesson," *City Journal* (Autumn 1997), pp. 14-29.

230 parental rights: In 2001, a Parental Rights Amendment was offered to the education bill being considered by the U.S. Congress, which sought to give parents the right to access and inspect their child's textbooks and other curriculum materials

and to shield the child from invasive personal questions and medical examinations at school. Senator Edward Kennedy of Massachusetts was among those who attempted to block such an amendment, which rightly aimed to reinforce parental responsibility. Reported at CNSNews.com on November 7, 2001.

231 2001 PBS documentary on history of American schooling: "School: The Story of American Public Education."

231 "Charter schools are public schools": Diane Ravitch, "Our School Problem and Its Solutions," *City Journal* (Winter 1999), pp. 39-40.

231 2,000 charter schools: For data on charter schools, see Chester E. Finn, Jr., and Kelly Amis, *Making It Count* (Washington, D.C.: Thomas B. Fordham Foundation, 2001), p. 31, and Center for Education Reform, "Survey of Charter Schools 2000-2001," May 2001.

232 15-20 percent of school-age population in charters: Chester E. Finn, Jr., "What Lies Ahead for Charter Schools?," *The Education Gadfly* 1 (October 24, 2001).

232 statistics on charter schools in Arizona and other states: "Survey of Charter Schools, 2000–2001," *op. cit.*, and Center for Education Reform, "Charter School Laws: Ranking Scorecard," May 2001.

232 half of all charters in U.S. have needed approval from local school boards: "Charter School Laws: Ranking Scorecard," *op. cit.*

232 problems in creating "break the mold" schools: On the problems experienced by charter schools, see Finn, "What Lies Ahead for Charter Schools?," *op. cit.*, and Chester E. Finn, Jr., Bruno Manno, and Gregg Vanourek, *Charter Schools in Action: Renewing Public Education* (2001).

232 "parents and children in Elk Grove Township": "Declaring War on School Choice," *Chicago Tribune* editorial, January 24, 1999.

233 "a junior Princeton Academy" catering to immigrant families: Based on a phone interview I conducted with the principal on November 13, 2001.

233 vouchers in higher education vs. K-12 education: On the general subject of vouchers, see John Chubb and Terry Moe, *Politics, Markets, and America's Schools* (Washington, D.C.: Brookings Institute, 1990), and "Questions on School Choice," special issue of *Policy Review* (January-February 1999).

234 voucher experiments in Milwaukee, Cleveland, and Florida: After visits to four voucher-supported schools in Milwaukee and Cleveland, one observer's verdict was "a straight A." Sol Stern, "The Schools That Vouchers Built," *City Journal* (Winter 1999), pp. 14-25. Findings showing gains in publicly funded as well as privately funded voucher programs are reported in Jay P. Greene, "The Surprising Consensus on School Choice," *The Public Interest* (Summer 2001); an expanded version of the article appears in Paul E. Peterson and Donald E. Campbell, eds., *Charters, Vouchers, and Public Education* (Washington, D.C.: Brookings Institute, forthcoming). Also, see Paul E. Peterson and Jay P. Greene, "What Cleveland Teaches About School Vouchers," *Wall Street Journal*, May 7, 1990, and "Voucher Programs in Three Cities Show Gains for Blacks," Program on Education Policy and Governance, Harvard University, 2001 Annual Report.

234 Supreme Court voucher ruling: *New York Times,* June 28, 2002.

234 support for vouchers at 34 percent in 2001: Andrea Billups, "In Poll, Schools Earn Good Grades," *Washington Times*, August 23, 2001. Some observers have questioned the wording of the survey items in these polls. Opinions may vary significantly around the country. For example, in Dayton, Ohio, 73 percent of respondents indicated recently they supported vouchers. See Chester E. Finn, Jr., "Education in Dayton," *The Education Gadfly*, 1, November 1, 2001. Some conservatives prefer tuition tax credits to vouchers, since vouchers may come with federal strings attached to them, while tax credits may entail less government intrusion into private schools. See Sarah Wildman, "Credit Is Due," *The New Republic* (February 26, 2001), and Finn and Amis, *Making It Count, op. cit.,* pp. 32-33.

234 Floyd Flake: See Floyd Flake, "Gore's Achilles' Heel," *New York Times*, June 25, 2000, and William Raspberry, "Solidly for Vouchers," *Washington Post*, August 6, 2001. The Joint Center for Political and Economic Studies has found that "57 percent of blacks support vouchers." Reported in *The Economist*, March 10, 2001.

235 "poorest Americans attending the worst public schools": Arthur Levine, "Why I'm Reluctantly Backing Vouchers," *Wall Street Journal*, June 15, 1998. Even the liberal *Washington Post* gave guarded support for the Supreme Court voucher decision in an editorial published the day the verdict was announced, June 27, 2002.

235 private school enrollments jump 19 percent: Margaret Talbot,

"Class and the Classroom," *The Atlantic Monthly* (February 2001).

235   Hawaiian private schools: "In Hawaii, Public Schools Feel a Long Way from Paradise," *New York Times*, October 12, 2001.

235   statistics on homeschooled children: Margaret Talbot, "The New Counterculture," *The Atlantic Monthly* (November 2001). A 1999 U.S. Department of Education study estimated 850,000.

235   "juggernaut": David W. Kirkpatrick, "The Home Schooling Juggernaut," in *Selected Readings on School Reform* (Fall 2001), published by the Thomas B. Fordham Foundation, pp. 42-43.

236   homeschooler SAT and ACT scores: "Class of Their Own," *Wall Street Journal*, February 11, 2000.

236   seamless K-16 system: Governor Paul Patton of Kentucky, chairman of the National Commission on the High-School Senior Year, formed by the U.S. Department of Education in 2000, has said that the entire educational spectrum "must be a seamless, unified system stretching from preschool to postsecondary education, with smooth transitions in which students master at each grade what they will need to succeed in the next." Quoted in Alex P. Kellogg, "Report Finds the Majority of U.S. Students Not Prepared for College," *Chronicle of Higher Education* (October 5, 2001).

237   grade inflation at Harvard: In 2001, under the glare of embarrassing publicity, Harvard's new president, Lawrence Summers, asked professors to "undertake a 'careful review' of their grading habits to help reduce grade inflation." More university leaders should be doing likewise, especially in schools of education. See Patrick Healy, "'Careful Review' of Grading Urged at Harvard," *Boston Globe*, November 14, 2001.

237   affirmative action overrides SAT scores and class rank: Two former chairs of the undergraduate admissions committee at UCLA recently took the unusual step of writing a member of the Board of Regents of the University of California, raising alarm bells about how, under the new admission procedures adopted by the university, "reduced weight is assigned to academics, in favor of various non-academic criteria." Letter from Prof. Mathew Malkan and Prof. Stephen Jacobsen to Regent Montoya, dated November 14, 2001 Also, see "Admitting Error," *The New Republic* (December 27, 1999), and Dan Seligman, "Mr. Diversity," *Forbes* (November 26, 2001), a profile of Lee Bollinger, the past president of the University of Michigan and the new president of Columbia University, who has argued that admissions using race as an important criterion inevitably produces

better education, a claim that is supported by little empirical evidence.

237   fluffy "general education" requirements: The sources of these stories are Tony Mecia, "Is It Weird? You May Get College Credit," *Campus* (Spring 1997), William Simon, "The Dumbing Down of Higher Education," *Wall Street Journal*, March 19, 1996, "How To Be Gay," an e-mail sent to me by the National Association of Scholars, August 13, 2001, and "U. of Chicago President, Who Sought to Revise the Core Curriculum, Will Return to Teaching," *New York Times*, June 5, 1999.

237   "select texts with plenty of cartoons": In "If It Pleases the Class," *Chronicle of Higher Education* (June 4, 1999), Lawrence Douglas and Alexander George, two professors at Amherst, offer a take-off on a piece by Glenn Altschuler of Cornell, entitled "Let Us Edutain You," that had appeared in the *New York Times*.

237   flow of beer: This statistic is cited by Chester Finn in "The High Price of College Sports," *Commentary* (October 2001).

237   "pigskin and sheepskin collide": Jere Longman, "At Oregon, Pigskin and Sheepskin Collide," *New York Times*, October 20, 2001.

237   cheating at University of Virginia: The University of Virginia was rocked by scandal in 2001, when 122 students were accused of cheating on term papers they had submitted in an introductory physics course. The physics professor, ironically, used a computer program to detect the plagiarism. *New York Times*, May 10, 2001.

237   videotaped lectures: Leila Jason, "Web Videos Make It Easier to Skip Classes," *Wall Street Journal*, August 22, 2001.

237   "That the university is exceedingly": Robert Weissberg, "Bending Over to Move Forward," paper given at the annual meeting of the National Association of Scholars, New York City, January 17, 2001. Also, see concerns about decreased classroom civility discussed in the *Chronicle of Higher Education* (March 27, 1998).

238   Things aren't quite this bad: Portland State University has built and exported an entire gen-ed curriculum around active and cooperative learning, despite faculty concerns that it is "shallow," "superficial," too "process-oriented," and designed to "accommodate the weakest students." "An Emulated General-Education Program Finds Itself Under Attack at Home," *Chronicle of Higher Education* (July 28, 2000).

238   "89 percent said cheating": Mona Charen, "High-Achieving Teens Admit That Cheating Is Common," *St. Louis Post-Dispatch*, January 28, 1996.

238   "less than 5 percent" and "62 percent of 10th graders": Reported in John H. Bishop, et al., "Secondary Education in the United States: What Others Can Learn from Our Mistakes," a 2001 study published at Cornell University.

238   "increasingly disengaged from the academic experience": John Leo, "No Books, Please: We're Students," *U.S. News and World Report* (November 2, 1995), p. 24.

238   "while 70 percent of today's high-school graduates": Kellogg, *op. cit.*

239   "noticed the quality of writing had declined": "Grammar Now Required for English Majors," *The Current*, October 21, 2001.

239   "writing caution": The writing caution I append to my syllabi has been borrowed with the permission of Professor Ron Christenson of Gustavus Adolphus College.

239   inattention to teaching on the part of university faculty: These are detailed in Charles Sykes, *Profscam* (Washington, D.C.: Regnery Gateway, 1988).

240   "As we enter the new": Frank H.T. Rhodes, "A Battle Plan for Professors to Recapture the Curriculum," *Chronicle of Higher Education* (September 14, 2001), p. B7.

240   "an alliance between alert parents": E-mail communication to me on October 28, 2000.

240   teaming content experts with pedagogical specialists: Among the K-12 educators who have stressed the need to link pedagogical process to solid disciplinary content is Sam Wineburg. See Sam Wineburg, *Historical Thinking and Other Unnatural Acts* (Philadelphia: University of Temple Press, 2001). Also see the reference to Lee Shulman in Chapter 7.

241   national conversation on education put on hold after September 11 terrorist attack: Earlier in 2001, a CNN-USA Today-Gallup poll revealed education to be the highest priority identified in a nationwide survey. Where only four in ten said Washington's main focus should be keeping America prosperous, providing military security, and dealing with energy problems, five in ten said improving education deserved top priority. *Dallas Morning News*, February 13, 2001. On how the events of September 11 placed education issues on the back burner, see "Crisis Shelves President's Focus on Education," *Education Week* (September 19, 2001) and "National Education Talks Languish in Shadow

of War," *New York Times*, October 10, 2001. It is testimony, however, to the continuing importance of education issues that, after September 11, the American political system remained focused enough to pass the "No Child Left Behind Act."

Index